A PLUME BOOK

OTHER PEOPLE'S MONEY

CHARLES V. BAGLI is a *New York Times* reporter who covers the intersection of politics and real estate. He has written about the sale of high-profile buildings, political contributions of the real estate industry, the battle to build a two-billion-dollar stadium for the Jets, bid rigging in the construction industry, payoffs at the tax assessor's office, and a Sutton Place co-op that turned public land into a private park. He has worked for the *New York Observer*; the *Daily Record* of Morristown, New Jersey; *The Tampa Tribune*; and the *Brooklyn Phoenix*. He lives with his wife in New Jersey. They have two daughters.

Praise for *Other People's Money*

"It's been said that journalism is the first draft of history, but with his upcoming book *Other People's Money*, *New York Times* reporter Charles Bagli writes the most authoritative account yet of the failed Stuyvesant Town-Peter Cooper Village deal and the housing crises that rocked the world."
—*The New York Observer*

"The reader interested in New York real estate history, its moneyed elites, or even the self-contradictory aspects of social investment should find ample material for reflection and enjoyment in Bagli's account." —*Publishers Weekly*

T0176236

"Bagli's sourcing is impressive, and readers will welcome his ability to make arcane investment dealings comprehensible."

—*Kirkus Reviews*

"[An] entertaining dissection of the disaster."

—*The Wall Street Journal*

"*Other People's Money* delivers one of the great untold stories of the financial crisis—how greed, arrogance, and the distorted incentives of the commercial real estate market helped drive our nation's economy off a cliff. Told through meticulous reporting of what was arguably the worst real estate deal of all time, in this vitally important book Bagli demonstrates how the well-heeled and well-connected walked away relatively unscathed from the wreckage that they created, leaving a devastated middle class holding the bag yet again."

—Neil Barofsky, *New York Times* bestselling author of
*Bailout: How Washington Abandoned Main Street
While Rescuing Wall Street*

"Charles Bagli does for the politics and economics of urban real estate finance what Jane Jacobs did for urban street life. Bagli's new book, *Other People's Money*, uses the sale of a major housing complex on Manhattan's Lower East Side, Stuyvesant Town-Peter Cooper Village, to demonstrate how contemporary real estate speculators deploy international finance and local politics to change the housing options of more ordinary city dwellers. Bagli, a talented journalist, makes the street-level impacts of abstract global finance easily understood."

—Elliott Sclar, professor of urban planning,
Columbia University

"*Other People's Money* is a terrific book. With remarkable textual clarity and a fine-tuned dramatic sensibility, Charles Bagli has re-created the extraordinarily high stakes poker game that was the largest real estate deal in U.S. history. His characters include the biggest real estate players on the planet as well as middle-class residents desperately holding on by their fingertips to the only housing they can afford. A truly epic tale, one that systematically demonstrates the logic (and illogic) of the real estate bubble that set the stage for worldwide recession and that reveals the wild, unforgiving nature of twenty-first-century capitalism. It's a powerful story and a great read."

—Rick Fantasia, coauthor of *Hard Work: Remaking the American Labor Movement* and professor of sociology at Smith College

"*Other People's Money* is an absolutely fascinating microcosm of the real estate market gone horribly wrong, with an eye toward the larger picture—and a siren warning that the real estate industry still hasn't learned from the catastrophic lessons of the past."

—*Midwest Book Review*

"[*Other People's Money*] expertly recounts the financial euphoria that gripped the market and threatened the most significant middle-income housing development in Manhattan."

—*New York Law Journal*

"*New York Times* reporter Charles V. Bagli tells the horror story [of Stuyvesant Town-Peter Cooper Village] with clarity and authority in *Other People's Money*."

—*Bloomberg*

"Right from the start the reader is the fly on the wall as negotiations between real estate execs, brokers, and attorneys are played out."

—*Town & Village*

"Engrossing . . . Bagli is a meticulous, evenhanded guide into how the deal went down."

—*The Cleveland Plain Dealer*

"[Bagli's] reporting is excellent, his writing clear, his exploration of the greed . . . of the principals thorough."

—*InfoDad*

"An absolute must-read."

—Institutional Real Estate, Inc.

OTHER PEOPLE'S MONEY

Inside the Housing Crisis and the Demise of
the Greatest Real Estate Deal Ever Made

CHARLES V. BAGLI

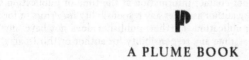

A PLUME BOOK

PLUME
Published by the Penguin Group
Penguin Group (USA) LLC
375 Hudson Street
New York, New York 10014

USA | Canada | UK | Ireland | Australia | New Zealand | India | South Africa | China
penguin.com
A Penguin Random House Company

First published in the United States of America by Dutton,
a member of Penguin Group (USA) Inc., 2013
First Plume Printing 2014

REGISTERED TRADEMARK—MARCA REGISTRADA

ISBN 978-0-14-218071-6

Printed in the United States of America

Ellie, Nikki, and Katy,
you're my electricity.

Dad, you always said:
If you want it done right, do it yourself.
I did.

Contents

The Poster Child of the Real Estate Bubble

October 16, 2006, 5:01 P.M.

Rob Speyer had spent hours pacing the small conference room near his office on the seventh floor of 50 Rockefeller Plaza, trading locker-room jibes and stories about real estate deals with Paul A. Galiano and Fred Lieblich, when the telephone finally rang.

Speyer, a thirty-seven-year-old with a marathoner's lanky build; sandy, close-cropped hair; and a machine-gun laugh, was the heir apparent to Tishman Speyer Properties, an international real estate company that operated on four continents and controlled some of New York City's most enduring icons, from Rockefeller Center to the Chrysler Building. For ten weeks, he and his colleagues had labored over a bid for a property whose size was almost unimaginable in densely packed Manhattan: Stuyvesant Town-Peter Cooper Village, a complex of 110 buildings with 11,232 apartments spread across 80 contiguous acres south of midtown, overlooking the East River.

Galiano, at forty-one years old, was Tishman Speyer's intensely focused co-chief of acquisitions. Lieblich was president of BlackRock Realty Advisors, forty-five years old and a partner in the prospective deal. They had formed a friendship with Speyer as they read the financial history of the rental complex and engineering assessments supplied by the seller, Metropolitan Life Insurance, or as it is known today, MetLife. By noon that day, they submitted their offer. They were up against an international who's who of real estate and finance that had gathered in New York for what promised to be the biggest real estate deal in history. Aside from New York's real estate royalty, like the Durst, Rudin and LeFrak families, there was the emir of Qatar; the Rothschilds and the Safras; the mysterious billionaire investor Simon Glick; the irascible Steve Roth of Vornado Realty Trust; Stephen Ross, a builder active in New York, Florida, Las Vegas and Los Angeles; the government of Singapore; and the Church of England, not to mention the many pension funds and private equity firms that had raised tens of billions of dollars to invest in real estate and other assets. Nearly a dozen rival bidders from around the globe were gathered in similar rooms high above Manhattan waiting to learn whether their multibillion-dollar offers had won the day and if they would spend the night negotiating contractual details of what would be the largest transaction in American real estate history.

The stark white walls of the Tishman Speyer conference room yielded nothing as the hours ticked by. One minute Speyer exuded the cocky confidence of a tycoon who prowled the world making deals, the next he wondered what might have gone wrong as a dark cloud of self-doubt descended over the conversation.

They had spent the afternoon of October 16, 2006, talking about anything but the call they desperately hoped would come. Adrian Fenty, who was running for mayor in Washington, DC, where the Speyers owned more than two dozen office buildings, popped into the room for a minute to say hello. He asked what was going on. Speyer explained it was "a fairly momentous day"; they were waiting to see who had won the bidding war. "I just came from Apollo's office," Fenty said with a chuckle, referring to Apollo Real Estate Advisors, Speyer's primary rival for the property. "They told me the same thing."

Then with the evening shadows gathering over Fifth Avenue, the phone rang a second and third time. Speyer snatched up the receiver and heard the voice of Darcy A. Stacom, the real estate broker conducting the multibillion-dollar auction of Stuyvesant Town-Peter Cooper Village.

Stacom, who was forty-six years old and a rare woman in the testosterone-fueled world of high-stakes real estate deals, quickly got to the point: "C'mon down to Two Hundred Park, now." But she warned, "Don't bring your whole team together. Come in ones and twos in case any reporters have staked out the lobby of the building." Two Hundred Park housed MetLife's law firm, Greenberg Traurig, and at the top, MetLife's ornate, old-world boardroom.

Stacom had not offered him congratulations, but Speyer knew what the call meant: If they could get through what promised to be hours of arguing over the final terms of the contract, Stuyvesant Town-Peter Cooper was his. He let out a yell as he put the phone down, almost simultaneously pumping his fist and hugging Galiano. Speyer turned and embraced Lieblich, who headed the real estate arm for one of the world's largest investment management firms for pension funds, institutions and high-net-wealth individuals.

Speyer and Galiano took the elevator to the ground floor and marched out the Fifth Avenue doors of the building, past the fifteen-foot bronze statue of a heavily muscled Atlas carrying the world on his shoulders. Speyer was under his own mythic strain and would remember little of the eight-block walk downtown.

Although not nearly as glamorous as Rockefeller Center, Stuyvesant Town held a pride of place in the minds of many New Yorkers. Stuyvesant Town, and its sister complex Peter Cooper Village, was unlike the real estate properties that seemed to trade like pork bellies on a daily basis in cities from Atlanta to Los Angeles, Boston to Dallas and Seattle during what was now a five-year-old real estate boom like no other in its intensity. Stuyvesant Town-Peter Cooper Village covered eighteen blocks of some of the most valuable real estate in the world.

The two complexes, which were erected by Metropolitan Life in what was once known as the Gas House District, were an urban version of Levittown, an inspiration for housing in the 1950s and 1960s that broke up the street grid rather than conformed to it, while keeping city life affordable to the middle class.

In the 1960s, Stuyvesant Town begat LeFrak City, a complex of ten eighteen-story buildings on forty acres in Corona, Queens, and Co-op City, a sprawling complex of 15,372 units in 35 high-rise towers and seven clusters of town houses spread across 320 acres in the Baychester section of the Bronx. Architecturally it was a failure. The red brick buildings were uniformly plain and looked more like the low-income housing projects nearby, the Jacob Riis, Lillian Wald and Alfred E. Smith Houses. But the buildings occupied neatly landscaped real estate on the East Side. In 2006, there were not eighty, or even twenty, contiguous acres available anywhere else on the thirteen-mile-long island of Manhattan, no matter what the price.

And Stuyvesant Town-Peter Cooper Village, despite its blandness, had been a safe, leafy oasis for thousands of middle-class firefighters, nurses, union construction workers, civil servants, writers, police officers, secretaries and even a few judges for nearly sixty years. For many New Yorkers, the complex had become a cherished landmark akin to the Empire State Building, the Statue of Liberty and Rockefeller Center. Early in their careers, Mayor John V. Lindsay, sportscaster Howard Cosell, reporter Gabe Pressman and presidential adviser David Axelrod had made their homes there. So had author Frank McCourt, mystery writer Mary Higgins Clark, actor Paul Reiser, operatic soprano Beverly Sills and Knicks basketball star Dick Barnett.

In 2006, hundreds of original tenants, many of whom had moved to Stuyvesant Town when it opened in 1947, were still living there. Thousands more had grown up in those twelve- and thirteen-story buildings and were now raising their own families in Stuyvesant Town-Peter Cooper Village.

"It's one of the most unique assets in the city," said Lieblich, who had himself lived in Stuyvesant Town when he was a MetLife executive in the 1990s. "A lot of people know of it. There's a lot of fond memories."

As Rob Speyer entered 200 Park Avenue, a fifty-eight-story skyscraper looming over Grand Central Terminal that had once been known as the Pan Am Building, he paused, noticing a handmade sign Scotch-taped to a storefront window promoting a sale. Tishman Speyer had bought the tower from MetLife eighteen months earlier for $1.72 billion, the highest price ever paid for an office building. The makeshift placard was just the kind of seedy thing that he had been trying to eliminate since taking control of the property. Shake it off, Rob said to himself, focus on the task at hand. He was up against eight other buyers who, in preparation for a bidding war, had collectively lined up a staggering $50 billion from money center banks, insurance companies, pension funds and private investors.

Every day seemed to bring another record real estate deal somewhere in the country and the prospect of windfall profits. The December 2004 sale of the 110-story Sears Tower in Chicago for $835 million had set a local record, despite the building's sizable vacancy. Maguire Properties, a publicly traded real estate investment trust, paid $1.5 billion for 10 office buildings in the Los Angeles area, thereby doubling the size of its portfolio and solidifying its position as the top landlord for first-class office space in Southern California. In the biggest retail deal of 2005, a joint venture of Regency Centers Corporation and Macquarie CountryWide Trust paid $2.7 billion for 101 shopping centers in 17 states and the District of Columbia.

Buyers jostled in line for bulk purchases of hotels, shopping malls, casinos, office buildings, apartment complexes and raw land. Prices accelerated far faster than rents, even as profit margins got thinner. Expectations were that prices would climb still higher. It was as if the markets had broken loose from their tether to the boom-and-bust nature of capitalism. At least that is the way the lenders acted, as well as the rating agencies whose job it was to judge the viability of the financial architecture underpinning the deals. And nowhere was the real estate market as hot as it was in New York.

That summer, Beacon Capital Partners, in partnership with Lehman Brothers, outbid thirty rivals when it paid $1.52 billion for 1211 Avenue of the Americas, a thirty-three-year-old, forty-four-story office tower whose prime tenant was News Corporation, the mass media conglomerate headed by Rupert Murdoch. At $800 per square foot, analysts expected Beacon to lose money, at least in the short term, because the mortgage payments were likely to exceed cash flow from the building. But Beacon, like many investors, was supremely optimistic about the future and it was determined not to lose out again. Previously, Beacon had been an also-ran in the bidding for twenty-three-story 522 Fifth Avenue, at Forty-Third Street, a prize captured by Broadway Partners with a bid of $420 million.

Speyer and Galiano settled into a small fifteenth-floor conference room off the main reception area at Greenberg Traurig, soon to be joined by Tishman Speyer's lawyer, Jonathan L. Mechanic, and two associates. Stacom, whose blond hair floated halfway down her back and who had a fondness for dangling costume jewelry and Technicolor clothing, was already present with her partner William M. Shanahan, the numbers specialist for the duo. In a conference room down the hall sat Robert R. Merck, a senior managing director and chief of MetLife's real estate investment unit; David V. Politano, who oversaw MetLife's real estate investments in the Northeast; and their coterie of lawyers. The insurer was selling the sister complexes as a single real estate asset.

Much of the contract had been marked up and completed in the course of the bidding, but now the lawyers would take over, hammering out language that would cover every possible contingency. The shuttling between the two rooms went on through the night, as lawyers for Tishman Speyer and MetLife inserted clauses to protect their clients against any possible trouble.

In between, Speyer, Lieblich, Galiano and other executives in the conference room debated the latest revisions. During the prolonged interludes, they played poker, five-card draw. One of the young associates from Mechanic's law firm cleaned up, even as the others teased him about how his skinny black suit and tie made him look like a member of the late-1970s New Wave group Devo.

Finally, at about nine thirty in the morning on October 17, they finished. Speyer had a $400 million nonrefundable deposit wired to MetLife for the biggest real estate deal of all time. He and his partners agreed to pay an astounding $5.4 billion—$70 million more than the number two bidder—for a single asset.

But that was not the total price tag. When all the acquisition costs were tallied, the sum would total $6.3 billion. Ultimately, the money would come from banks, foreign and domestic pension funds, a foreign government and the Church of England. A tiny fraction of the money would come out of the well-lined pockets of Tishman Speyer or BlackRock. Both firms traditionally bought property with what is known in the business as OPM (other people's money). They largely made their money on fees—asset fees, management fees, partnership fees, construction fees—while putting up only a sliver of equity, if that. Of course, no pension fund or wealthy family would invest with Tishman Speyer or BlackRock simply for the privilege of paying fees if the firms did not consistently generate annual returns on the order of 20 percent. Of the total cost of $6.3 billion, Tishman Speyer put up only $56 million of the firm's own money, less than 1 percent of the winning bid, with another $56 million coming from their longtime partner, the Crown family of Chicago.

The deal immediately created a media storm of headlines

around the world, generating editorial comment from the Agence France-Presse, the *International Herald Tribune*, National Public Radio and Bill Maher at HBO.

The *New York Post* put it succinctly: "$5.4 Bil Stuy Town Deal Shatters Record." Rob told the tabloid that "the opportunity to buy 11,000 units in Manhattan is what you live for."

Elated but tired, Rob called his father, the real estate magnate Jerry I. Speyer, to deliver the news in a voice scratchy with fatigue. The elder Speyer congratulated him, heaping praise on a son who had forsaken a career in journalism to join his empire a decade earlier. Now his son was debuting on a very public stage.

"It's a dream come true," confided the elder Speyer, whose powerful reach extended from his company to the Federal Reserve Bank of New York, the Council on Foreign Relations, the Museum of Modern Art and the New York Yankees. He helped Michael R. Bloomberg successfully clear the legal and political hurdles to run for a third term as mayor in 2009 and both he and his son were close to Andrew Cuomo, who would become governor in 2010. "I expect he'll be far more successful than I was," Jerry Speyer said of his son. "He has great vision, wonderful people skills, and above all, he loves what he does."

The two men quickly divided up a list of courtesy calls, with Jerry taking Mayor Michael R. Bloomberg and Rob reaching out to Daniel R. Garodnick, a lifelong resident of Stuyvesant Town-Peter Cooper Village and a newly elected city councilman. Rob assured Garodnick, "There will be no dramatic shifts in the community's makeup, character or charm."

But Garodnick did not greet the news with the same breathless enthusiasm as the *New York Post*, Wall Street, city hall and the Speyers' fellow private equity moguls, who never seemed to want for cash for the next deal. Sure, MetLife would make

$3 billion after taxes, fourth-quarter profits would soar and its stock would hit a fifty-two-week high. Mayor Bloomberg would endorse the Speyers' takeover and Robert White, founder of Real Capital Analytics, a research and consulting firm, would declare Stuyvesant Town an "irreplaceable property," saying, "It would be impossible today to get a property of that scale in an urban location."

Garodnick, a smart, handsome, dark-haired lawyer who had grown up in the complexes, was not concerned about corporate profits. For nearly sixty years, Stuyvesant Town-Peter Cooper Village represented a relatively affordable opportunity for construction workers, firefighters, designers, small-business owners and others to live in ultra-expensive Manhattan and raise their children. But all that seemed to be in jeopardy during this real estate boom in 2006. The "average" two-bedroom, one-thousand-square-foot condominium in many Manhattan neighborhoods was selling for more than $1.2 million. Residential life in the borough was drifting increasingly outside the grasp of middle-class families.

Garodnick worried that the extraordinary price paid by the Speyers would force them to oust longtime residents in favor of younger, more well-heeled tenants willing to pay rents that were 30, 40 or 50 percent higher. He was at his office at 250 Broadway, across from city hall, when Rob Speyer called. The two men had never spoken before.

Unlike the other bidders, Speyer had not contacted the tenant association or Garodnick prior to buying the complex. Speyer was both cordial and polite, telling the councilman that Tishman Speyer had no plans to make radical changes in the way Stuyvesant Town was run. He assured Garodnick that his intention was to be a proper steward of the property and to do right by the twenty-five thousand current residents.

Garodnick was encouraged. Tishman Speyer, after all, had a well-burnished reputation and might be a better landlord than some of the other bidders. But after an exchange of pleasantries, he asked about specific terms. He asked what his plans were for preserving the long-term affordability of the complexes. He felt Rob avoided the question other than to say he was open to any ideas.

"I thought, 'This is going to be a problem,'" Garodnick recalled. "I wanted to hear their plan for long-term affordability, and he didn't have one. Their plan was the opposite of long-term affordability. He said there wouldn't be any major changes, but when we saw him raining legal notices on tenants we realized we were in for a struggle."

Rob Speyer's relationship with Garodnick would be a source of endless frustration. The son of a lawyer and a public school teacher, Garodnick's life and career were inextricably bound to Stuyvesant Town, where legions of MetLife security guards shooed children off the carefully cropped grass, while the playgrounds offered seemingly endless rounds of kick ball, punch ball, basketball and baseball. As a teenager, one neighbor in his building taught him gin rummy and another tutored him in Spanish. He couldn't imagine a better place to grow up.

There was, however, an original sin in the creation of this idyllic community back in the 1940s. After razing an entire neighborhood of hundreds of tenements, factories and shops, MetLife by 1947 displaced more than ten thousand city residents, most of whom were forced to seek shelter in substandard housing else-where in Manhattan because they could not afford even the reasonable rent at the new complexes. Moreover, MetLife very publicly refused to rent apartments to African-American and Hispanic families. A remarkable group of tenants and their sup-porters battled MetLife's discriminatory policies in the late 1940s, disrupting the regimented environment established by the insurance company. But it would be more than twenty years before more than a handful of minorities could call it home.

The twenty-five thousand tenants ranged from the now-elderly residents who moved into the complexes on opening day in 1947, to second-generation families, workers from nearby hospitals and newcomers with tots in tow, as well as recent graduates of New York University. The vast majority of resi-dents were protected by the city's rent regulations, which lim-ited rent hikes in any one year. That was what made Stuyvesant Town affordable for a middle-class couple raising children in Manhattan. In 2006, rent regulations were the fiercely guarded salvation of the original residents, many of whom lived on fixed pension and social security benefits.

While many of his contemporaries were playing basketball at Playground 9 or rounding the bases during a Little League game, Garodnick had spent hours in the smoky rooms of the Jefferson Democratic Club on East Twenty-First Street, across First Avenue from Stuyvesant Town-Peter Cooper Village. His desire to run for public office was born in those rooms on open-house nights, when local residents would arrive desperate for help with problems large and small. He recognized that his po-litical ambitions were tightly woven into the complex, whose residents voted in large numbers and almost always Democratic.

In the days after buying the complex, Rob Speyer also put in a call to Alvin D. Doyle, the tall, burly man with a salt-and-pepper brush mustache who headed the Stuyvesant Town-Peter Cooper Village Tenants Association. Like Garodnick, Doyle was a lifelong resident of the complexes. His mother and father, a newspaper reporter and a returning World War II veteran, were among the complex's original tenants.

Doyle's friends sometimes kiddingly called him "Fidel." He did not get the nickname because he delivered fiery, three-hour diatribes on the tenants' inevitable triumph over powerful landlords. It was simply a reference to his sixteen-year tenure as president of the tenants association, no easy task in a complex with 25,000 residents and perhaps 25,001 different opinions. But his calm, cautious and soft-spoken demeanor inspired trust and gave him the ability to bridge the gap between militant and more timid tenants.

He and Garodnick formed a Mutt and Jeff team on behalf of the tenants, with Doyle towering over the smaller Garodnick, who was nonetheless the more voluble character in this duo. On a brilliant fall afternoon a couple of years ago, Garodnick had stood next to a card table covered with leaflets on the grassy oval at the center of Stuyvesant Town, answering questions from dozens of tenants about the fate of the complex. As Garodnick patiently responded to every query, Doyle sat on a bench fifty feet away, consciously avoiding the spotlight. "I try to avoid it," Doyle explained. "I always thought you could get more done behind the scenes than you can get done in the spotlight."

Garodnick and the tenants association, its ranks ballooning with residents' fears of rent hikes and evictions, had enlisted support from New York's political establishment, including United States senators Charles Schumer and Hillary Clinton, Congresswoman Carolyn Maloney and city council speaker

Christine C. Quinn. Their political muscle helped the tenants association submit its own $4.5 billion bid for the property, despite MetLife's initial desire to lock them out of the sale process.

In a city of renters, the real estate boom in the early 2000s was prompting not only poor and working-class but also middle-class New Yorkers to wonder how much longer they could afford to make their home in one of the five boroughs. The real estate titans who had spent billions grabbing glamorous landmarks like the General Motors Building in New York and the Sears Tower in Chicago or building glassy condominium towers had turned their attention to brick, "meat-and-potatoes" tenements, unabashedly paying previously unheard of prices to unlock future profits as they accumulated thousands of apartments and boosted rents from New York to Chicago and San Francisco. In 2006, Mayor Michael R. Bloomberg would declare that MetLife had every right to sell Stuyvesant Town to the highest bidder, despite the very real public investment in the project by an earlier mayor, Fiorello H. La Guardia.

But many others decried the fact that easy credit and the real estate boom had turned a valuable urban resource, housing built with a sizable public investment for the middle class, into a commodity no different than corn futures. "Stuyvesant Town was a national model for middle-class people in an urban setting," said John H. Mollenkopf, director of the Center for Urban Research at the Graduate Center of the City University of New York. "It wouldn't have happened without eminent domain and favored tax treatment. It's disingenuous to say there's no public interest in what happens to housing."

Senator Charles Schumer sounded a similar theme when he addressed a tenant rally on the steps of city hall before the first bids were submitted. "When MetLife hung the 'for sale' sign on the doors of Peter Cooper Village and Stuyvesant Town, all New Yorkers, particularly those in the middle class, should have been troubled by the news," he said. "We need to do everything to preserve this vital stock of affordable housing."

The speculators and their Wall Street financiers, however, turned even their plain brick buildings into another commodity ripe for speculation. Perhaps the stage was set not long after MetLife converted in 2000 from a mutual company owned by policyholders to a corporation owned by stockholders with a keen eye on the bottom line. It was then that a plaque commemorating the vision of Frederick H. Ecker disappeared from the oval at the center of Stuyvesant Town. Ecker was the MetLife chairman who led the effort to build Stuyvesant Town and tens of thousands of other apartments in New York, Virginia and California for the middle class. The plaque's inscription harkened to a bygone era when Ecker and MetLife conceived of a project where "families of moderate means might live in health, comfort and dignity in park-like communities and that a pattern might be set of private enterprise productively devoted to public service."

So after a visit to see Rob Speyer at Tishman Speyer's impressive offices at Rockefeller Center, Doyle experienced as ominous a feeling as Garodnick had about the future of Stuyvesant Town and the tenants. Speyer asked Doyle and several other tenant leaders who were at the meeting to put aside their misgivings. "In another year, you guys will be happy how we turned things around," he said. "We pride ourselves on service."

Although Speyer exuded the confidence of a successful businessman, he did not allay their fears. "Other than saying he would turn the place around, he did not make any comments about searching for ways to keep the place affordable," Doyle recalled years later. "He really couldn't do that because he had to make the mortgage payments. We were cognizant of that fact."

From the beginning, Rob Speyer and the tenants were locked in a battle in which neither side ever spoke the same language as the greatest real estate deal of all time devolved over three years into one of the biggest business failures of all time. The tenants would file lawsuits, attack Rob Speyer for trying to evict what he claimed were unlawful tenants and even scorn his $19 million beautification program that introduced more trees, shrubs and perennials to the grounds.

At the same time, as tenants died or moved away, Speyer and his partners converted previously rent-regulated apartments to market rents, thus generating desperately needed revenue. They could not, however, convert enough apartments fast enough to cushion the crushing debt they had placed on the property. The legal battles, the landscaping and the conversions, which required more than $50,000 per apartment for installing granite countertops, stainless steel appliances and other renovations, all cost money, lots of it.

Instead of appreciating rapidly as his business plan predicted, the estimated value of Stuyvesant Town-Peter Cooper Village plummeted. In October 2006, Tishman Speyer and BlackRock valued the properties at $6.3 billion. Within two years, it was valued at $1.9 billion after the collapse on Wall Street in September 2008. The subsequent recession wiped out billions of investors' dollars. Rob Speyer and other moguls who bought and sold properties between 2005 and 2008 blame their gut-wrenching troubles on one of the most severe recessions in the country's history and a sharp 20 percent decline in the average rent in Manhattan.

After all, Tishman Speyer was in good company with other commercial and residential landlords who expanded rapidly in this period only to default on tens of billions of dollars in loans. Maguire Properties, once a dominant developer in Southern California, was crippled by the demise of the subprime mortgage industry in Orange County. In New York, the real estate mogul Harry B. Macklowe lost seven office towers he bought from Blackstone, along with the General Motors Building and much of his empire, after he was unable to refinance the $7 billion in short-term, high-interest debt he used to buy them. Well-regarded companies like the Extended Stay Hotels chain and the national shopping center developer General Growth Properties, which owned the South Street Seaport in New York, the Faneuil Hall Marketplace in Boston and Ala Moana Center in Honolulu, tumbled into bankruptcy under the weight of their recently accumulated debts.

But the Stuyvesant Town-Peter Cooper Village deal became the poster child for the first great economic bubble of the twenty-first century, a period in which tens of billions of dollars from insurance companies, pension funds and sovereign funds poured into real estate deals in every part of the country with the expectation that prices and values would soar forever, or at least until the property could be sold at a fat profit.

The collapse of the Stuyvesant Town-Peter Cooper Village deal and a legion of other celebrated deals from that era were brought on by far more than the vagaries of the real estate market.

Buyers were indiscriminate. They wanted trophy office buildings, see-through glass apartment towers designed by starchitects, shopping centers, golf courses and even a bunch of red brick tenement-like buildings at Stuyvesant Town.

The $6.3 billion acquisition, like so many at the time, required a financial leap of faith and a total disregard for worst-case scenarios by buyers, lenders and investors. Buyers once priced properties based on a multiple of existing cash flow. By that calculus, real estate experts said that the two Manhattan complexes would have generated a $3 billion or even $3.5 billion price. But buyers were operating in the Wall Street casino.

Buyers were looking to the future, building models of anticipated cash flow. Tishman Speyer and BlackRock's winning $5.4 billion bid, and even the tenant association's own $4.5 billion offer, reflected the new math. They did not expect a profit for years to come. The business plan projected that income would triple to $330.9 million by 2011, mainly by converting rent-regulated apartments to market rents. But almost every single assumption in their pro forma calculations proved wrong. Net income amounted to only $138 million in 2009, less than half the $284.4 million in annual loan payments on the $4.4 billion in debt ladled onto the property.

Wall Street was only too happy to fuel a speculative deal that required lenders and investors to believe that everything would go according to plan. Everyone was in on it. For a fee, the banks provided billions of dollars in mortgages for property with cash flow that did not even begin to cover the payments on interest-only loans. Instead of holding the loans on their balance sheets, Goldman Sachs, Lehman Brothers, Merrill Lynch, Wachovia and other banks bundled a set of individual mortgages and transferred them to a trust, which issued bonds or securities. The securities, in turn, got a seal of approval from Fitch Ratings, Moody's Investors Service and Standard & Poor's, bond rating agencies paid by the banks, and were sold to investors for still more fees. With no stake in the mortgage, the banks had little financial incentive to ensure that the deal made sense and the borrower could repay the debt. Instead of profits, the biggest real estate deal in history ended in default, which, if you were objectively looking at the deal at the time it was made, was the most likely outcome by far.

The apartment complexes, hotels, shopping centers and golf courses financed and refinanced during the boom ultimately changed hands after emerging from bankruptcy court. But deals like the one at Stuyvesant Town-Peter Cooper Village also tore at the social fabric of cities like New York, where working and even middle-class tenants increasingly found themselves priced out of a market as longtime affordable havens became targets of speculation. The pension funds that poured money into Stuyvesant Town-Peter Cooper Village essentially cooperated in displacing residents who were very much like their own pensioners: municipal clerks, teachers, police officers and small-business owners. The tenants in New York and investors from Florida to California, England and Singapore would feel the consequences from a roller-coaster ride in real estate values that would rival anything at a Coney Island amusement park. The losses by public employee pension funds would ripple into city budgets and the lives of retired teachers whose retirement funds faced life-altering shortfalls.

The story of New York City throughout the centuries is by and large the story of real estate. Even the epic social history of Stuyvesant Town-Peter Cooper Village and the extraordinary financial deal of 2006 fit into that story line. But, as we shall see, the Wall Street financiers and many deep-pocketed investors could be a forgiving bunch. Especially when the deals are done with other people's money. Even as Jerry and Rob Speyer wrote off their $56 million investment in Stuyvesant Town-Peter Cooper Village and walked away from the property in 2010, their company had already raised over $2 billion for a new real estate fund. A company spokesman was emphatic: the default had no effect on Tishman Speyer. Their partner also came out unscathed. By the last quarter of 2010, BlackRock, the world's largest asset manager, reported record earnings.

CHAPTER ONE

"Negroes and Whites Don't Mix"

On April 18, 1943, New York Mayor Fiorello H. La Guardia opened his regular Sunday-afternoon radio broadcast on WNYC with what he acknowledged was tough talk about speculators and food chiselers. He was unsparing in his vitriol for anyone who would overcharge for produce, potatoes, pork, eggs and butter in a city whose citizens were struggling to make ends meet while war raged in Europe, North Africa and the Pacific.

His own inspectors had found a half-smoked ham, shank end, bone-in, selling for fifty-nine cents a pound, seventeen cents a pound above the price ceiling set by wartime regulators. And to make matters worse, he said the ham was short-weighted. It was but one of three hundred and eighty-eight violations uncovered by the city's Department of Markets. Three hundred and seventy-eight violators had already paid their fines, the mayor assured his listeners.

"Anyone who willfully and intentionally and deliberately chisels or profiteers on foods is just a bad citizen," La Guardia warned. "He's a disloyal citizen and we won't have him in our midst and we don't want him in business."[1]

He also had a word of advice for frugal housewives looking to save every penny they could: save your egg box so you can bring it back with you to the store. The grocer was allowed to charge two cents for either the egg safety box or the regular square box.

Midway through the broadcast, La Guardia turned to the problem of housing, a topic of immense interest to the many New Yorkers desperate for a place to live. During the race to build the world's tallest building in the 1930s, New York saw the rise of skyscrapers, from the seventy-story office tower at 40 Wall Street downtown to the seventy-story 30 Rockefeller Plaza, the seventy-seven-story Chrysler Building, the one-hundred-and-two-story Empire State Building. Even by the 1920s, New York had nearly a thousand buildings eleven to twenty stories tall, ten times as many as Chicago, and fifty-one between twenty-one and sixty stories. They were clustered in midtown, especially around Grand Central Terminal, and downtown.

But they loomed far above the cramped, low-slung four-, six- and ten-story buildings in which most New Yorkers lived. The garment factories, warehouses and tenements that squatted on the West Side, from Hell's Kitchen to Chelsea, served the rail lines and the bustling piers along the waterfront. On the Lower East Side, tens of thousands of factory workers made their homes in cramped, old-style tenements where light and sanitary conditions were often hard to come by. And there never seemed to be enough housing for the steady stream of immigrants who made their way year after year to what was then a largely blue-collar city.

With vacant apartments a rarity throughout the city, couples across all class lines were forced to double up with their families and friends, some in substandard housing. La Guardia had a very personal and deeply held commitment to improve the city's housing stock that was rooted in the death by tuberculosis of his first wife, Thea, and their only child in 1921. By 1943, his administration had outlined a $110 million program to build modern apartments for low-income tenants as soon as the war ended.

But what he wanted to talk about that day was an unprecedented plan for a nicely landscaped, middle-class community in a dilapidated corner of the city known as the Gas House District, a drab, eighteen-block stretch from Fourteenth to Twentieth Streets, between First Avenue and Avenue C, filled with factories, bathhouses, flimsy tenements, small businesses and the gas tanks that lent the neighborhood its distinct and unpleasant odor. La Guardia and his building czar, Robert Moses, had spent several disappointing years trying to find a willing partner among the city's powerful financial institutions who could match his grand vision. Now he had one: Frederick H. Ecker, the seventy-five-year-old chairman of the world's largest insurance company, Metropolitan Life.

"Today I am very happy to announce a rehabilitation of a real blighted area in Lower Manhattan," La Guardia told his radio audience. "There will be a reconstruction of this area as a residential community."[2]

Metropolitan Life, the mayor said, would redevelop the seventy-two-acre site, building thousands of apartments for twenty-five thousand middle-class residents, nearly three times the number of people then living in the area. The mayor reassured existing residents that there would be "no dispossessing or no tearing down of existing buildings during the war." Construction would start afterward. The city would accommodate low-income tenants at municipal housing projects and assist higher-income residents in finding suitable apartments elsewhere.

Metropolitan, as it was then known, would soon christen the project Stuyvesant Town, a historical reference to old New York and the farm nearby that Peter Stuyvesant III, great-grandson of the Dutch governor, had carved out of the quiet woodlands in the late 1700s.

That same day, Ecker, a small, stocky man who wore wire-framed glasses and a precisely clipped mustache, told reporters that the plan was a step in the direction of a new Manhattan, "one in which wholesomeness of residential environment will combine with existing convenience to anchor families, especially those with children, to this borough."

At a cost of up to $50 million, the insurer planned to erect thirty-five thirteen-story buildings on lushly landscaped terrain with trees, playgrounds and paths, "such as many suburbs do not possess." Its proximity to midtown offered walk-to-work possibilities, added a press release from Metropolitan.

There is "an opportunity for private investment that will restore the residential values of the land," Ecker said. "Reconstruction can be accomplished on a sound, economic basis. It should have the effect of protecting Manhattan's position as a borough in which families with children can enjoyably and profitably live. It should promote the welfare of the city as a whole." [3]

La Guardia concluded his housing announcement by thanking Ecker and taking a jab at the city's other insurance companies, which had resisted his pleas to address the city's housing crisis. He thanked Metropolitan for providing "this very useful housing unit for our city. . . . It is not only a vision, it is prudence and good business and may I say in all kindliness to the New

York Life and Equitable Life and Mutual Life, that they should look into this housing proposition and the advantages it offers and they should also provide as much at least as the Metropolitan Life is doing in the area I have just described."[4]

The other insurers would never match Metropolitan's investment in urban housing. But now that La Guardia had finally found a willing partner he did not want to waste any time. Prior to the announcement, he and his aides drew up a schedule that set a record for municipal planning even by 1940s standards. It called for the planning commission to assess and approve the project in early May and the city's powerful Board of Estimate to give a final stamp of approval two days later, less than two months after Stuyvesant Town was first announced to the public.

Moses warned La Guardia in a memo that the development could be slowed by "some pretty mean critics on the outside—the real radical housing boys, who don't want private capital horning into their field."

The next day the mayor was unequivocal in his instructions to city officials. "I want no controversy on this subject," the mayor wrote in a terse note to city planning commissioner Edwin A. Salmon, five days after his radio show. "This is not Washington. This is New York. There will be no disagreement on this."[5]

But critics descended on La Guardia, Moses and Metropolitan and slowed their fast-paced schedule, albeit only by weeks. Urban planners and civic groups blasted the project for its unprecedented level of subsidies in the form of free public land and property tax breaks, its design as a "medieval walled city" and the lack of community facilities at a complex as large as Peekskill, New York, or Danbury, Connecticut. In order to gain maximum control over the property, Ecker did not want any public facilities—schools, churches or libraries—within its boundaries that might attract outsiders and the poor people who lived south of the complex, on the Lower East Side.

Ecker was not interested in flamboyant architecture. His architects designed buildings less for their aesthetic qualities than for practical economics. At twelve and thirteen stories, the buildings were more than twice the height of most tenements on the nearby Lower East Side. But the height allowed for more apartments, and a greater rent stream, to share the cost of creating the complex. The unrelenting uniformity of the buildings allowed construction to proceed swiftly and economically.

City officials agreed to provide what would become one-fifth of the land and to freeze property taxes for a quarter-century at relatively low pre-demolition levels, allowing MetLife to save millions of dollars a year. Most important, the city would use one of its most sweeping powers, eminent domain, to condemn land that MetLife could not purchase from private owners. Traditionally, cities and states used eminent domain to acquire property for schools, hospitals, highways and other public uses. Critics were alarmed that La Guardia had expanded the use of the power to benefit a wealthy corporation.

The debate exploded after Ecker publicly revealed exactly who would not be eligible for his company's grand version of suburban living within the urban grid. As he left a city planning commission hearing on May 19, 1943, he told a reporter for the *New York Post* that Negroes would be barred from Stuyvesant Town. "Negroes and whites don't mix," he told the reporter. "Perhaps they will in a hundred years but they don't now. If we brought them into this development, it would be to the detriment of the city, too, because it would depress all the surrounding property."[6]

Time and again, Ecker would say his position was a product of "business and economics, and not of racial prejudice."

By June, a young city councilman and minister from Harlem, Adam Clayton Powell, called for La Guardia's impeachment over Metropolitan's discriminatory policies at the city-backed Stuyvesant Town project before a roaring crowd of twenty thousand at the Freedom Rally in Madison Square Garden.

Ecker, like many employees at the Metropolitan, was a lifer who worked at the company for his entire career. Born in 1867 in Phoenicia, New York, a small village in the Catskills, he was the son of John Christian Ecker, a decorated Civil War veteran, and grandson of Jacob P. Ecker, a staff officer for one of Napoleon's generals. He graduated from public school in Brooklyn at fifteen and went to work for a law firm in the same downtown building at Park Place and Church Street that served as the home office for Metropolitan Life, a firm that had been founded in two rented rooms in a building on Broadway in Lower Manhattan the same year he was born.

Impressed by the prosperous appearance of the insurance executives, Ecker wrote a letter to Metropolitan asking for a job. "Knowing that you know of a situation for a boy," he wrote to an assistant to the president of the insurance company, "and being desirous of obtaining one, I will with your permission apply for it.

"I would like to get a position where I would have a good chance of advancement," he added.[7]

Ecker landed a job in the mailroom, paying $4 for a fifty-four-hour week, less than what he was getting at the law firm. But he was looking to the future. Metropolitan had grown swiftly since its early days insuring Civil War sailors and soldiers against disabilities due to wartime wounds and accidents and a searing recession that nearly crippled the company. But it soon focused on providing life insurance expressly for the middle class.

A tiny company, Metropolitan initially had to contend with the industry's Big Three: Equitable Life Assurance Society of the United States, New York Life Insurance and Mutual Life Insurance of New York. The company adopted a British program of selling "industrial" or "workingmen's" insurance policies, an area largely ignored in the United States because of the necessity and expense of sustaining an army of agents to sell policies door-to-door and to make the weekly rounds collecting five- and ten-cent premiums. Under Ecker's leadership, Metropolitan sold policies to both white and black families. Despite having more than one hundred thousand policyholders in Harlem alone, however, the company's workforce was entirely white.

The company imported English agents to train its workforce and was soon signing up seven hundred new policies a day. By the turn of the century, Metropolitan dominated industrial insurance, claiming 49 percent of the American market. By 1920 it had surged ahead of the "Big Three" in terms of assets under its control.

The methodical, soft-spoken Ecker rose rapidly within the Metropolitan. At twenty-five, Ecker ran the company's bond and mortgage department. Fourteen years later, in 1906, he was chief financial officer, overseeing all of the company's assets. He was elected vice president in 1919, president in 1924 and chairman in 1936.

Although Ecker could shoot a round of golf under 100, he was a man who lived to work. "I don't think anybody yet has invented a pastime that's as much fun, or keeps you as young, as a good job," he once told an interviewer.[8]

"Some people talk nowadays as if work is just something to be endured for the leisure it buys us," Ecker added. "I look at it just the opposite. I would be willing to endure quite a bit of leisure, if I had to, for the pleasure of working."

It was Ecker who led the giant insurer into real estate development. Like other insurance companies, Metropolitan invested in commercial and residential mortgages. But during the depression of 1893, Metropolitan got stuck with wide swaths of urban real estate, after it was forced to foreclose on scores of bad loans. Ecker, then in the real estate department, made a reputation for himself by rehabilitating and selling foreclosed properties. Over time, he was put in charge of the company's entire real estate portfolio and became an expert on building construction, market trends and real estate values.

In the early 1920s, Ecker and Metropolitan were ready to get involved in development. Their decision was spurred by the passage of new state laws designed to address a chronic housing shortage that had plagued the city since the end of World War I by encouraging insurers to invest a portion of their assets in housing production. Under the laws, new housing complexes were exempt from real estate taxes for ten years as long as the rents did not exceed $9 per month per room.

Metropolitan plunged in, spending $7.5 million to buy three

sites in Long Island City, Queens, to build 54 five-story walk-up apartment buildings with 2,125 apartments. A shrewd businessman, Ecker focused on locations easily accessible from Manhattan. Given the size of the project, Ecker also sought to achieve an economy of scale, while providing better housing for the middle class.

He imported brick from the Netherlands and Belgium at two-thirds the cost of local brick and purchased bathtubs at below-market prices. The buildings may not have been architecturally striking, but the apartments, though small, had a standard size and were designed to provide generous natural light and cross-ventilation, two things sorely missing in much of the city's older housing stock. Rents, at $9 per room, included two items not ordinarily found in mass housing: steam heat and hot water.

The apartments were an instant hit and filled quickly when they opened in 1924. During the Depression, Metropolitan was forced to drop the rent to $8.35 a room in order to maintain a high occupancy rate. In other words, tenants paid $36 a month for a two-bedroom apartment with a kitchen and bath. Still, the company noted, Ecker's Long Island City apartment buildings generated an impressive return of 8 to 9 percent, before depreciation, during the ten-year tax exemption.

Ecker's twin goals of public good and corporate profit were consistent with the company's long-standing philosophy. Dating back to its early years, Metropolitan saw the fortunes of the company as inextricably linked to the health and welfare of the middle class and the national economy. As a result, Metropolitan engaged in public health campaigns, including a seven-year demonstration project against tuberculosis in Framingham, Massachusetts, that enlisted every local club, church and civic organization in a successful effort to reduce the ravages of the country's number one killer.[9]

It encouraged healthy exercise among its employees, building one of the first gyms for office workers at its newly established headquarters on Madison Avenue and Twenty-Third Street. The company also issued a steady stream of pamphlets for its employees and policyholders covering everything from clean milk and personal hygiene to citizenship. Given that Metropolitan insured one out of three urban residents, *Business Week* concluded dryly that the "provision of better living conditions for city folks must accordingly improve the company's mortality experience and annual earnings."

During the Depression, Ecker negotiated two of the largest mortgages ever made, a $27.5 million loan to finance construction of the Empire State Building in 1929 and a $44.9 million mortgage for John D. Rockefeller Jr.'s vast office complex, Rockefeller Center, in 1931. The company went on to place 51 percent of its total assets in government bonds during World War II, making it the largest private contributor to the war effort.

But housing development held a special allure for Ecker. *Fortune* magazine described his approach this way in a 1946 article: "A great many years ago Mr. Ecker became intrigued with the idea that if life insurance funds could be made available for housing projects so planned as to eliminate the speculative element, Metropolitan might gain an advantageous new field for the investment of funds and at the same time be making an additional contribution to public welfare by supplying an existing need in housing—to say nothing of stimulating employment via the building industry."[10]

Fresh from his success building apartment buildings in Queens, Ecker and Metropolitan embarked in April 1938 on a more audacious plan to create the largest housing project ever built by the federal government or private enterprise, Parkchester. Ecker announced that Metropolitan had bought 129 acres in the East Bronx, most of it from the New York Catholic Protectory, in order to build 171 buildings, with 12,271 apartments.

"The area acquired is one of the largest single undeveloped properties within the greater city," Ecker said in describing his evolving vision of housing development. "Its size will permit the planning of a completely balanced community containing all facilities for family life, including necessary stores, schools, churches, parks, playgrounds and opportunities for recreational and social life. The development will be the largest integral housing project so far planned and built in this country. It will not only help in supplying the existing need for housing at moderate rents, but it will provide continuous employment to the building trades and construction industry for three years."[11]

Again, Metropolitan's venture was fueled with substantial government assistance, something rarely mentioned in modern accounts or when the company later moved to sell the properties. This was a joint effort by the private sector and government. The city granted Metropolitan substantial subsidies and incentives in order to get the company to build badly needed housing for the middle class, while the La Guardia administration and the federal government built housing projects for poor and working-class residents. The company, in turn, was able to make a tidy profit addressing a social problem. The legislature in 1938 amended state insurance statutes, permitting life insurance companies to invest up to 10 percent of their assets in housing construction. The insurers could create a limited-profit corporation to build the housing in return for special tax breaks.

In anticipation of the legislation, Metropolitan announced that it was willing to invest $100 million in housing.

Fortune estimated that Metropolitan earned a net return of 4 percent, after amortization, on its $62 million investment at Parkchester, better than the 3 percent generated by many of the company's bonds and other investments.[12]

"From the investment standpoint, Metropolitan's housing projects are attractive because they have enabled the company to put a small portion of its assets (3 percent presently, with a legal maximum of 10 percent) into properties that have been handsomely hedged against obsolescence and deterioration and afford excellent prospects of netting 4 percent for many years to come."[13]

It's no wonder that La Guardia and Moses would form what would become known decades later as a public-private partnership with Metropolitan. Ecker was at the helm of the country's largest private corporation and the world's largest life insurance company, with $6 billion in assets and 31 million policyholders. Under his leadership, Metropolitan was in the midst of its own residential building boom at a time when there was little new construction anywhere else in the country. Moses, the city's master builder, who did not tolerate critics or fools, once described Ecker as "exceedingly able, experienced, shrewd, hardboiled and conservative."[14]

Not only had Ecker completed Parkchester, which had 30,000 residents, a larger population than Elkhart, Indiana; he announced plans for Parkmerced, 3,483 apartments on 206 acres near Lake Merced in San Francisco; Park La Brea, 4,253 apartments in a series of buildings stretching across 173 acres of what is now the Miracle Mile district in Los Angeles; and Park-fairfax, 1,684 town house units on 202 acres outside Washington, DC.

La Guardia also set a torrid pace when it came to building housing for the city's poorest citizens. He used city, state and federal funds to build 14 low-rent housing projects for 17,040 families at a cost of $90.4 million in the decade between 1934 and 1943. As the city evolved, he wanted to replace dangerous, substandard housing as well as the warehouses and factories that served the now-defunct piers on the East Side. He vowed that his postwar housing program, which included the Jacob Riis Houses, the Lillian Wald Houses on the Lower East Side and the Alfred E. Smith Houses in the shadow of the Brooklyn Bridge, would "put every city in this country to shame."

But his ambitions extended beyond that. What he had in mind was not simply erecting a housing development in a relatively remote part of the Bronx. La Guardia wanted to clear away broad swaths of the city's slums and anchor the middle class to the urban core. He was convinced that he needed the private sector to do it. The La Guardia administration had sponsored a series of state laws, including the Redevelopment Companies Law of 1942, that sought to encourage savings banks and insurance companies to get into the housing business. Moses spent three fruitless years wooing insurers, before lengthy negotiations with New York Life president George L. Harrison collapsed. The company's board voted against taking on the risk of housing development, despite the company's having lobbied for the Redevelopment Companies Law.[15]

La Guardia and Moses turned to Ecker at Metropolitan, who proved to be more receptive. But Ecker wanted certain economic assurances before he would agree to a deal. So Moses went to the state legislature in March 1943 with an amendment to the recently adopted Redevelopment Companies Law that was specifically tailored to assuage Ecker and guarantee a deal to build Stuyvesant Town.

Under the new legislation, the La Guardia administration granted Metropolitan a heavy platter of benefits. The city agreed to limit public oversight, to use the power of eminent domain on behalf of Metropolitan to acquire the land and to give Metropolitan unprecedented control over the selection of tenants. The amendment granted project oversight to the state superintendent of insurance and the city's Board of Estimate, leaving the City Planning Commission with only a minor role. The city also contributed nearly twelve publicly owned acres, or 19 percent of the total land, for the project.

It provided a twenty-five-year tax exemption worth an estimated $53 million. During the twenty-five-year exemption, which froze the tax assessment at pre-demolition levels, $13.5 million, Metropolitan agreed to limit its annual profit to 6 percent and to set monthly rents at $14 per room.

Critics like Charles Abrams, a housing reformer and a prominent civic leader, excoriated the mayor for his "lavish" gifts to Metropolitan.

"With all this expenditure," Abrams wrote in *The Nation*, "not a single slum dweller is actually to be rehoused. The present residents of the area are to be crowded into other slums, making them more profitable for the owners and stabilizing the mortgages of the very institutions which are most vociferous in acclaiming the Stuyvesant Town formula. All the city gets in return is a walled-in town . . ."[16]

At the time the legislation was approved, La Guardia confided that he had doubts about the provisions that ceded so much authority to Metropolitan. Moses convinced La Guardia that he needed the private sector for slum clearance, and after years of failed efforts to engage the city's powerful insurance companies in building middle-class housing, the mayor was unwilling to accept defeat. "The purpose of the bill, however, is of such great importance that I have resolved the doubt in favor of the bill," La Guardia continued. "The immediate practical problem is housing or no housing. The answer is in favor of housing."

La Guardia, Moses and Ecker set a speedy timetable for the project because the negotiations for the deal had already taken place in complete secrecy and La Guardia, who ran a powerful mayoralty, had lined up the votes with the help of Moses, the parks commissioner and the city's chief planner and construction coordinator, whom few councilmen dared to cross for fear of losing a favorite public project in their district.

Yet, after it was announced, Stuyvesant Town came under immediate attack. Some property owners filed a lawsuit in state supreme court claiming that the government's use of eminent domain to take private property on behalf of a private developer was unconstitutional. Few civic groups, unions or tenant organizations, however, challenged the notion of slum clearance, which required the demolition of five hundred buildings in the Gas House District and the displacement of hundreds of businesses and eleven thousand working-class tenants, in favor of a middle-class development. The project site stretched over eighteen city blocks, from Fourteenth Street to Twentieth Street, between First Avenue and Avenue C.

Abrams, an influential figure in New York's civic circles, continued to rail against the public-private partnership, which, he argued, amounted to a public subsidy for private profit, given the lavish concessions awarded to Metropolitan. Further, he said, the incentives were also a public subsidy for housing discrimination.[17] His argument against public-private partnerships, as well as the use of eminent domain on behalf of a private party, is as familiar today as it was in the 1940s.

Abrams highlighted the dangers of business that "assumes the function of a body politic without being responsible for the social obligations to which a body politic is subject" during Housing Week in May 1944.

The opposition, including the Citizens Housing Council, an advocacy group formed in 1937 that included housing experts, civic reformers, builders and landlords, listed a series of "undesirable elements," including the density of the project and the lack of a public school, as well as the extraordinary level of benefits—eminent domain and valuable, long-term tax exemptions—granted to a private company. The group, which later changed its name to the Citizens Housing and Planning Council, questioned why the La Guardia administration had expanded the city's list of redevelopment areas to include the land sought by Metropolitan north of Fourteenth Street. In a city where much of the housing consisted of four-to-six-story tenements, critics said Stuyvesant Town would be uncomfortably crowded, at 445 to 594 persons per acre, depending on how you counted, compared with the city's maximum allowance of 416 per acre.

The Housing Council and the American Civil Liberties Union, the Citizens Union, the American Labor Party, the American Jewish Congress, various unions and the NAACP also objected to Metropolitan's plans for a segregated complex. Ecker met privately with Harold S. Buttenheim and other members of the Housing Council on May 10, when he gave an inkling of the company's approach. Asked why Metropolitan had not included a school within the complex, Ecker stated, as Buttenheim later revealed, that "as one of the determining factors, that the Company desires to restrict the use of the entire area to its own tenants to the greatest extent practicable, and that if there were a public school in the project the City would allow some children, including Negroes, to attend from outside the area."[18]

Stanley M. Isaacs, the city council's sole Republican and a leading member of the City-Wide Committee on Harlem, testified at the hearing that the project would create a "medieval walled city privately owned, in the heart of New York," a phrase that was quickly adopted by the opposition and newspaper headline writers. Prentice Thomas of the NAACP declared at the hearing that unless a nondiscriminatory clause was written into the contract his organization would oppose the project.[19]

The next day, May 20, the Planning Commission voted five to one in favor of Stuyvesant Town, with the sole opponent, Lawrence M. Orton, saying he would have voted with the majority if Metropolitan had included a school.

Two weeks later, the city's Board of Estimate voted eleven-to-five in favor of Stuyvesant Town, after a raucous three-and-a-half-hour hearing in which twenty-four opponents argued that Metropolitan should be blocked from discriminating against Negroes because Stuyvesant Town was a public project by virtue of receiving a twenty-five-year tax exemption and the right of eminent domain. Assemblyman William T. Andrews read into the record a letter from George Gove, Metropolitan's director of housing, stating that "no provision has been made for Negro families" in the project.[20]

Henry Epstein, a former state solicitor general, predicted in

1943 that Stuyvesant Town would be "a new style ghetto" if it was permitted to exclude tenants based on race. "Today, with Stuyvesant Town, it will be the Negroes, the next day the Jews, the next day the Catholics and the next the undesirable aliens, whoever they wish to call them. This is what Hitler stands for, the superiority of one race against the other."[21]

For his part, Ecker rejected the notion that his policy was the result of racism. "Today, it is my personal opinion that an invitation to Negroes to apply for apartments in a neighborhood which is, and always has been, occupied by white people will result in depreciation of the property and neighborhood, serious differences between and among tenants and unfortunate incidents which would imperil the investment in the enterprise and its financial security."[22]

The battle galvanized residents of Harlem, which, like Detroit, Boston, Chicago and other cities, was in the midst of a great migration of African-Americans from the South to the North, where they hoped to find jobs and prosperity. The *Amsterdam News*, a black weekly based in Harlem, noted that Metropolitan had long scorned Negroes, well more than two million of whom held life insurance policies with the company. Yet, the insurer did not employ any Negro sales agents at its thirteen hundred offices, not even the one in Harlem where there were one hundred thousand policyholders.

Publicly, Moses was largely silent on the issue of racial discrimination, preferring to cast the battle as one between the pragmatists who sought to transform the slums versus the impractical or dishonest dreamers who opposed discrimination. "Those who would insist upon making projects of this kind a battleground for the vindication of social objectives, however desirable, and who persist in claiming that a private project is in fact a public project, obviously are looking for a political issue and not for results in the form of actual slum clearance.

"If the city were to insist upon ideal conditions, this project would be wholly unsound from the point of view of prudent investment."[23]

Throughout his career, Moses had at the very least accepted, if not promoted, racial discrimination in the building and operation of city and state parks. He had also blocked public works projects in Harlem. In the Stuyvesant Town fight, he privately advised the insurance company on how to defend itself against several lawsuits. At the same time, Moses blamed not Ecker but his advisers for Metropolitan's racial policy. He told New York lieutenant governor Frank C. Moore that his friend Ecker might be persuaded to relent on the "discrimination question" at Stuyvesant Town. He suggested that Ecker had "some very poor advisers," namely his son and heir apparent, Fred Ecker Jr., and George Gove, Metropolitan's executive vice president.[24] But there is no evidence that Moses himself ever pressed Ecker on the issue.

During the Board of Estimate meeting, only Ecker and Moses, who both dismissed their critics as demagogues and leftists, spoke in favor of the project. Moses downplayed the subsidies for Metropolitan, saying the concessions were "the minimum inducements necessary" to attract private capital to engage in slum clearance. He offered a take-it-or-leave-it proposition.

"If you don't want this contract," said the combative Moses, "I can assure you that it will be the last opportunity we'll have to attract private capital. It will mark the death knell of slum clearance by private enterprise."[25]

The *New York Times* and the *New York Herald-Tribune* concurred in subsequent editorials, without mentioning the color line imposed at the complexes. "Stuyvesant Town by now is presumably a closed subject, and closed the right way, too, in the opinion of a good many of us," the *Times* said. "The heart of the matter was expressed by Robert Moses, who has a habit of going to the heart of a good many things. Do we want to enlist private capital in behalf of slum removal and rehousing, or don't we."[26]

It certainly seemed as if the issue of racial discrimination was a closed subject. The state's highest court, the court of appeals, ruled in favor of Stuyvesant Town, rejecting a lawsuit brought by property owners claiming that the Redevelopment Companies Law was unconstitutional. A second lawsuit, brought by the Citizens Housing Council and other civic groups, including the United Tenants League of Greater New York, the ACLU and the Congress of Industrial Organizations, met a similar fate.

Many of La Guardia's supporters found his support for discrimination at Stuyvesant Town puzzling. La Guardia, who was well-known in civil rights circles locally and nationally, certainly did not fit the picture of a Southern segregationist. In June 1942, he had been instrumental in getting President Franklin D. Roosevelt to issue Executive Order 8802, the Fair Employment Act, which banned discriminatory employment practices by federal agencies and all unions and companies engaged in war-related work. And almost 15 percent of the tenants at the city housing projects built by La Guardia were black, although African-Americans comprised less than 7 percent of the population.

Even as Adam Clayton Powell very publicly condemned La Guardia as a hypocrite, Walter White of the NAACP sent a "personal and confidential" letter to La Guardia that desperately sought to understand the mayor's reasoning.

> Dear Mayor La Guardia:
>
> I wonder if you would let me know your reasons for approving the Stuyvesant Town project? I am sure they must be good ones and I know personally that they are honest ones.
>
> Deputy Mayor McGahen's casting of your three votes announcing your approval of the project, which, as you know proposes to exclude Negroes, puzzles me. Knowing of the long-time friendship which you and I have enjoyed, a number of people have asked me about your position on this project. I have refrained from expressing any opinion until I could first learn from you your reasons for approval. If you would rather I come in to talk with you, let me know and I will arrange my schedule accordingly.
>
> That was a swell party you and Mrs. La Guardia gave yesterday. I enjoyed it as did Gladys.[27]

There is no question that on the eve of signing a contract for Stuyvesant Town with Ecker, La Guardia was burning with the friction between his progressive personal beliefs and Ecker's discriminatory policies. The nation's simmering racial tensions were further brought into relief by a series of riots in 1943, culminating on June 20 in Detroit, where forty people were killed and seven hundred injured during a conflagration that lasted almost two days and saw $2 million worth of property destroyed. New York did not escape the unrest. A white police officer shot a black soldier in uniform on a Harlem street corner two months later, touching off a riot in which six people died, hundreds were injured and many white-owned stores were laid in ruin.

In a letter to La Guardia dated July 26, 1943, Ecker was unwavering in his position that Metropolitan must control tenant selection. His words were couched in the polite language of a prudent banker rather than a bigot's vitriol. "We shall rent to applicants solely on the basis of the standard which must govern a fiduciary's prudent investment in the particular neighborhood in which Stuyvesant Town, Inc. is located."[28]

La Guardia responded in a letter five days later.

> I deem it proper at this time also, because of the discussion, statements and even gossip during the course of the consideration of this project, and at hearings and even in judicial proceedings, to say that I consider this particular project as having a certain public obligation different from and greater than a like project financed entirely by private funds without any tax exemption or right of condemnation or other privileges. The standards or conditions or requirements for tenancy in a housing unit aided by the City through statutory authorization, as is the case in Stuyvesant Town, must be applicable to all. In other words, any person meeting all the requirements should not be barred because of belonging to any particular racial group. There can be no discrimination in tenant selection based on prejudice or contrary to any provisions of our state constitution or state law. If, after operating of the Stuyvesant Town is started, there should be any litigation or proceedings for

> judicial adjudication on the question of barring ten-
> ants who are otherwise qualified solely because of dis-
> crimination or solely because of racial prejudice, you
> should know now that I will take a position as above
> indicated.[29]

The handwritten notation "Not sent" is scrawled across the top of the letter. But there was a lively exchange of back-channel communications between Ecker and La Guardia that ran through Moses, who strongly urged Metropolitan's chairman to resist the mayor's last-minute attempt to ban discrimination. The exchange suggests that La Guardia had second thoughts about sending his letter because he feared that Ecker would scuttle the entire deal. Ecker's response to the mayor's unsent letter came in the form of a five-page "draft" letter that was marked "Not sent by Mr Ecker." Both letters made their way into Moses's files.

Ecker, who began by acknowledging the mayor's letter, was irate that La Guardia sought to completely "change the contract and to impose new conditions." La Guardia, Ecker pointed out, had drafted legislation and urged the governor to sign it giving Metropolitan full control over tenant selection at Stuyvesant Town despite strenuous objections from "persons who de-manded that the law include a provision for public control over the selection of tenants, and a clause to prevent any possible discrimination."

Finally, he delivered a threat that La Guardia could not with-stand.

> Under these circumstances I am compelled to
> state to you that I cannot sign the contract between

the City and Stuyvesant Town Inc. since you have put
a cloud on the contract by your interpretation of
it . . . I believe I am not exaggerating when I say that
your action in this matter ends all possibility of investments by fiduciaries in slum clearance projects in
the City.[30]

Moses persuaded La Guardia not to renege on the contract.
But La Guardia did not completely forsake his principles. At
12:30 P.M. on August 4, 1943, he and Ecker came face-to-face
at a private ceremony at city hall to formally sign the contract
for the Stuyvesant Town project. It was there that La Guardia
delivered a verbal rendition of his letter, once again vowing that
in the event of any litigation he would take the position that
"there can be no discrimination in tenant selection based on
prejudice."[31]

Ecker shot back days later, saying that Metropolitan's position was that "Stuyvesant Town management must have complete freedom in the matter of the selection of tenants and that
the question was one of business economics, and not of racial
politics." Ecker was incensed by what he called La Guardia's
"change of attitude." Ecker went on to quote from a memorandum, submitted to Governor Dewey on La Guardia's behalf,
specifically stating that if the amendment to the state's housing
law contained a provision giving tenant selection to the city "no
company would operate under it." Further, Ecker said, Metropolitan "would not have proceeded with the matter and certainly would not have invested large sums in the acquisition of
real estate if [La Guardia] had not signed a memorandum indicating approval of the law" giving the company control over
tenant selection.[32]

La Guardia remained especially sensitive about the issue and the mere mention of Stuyvesant Town could drive him to distraction, Councilman Benjamin Davis recalled more than twenty years later. "It was as though he realized he had made a political mistake, but couldn't turn back for fear of losing face."

But if La Guardia was content to let the courts sort it out, Moses was an advocate for the defense, sending a steady stream of memos to Ecker and his counsel, Judge Samuel Seabury, advising them on a legal strategy in defending the company against charges of discrimination and the improper use of the powers of eminent domain. Government did not have a uniform policy when it came to race and housing, Moses wrote to Ecker: "Even the federal public housing officials recognize the color line in the South and provide housing for negroes as such."[33]

Still, early in 1944, Moses told Ecker that the state supreme court and the appellate division had dismissed most of their opponents' arguments, save for one issue: "equal benefit under the law is not being afforded to negroes because no projects for negroes under this law are being undertaken contemporaneously with the Stuyvesant Town project." Moses said that was why he had been urging Metropolitan to undertake housing projects in Harlem and Bedford-Stuyvesant, largely black neighborhoods in Manhattan and Brooklyn.[34]

Ecker, however, was reluctant in light of the pending litigation. He was also worried about how the broader public might perceive such a concession. "I should not like to appear to have been driven into such a position and in that I feel quite sure you will agree. . . . It should not appear, even by inference, that either we or the City admitted that the Redevelopment Law or the Constitution of New York would require private capital to match each White project with a Colored project," Ecker said in a February 25, 1944, letter to Moses.

But Moses kept at it. He assured Ecker that his suggestion that Metropolitan undertake a project in Harlem or Bedford-Stuyvesant was based "on a much sounder theory that colored areas are entitled at least to an experiment in this direction."[35]

La Guardia added his own plea, telling Ecker he was eager to see a privately built housing project started in Harlem "where conditions are particularly bad." He said that the city had planned any number of postwar public housing projects using city, state and federal loans and grants. Despite government efforts, the projects were unlikely to clear even 10 percent of the city's slums.[36]

At the same time, La Guardia signed a bill in June 1944 sponsored by city council members Stanley M. Isaacs and Benjamin J. Davis Jr., a Communist from Manhattan, opposing housing discrimination by barring tax exemptions for any privately financed housing that practiced discrimination. The law was carefully written, however, so that it did not apply retroactively to Stuyvesant Town, only to prospective projects.

Two months later, in August 1944, there was a breakthrough. Metropolitan had acquired the land for Stuyvesant Town, from Fourteenth to Twentieth Streets, but the company was not stopping there. Metropolitan was quietly buying up several blocks to the north for an additional housing development, although it would not be built under the Redevelopment Companies Law, so the insurance company would be paying full taxes. The new development, which would eventually be known as Peter Cooper Village, would wipe out a set of noxious gas tanks owned by the Consolidated Edison Company.

Unlike Stuyvesant Town, Peter Cooper would be built without public subsidies on land from Twentieth to Twenty-Third Streets, from First Avenue to East River Drive. Rents for the 2,495 apartments there would be somewhat higher. The living rooms would be larger and the apartments would include a second bathroom.

Metropolitan was also actively buying a twelve-acre parcel in Harlem with nearly a dozen crumbling tenements, junk shops, and factories for a new residential community. On September 17, 1944, La Guardia announced on his weekly radio program that Metropolitan planned to build "Riverton" for an estimated 3,400 people at an average monthly rental of $12.50 per room.

Riverton, with 1,232 apartments in seven 13-story buildings arranged around a 700-foot-long grassy mall, would be one-tenth the size of Stuyvesant Town and Peter Cooper Village. But like the projects on the Lower East Side, Riverton's buildings would be arrayed around a leafy, parklike setting. In paying tribute to Ecker as a "young man past 70 years of age" with a vision, La Guardia zinged the five "blind" men representing five financial institutions who had failed to follow Metropolitan's lead.[37]

Ecker told reporters that the project, initiated by La Guardia and under consideration for a year, would turn an unattractive corner of the city—from 135th Street to 138th Street, between Fifth Avenue and the Harlem River—into a community with a suburban atmosphere. "The project is of great importance, forming part of the rehabilitation program so essential to the future of the city," Ecker said.

"Riverton and Stuyvesant Town represent the first use of private capital for the rebuilding of obsolete city areas under the

Redevelopment Companies Law which has been described by the Court of Appeals as 'an effort by the Legislature to promote cooperation between municipal government and private capital to the end that substandard insanitary areas in our community may be rehabilitated.'"[38]

The separate-but-equal approach adopted by Ecker, Moses and La Guardia, who retired in 1945, divided the opposition. At an informal meeting of civil rights and tenant activists at the Society for Ethical Culture on West Sixty-Fourth Street, Charles A. Collier of the NAACP flatly opposed Riverton, which he described as a "Jim Crow housing project that will not only keep the Negro walled in but will delay his fight to live in the community of his choice as a citizen."[39]

Goode Harney of the New York Urban League argued that it was proper to condemn Stuyvesant Town, but protesting Riverton would confuse the issue. "People are so badly in need of housing in the area that they would still apply over our protest," he said. It would be better to encourage white people to apply to Riverton, he added.[40]

For its part, Metropolitan, bound by the new city law prohibiting housing discrimination, said Riverton would be open to everyone. Stuyvesant Town remained closed to Negroes.

CHAPTER TWO

Thirty-Six Million Bricks

In the fall of 1945, bulldozers, pile drivers and steam shovels rumbled onto the Stuyvesant Town-Peter Cooper Village site to begin demolition of over five hundred tenements, factories, warehouses and storefronts. Carmela Garcea, who grew up nearby on East Tenth Street, used to play amid the rubble as Metropolitan knocked down block after block of buildings. "We used to walk through the neighborhood," said Garcea, seventy-seven and still marveling at the thought of it in 2011. "It looked like a war zone. It looked bombed out when they got through with it."[1]

Metropolitan had acquired the land over two years, sometimes using intermediaries to mask their shopping spree so that property owners would not suddenly hike their prices. With the war winding down in Europe, the insurer judged that the moment had arrived to start building. Some 765,000 veterans returned to New York City, exacerbating the existing housing shortage. The veterans were living in trailers, tourist camps and Quonset huts, or doubled up with friends and relatives. Most of them could not afford to buy a house, which the city's Veterans

Service Center said would require an income of $90 a week, $34 more than the average among veterans. Metropolitan announced that it would give veterans a preference at all its housing developments.

Moses and Ecker had portrayed the area as a blighted neighborhood, where the population had tumbled from twenty-three thousand in 1910 to about twelve thousand in 1940, as the old tenements crumbled, businesses failed and the garment industry migrated from the Lower East Side to the West Side of Manhattan. The Hungarian, Russian, Italian and Polish residents were largely poor, paying less than $30 a month for a two-room, cold-water flat. One out of four residents was looking for work and those who had a job earned less than $200 a month, mainly working in the shipyards and other defense industries.

The Gas House District had the city's greatest concentration of substandard housing. Three-fourths of the apartments in the aging buildings on the site lacked central steam heat. Hot and cold running water was a luxury. The area had devolved into "obsolescence," Ecker told the Annual Conference of Mayors, echoing the same description of blight used by planners and promoters in knocking down the slaughterhouses and breweries north of East Forty-Second Street to make way for the United Nations.

Although few critics challenged the necessity of wholesale demolition and the removal of the residents, the neighborhood was not exactly a burned-out husk. There were 200 active businesses and 150 industrial firms. A new Coca-Cola bottling plant sat near the East River and Dowd's Lumber Yard was on Avenue A. The Dairyman's League Cooperative Association called the Gas House District home, as did the Goodman noodle factory; Bull's Head Horse Auction Company; the Mecca Theater; one Lutheran and two Catholic churches, including the seventy-two-year-old St. Mary Magdalen; two schools; and scores of other businesses and factories. It marked the beginning of a growing consensus among the city's real estate interests, civic groups and planners that industrial neighborhoods no longer belonged in Manhattan. Over the next half century, the fur district, the flower district, the printing district and much of the garment district would disappear, much like the Gas House District. Still, most residents of the Gas House District were reluctant to leave their homes, despite the planners' intentions. "My husband died here," one resident, Concetta Tornabene, told a *Herald Tribune* reporter, "and I want to die here too."

Tenants, who organized the Stuyvesant Tenant's League, protested their expulsion with a succession of rallies, which distressed La Guardia. In January 1945, residents of one section of the Stuyvesant Town site were warned to decamp by the summer. Metropolitan hired James Felt, a real estate executive, to set up the Tenant Relocation Bureau, which would assist residents with the enormous task of finding new housing. Felt quickly assembled a list of six thousand vacant apartments and hired a team of multilingual female interviewers who escorted families "around in a station wagon without cost to examine new apartments."[2]

The Relocation Bureau could do little for tenants who could not afford more than $10 a month in rent. The City Housing Authority could absorb only a handful of the tenants. A few families made their way to the Parkchester complex in the Bronx, where there was a waiting list of two thousand veterans. Felt acknowledged that "only a small percentage of the former site residents could afford Stuyvesant Town, where rents per room were about $14 per room, $8 more than the average rent in the district." Most tenants moved to surrounding neighborhoods to the north and south, where the housing was equally bleak.

"By and large, families dislocated by slum clearance and not provided for in public housing or given some other form of assistance in securing decent housing must find shelter in other slum areas," a report by the Community Service Society concluded. "Thus slum living is not eliminated for these families."[3]

By November 1, 1945, all but seventy-seven of more than three thousand families had moved without a single eviction, according to a report by the Relocation Bureau, which was regarded as an inexpensive success and adopted by successive slum clearance projects. Meanwhile, Metropolitan worked with Richmond Shreve, Irwin Clavan and Andrew J. Eken to design the uniform L- or cross-shaped red brick buildings at Stuyvesant Town and Peter Cooper Village. It was the same team that had worked on Parkchester and the Empire State Building.

About 5,000 steelworkers, masons, carpenters, plumbers and electricians swarmed over the site, driving 42,000 steel piles into the ground and ultimately laying 36.5 million bricks for the buildings symmetrically arrayed around a grassy oval. They carved pathways and playgrounds out of the gently sloping land, which was ultimately planted with sweet gums, Oriental planes, pin oaks, azaleas, rose mallow, bush honeysuckle, rhododendrons and snowballs. Within a year, Metropolitan was showered with more than 110,000 applications for the apartments in yet another indication of the city's desperate housing crisis.

With Metropolitan nearing completion of the first buildings at Stuyvesant Town and Peter Cooper Village in 1947, three black

veterans sued Metropolitan in June 1947, charging that its ex-
clusionary policies violated their constitutional right to equal
access under the Fourteenth Amendment. The lead plaintiff
was Joseph R. Dorsey of Harlem, a former army captain who
held a master's degree and worked as a social worker. Dorsey,
joined by Monroe Dowling, another former army captain, and
Calvin B. Harper, a disabled veteran from the Bronx, argued
that their existing apartments were unfit for habitation and that
they had tried unsuccessfully to find better housing closer to
work. The suit was sponsored by the American Civil Liberties
Union, the American Jewish Congress and the NAACP and
argued by Abrams, joined by Will Maslow and Thurgood Marshall, who would later successfully argue the landmark *Brown
v. Board of Education* case and become the first African-
American justice of the Supreme Court.

They argued that Stuyvesant Town was a private complex
built with extensive public support in the form of land, a generous tax exemption and the use of eminent domain, which con-
veyed a public purpose and a public use. Government limited
the profits and imposed a rent ceiling. Therefore, Metropolitan
was compelled to comply with the state and federal constitu-
tions, which guaranteed equal access to all citizens.

"If the nation's neighborhoods are to be marked off into areas
for the exclusive and the excluded, the involuntary ghetto will
have become an unalterable American institution," the suit
stated. "For, once the racial composition of the new neighborhoods is fixed, they cannot be easily changed, particularly if
they are as rigidly controlled as Stuyvesant Town would be with
all the freedom from public interference it asserts it has."

Metropolitan countered that the federal and state constitu-
tions had no bearing on the matter. "Stuyvesant is not exercising

any governmental power, nor is it acting as an agent or representative of the State or City," the company said. "It is exercising mere private rights in an undertaking which neither the State nor the City has the power to undertake."

Only days before the first tenants moved into Stuyvesant Town, Justice Felix C. Benvenga ruled in favor of Metropolitan, saying that designating the complex a public use did not make it a public project under state law. Benvenga wrote that the public use ended when the redevelopment project was completed. There was "no established civil right where the question of private housing accommodations were concerned," he said.[4]

"It may well be that from a sociological point of view a policy of exclusion and discrimination on account of race, color, creed or religion is not only undesirable but unwise," Benvenga continued. "But the wisdom of the policy is not for the courts."

The lawyers appealed to the state's highest court, which affirmed on July 19, 1949, that the state had no role in Stuyvesant Town. In a four-to-three decision, the court ruled that while the state played a role in helping Metropolitan clear the site, the state legislature had intentionally refrained from imposing any restrictions upon a redevelopment company in its choice of tenants, although the public housing law explicitly prohibited discrimination at state-constructed low-rent housing projects. The ruling noted repeated efforts by Moses and other city officials to fend off prohibitions against discrimination at the Board of Estimate.[5]

In his strongly worded dissent, Justice Stanley Fuld found that the city was wrong in approving the Stuyvesant Town contract in the first place, knowing that Metropolitan intended to bar Negroes. He referred to Stuyvesant Town as a "private barony" in the middle of Manhattan that should not be left free of constitutional safeguards. The Fourteenth Amendment proscribes discrimination in Stuyvesant Town and the state constitution also condemns it, he said.

"As an enterprise in urban redevelopment, Stuyvesant Town is a far cry from a privately built and privately run apartment house," Fuld concluded. "More, its peculiar features yield to those eligible as tenants tremendous advantages in modern housing and at rentals far below those charged in purely private developments. As citizens and residents of the City, Negroes as well as white people have contributed to the development. Those who have paid and will continue to pay should share in the benefits to be derived."

No sooner had the court of appeals issued its decision than a group of Stuyvesant Town tenants decided to take matters into their own hands with a direct challenge to Metropolitan on their home turf. A dozen Stuyvesant Town tenants, many of them veterans, had a year earlier formed the Town and Village Tenants Committee to End Discrimination at Stuyvesant Town, a group that would eventually swell to 1,800 members.

"It was a landmark in the struggle against segregation in this country," Lee Lorch, a vice chairman of the committee, recalled in 2011. An army veteran and a math professor, Lorch and his family would pay a high price for his role in this and other civil rights battles. "I thought then, and still do, that it was an important struggle worth any sacrifice in pursuing it."[6]

Lorch's fellow committee members included the chairman, Paul L. Ross, a former secretary to Mayor William O'Dwyer; Rabbi Daniel L. Davis, director of the New York Federation of Reform Synagogues; and Esther Smith, who wrote many of the group's letters and leaflets. The group also included Bill Mauldin, the cartoonist whose drawings of American GIs endeared him to a generation; Stefan Heym, author of the bestseller *The Crusaders;* and Lee Vines, the CBS radio announcer. It was a diverse group of liberals, civil rights advocates and Communist Party members, who played an energetic role among both New York City tenant and labor unions.

Edward A. Stanley, whose parents were original Stuyvesant Town tenants, recalls his father Stephen describing the picket lines and the chanting that enveloped the complex. "They had a song," said Stanley, who later was an NYPD detective in the elite bias unit, "that went: 'Stuyvesant Town is a grand old town; but you can't get in if your skin is brown.'"

Like many of his neighbors, Lorch had recently gotten out of the service, after serving as a corporal in the Army Air Corps in the Pacific. The only housing he and his wife, Grace, could find was half a Quonset hut at a veterans' housing project on Jamaica Bay in Brooklyn. It was a long subway ride from there to City College, where he taught mathematics. After getting a doctorate at the University of Cincinnati in 1941, Lorch had worked briefly for the National Advisory Committee for Aeronautics, a precursor of NASA, before resigning his draft-exempt job to join the army.

Lorch and his family were among the one hundred thousand applicants for apartments at Stuyvesant Town, which gave preference to veterans. They were happy to finally get an apartment, he said, but Metropolitan's racial policy was well-known. "There was no way of boycotting Metropolitan," recalled Lorch, who is white, "but going there carried an obligation to fight discrimination. That's the way a lot of people felt about it."

Not wanting to get too far ahead of their neighbors, the

committee drew up a survey designed to assess residents' views of Metropolitan's policy of barring black tenants at Stuyvesant Town. The activists were pleasantly surprised but a bit skeptical when their survey revealed that two-thirds of the twenty-five thousand residents opposed the segregated housing policy of the landlord. So they created a second poll, which produced the same results, and quickly gathered over three thousand signatures on a petition opposing the exclusion of Negroes and calling on Mayor William O'Dwyer to take all necessary steps to open apartments to Negro tenants who met the eligibility requirements.

The *Town & Village* newspaper, which has diligently reported the community news since Stuyvesant Town's inception, did a survey of its own with similar results. But the committee did come under attack from some readers of *Town & Village*, as well as Metropolitan executives, who insisted it was a Communist front group.

"If they want Negroes as neighbors we say let them move to Harlem," said one anonymous letter writer published in the *Town & Village*. "It is a shame we cannot keep them by themselves," wrote another. "When we signed our lease they did not say colored people would be accepted. Why don't they take a vote of all concerned."

Still other tenants were sympathetic to the activists but feared the repercussions if they were publicly associated with the antidiscrimination battle. "It was very unpleasant; they didn't want blacks to come in," recalled Elaine T. Haber, who moved into her Peter Cooper Village apartment in 1947 and still lives there today. "They wanted to keep it white." But she did not get involved out of a sense of self-preservation. Her first husband had died in 1950 and she was juggling two jobs to pay the rent. "We didn't want to risk being ousted. I think a lot of tenants felt as I did: There were people fighting the fight, let them continue."[7]

In a committee pamphlet entitled "What's wrong with this picture*," Leo Miller explained his reasoning. "In the Battle of the Bulge on December 18, 1944, the courage and sharp shooting of a Negro machine-gunner saved my life and a dozen other white GIs. Can anyone of us who live in T & V say he may not be my neighbor. . . . I can't."

In August 1949, Jesse Kessler, a committee member and a union organizer for Local 65 Wholesale and Warehouse Workers, offered his four-room apartment at 1 Stuyvesant Oval to Hardine Hendrix, a twenty-eight-year-old veteran and a fellow union member, while Kessler went away on vacation. An art student, Hendrix was living with his wife Raphael (Rae) and five-year-old son, Hardine Jr., in a cramped, rat-infested apartment in Harlem. They welcomed the move downtown, even temporarily.

The Hendrixes' appearance at Stuyvesant Town caused a sensation, but the insurance company was loath to risk a very public confrontation, especially since committee members, veterans and union activists often slept at the apartment to ensure that the Hendrix family would not be evicted without a fight. A New York Times reporter found that twelve of the Hendrixes' fifteen neighbors had no problem with African-Americans living in Stuyvesant Town. The Hendrixes, in turn, liked living in Stuyvesant Town even if they were the subject of occasional taunts from windows they passed or threatening phone calls.

"I can recall many nights my father left our apartment to stay at the Hendrixes', to protect them," said Karen Smith, whose father David was a jewelry worker. Her mother, Esther, a graphic designer who worked at home, was the committee's executive secretary and part of a core group of women who did the bulk of the organizing, Mr. Lorch said.[8]

Metropolitan kept a close eye on their critics, going so far as to send an employee undercover to an August 29, 1949 rally billed as "The East Side Welcomes First Negro Family to Stuyvesant." Daniel B. English, a Metropolitan executive in the company's publication division, wrote a six-page account of the affair, which he said was attended by about three hundred people and featured speeches from James E. Allen of the NAACP, Nathan M. Padgug of the American Jewish Congress, the Kesslers and Rae Hendrix, an organizer for the Domestic Workers Union. In his judgment, the meeting was designed to advance the cause of left-wing activists and the American Labor Party. Aside from a small number of Stuyvesant Town tenants and a sprinkling of Negroes, Mr. English reported, "Most of the audience seemed to me of Jewish appearance."[9]

Mr. English confided that he was forced to contribute money when a speaker called on the audience to stand and pledge a donation. "Your observer thought it politic to contribute $1 of Metropolitan money so he could sit down again!"

After Kessler returned from vacation at the end of August Dr. Lorch offered the Hendrixes his Stuyvesant Town apartment at 651 East Fourteenth Street. Metropolitan refused to accept Kessler's $76 rent check, which the activists suspected was a first step toward evicting him. Lorch, who figured he would face the same threat, was heading off to Pennsylvania State College, having lost his job at City College when the administration overruled his colleagues and refused to grant him tenure. Although City College denied that there were political reasons behind the action, Lorch's failure to get tenure was widely believed to be a reprisal for his Stuyvesant Town activism. More than twenty organizations called on City College to reconsider.

"It happens that he lives in Stuyvesant Town," Justice Hubert T. Delaney, one of the city's first black judges, said of Lorch. "It happens that he was vice president of a committee that got 3,500 signatures of tenants there who were opposed to the exclusion of Negroes. I get pretty sick and tired of having a man called a Communist just because he did a decent thing. I think we are giving Communists too much credit."[10]

Ross, chairman of the tenant committee, promised that their campaign would continue "until the Hendrixes and other Negro families live among us, not just as guests, but as permanent residents."

Rae Hendrix, who became active with the committee, insisted that Metropolitan should not issue any more leases at Stuyvesant Town until the complex was integrated. She told the *Amsterdam News* that "no more families should be housed until a certain number of Negro families are admitted." Metropolitan countered that that would be unfair to white families already on the waiting list. What was unfair, she responded, was "that Negroes have never been allowed the opportunity to apply."

Meanwhile, Lorch's career at Penn State came to a quick end the following spring, when, Lorch explained in a front-page article in the *New York Times*, a school official told him that Penn State would not renew his contract because his actions in permitting a Negro family to live as guests in his New York apartment were "extreme, illegal and immoral, and damaging to the public relations of the college." The school's decision sparked a protest from the American Association of University Professors over academic freedom, a campus rally of more than a thousand students and a letter of public support from a Princeton mathematician, Albert Einstein. Lorch, however, soon decamped to Nashville, for a teaching position at Fisk University.[11]

On the same day in June 1950 that the United States Supreme Court declined to review the Stuyvesant Town case, the court issued three decisions favorable to the civil rights movement. One prohibited the segregation of Negroes in railroad dining cars. The second barred the segregation of Negro students at the University of Oklahoma. The last case involved a student who was refusing to attend a new state law school for Negroes in Houston, Texas, demanding instead entrance to the University of Texas law school in Austin. The court ruled that the Negro school in Houston was not the equivalent of the university law school and therefore ordered his admission to the law school in Austin. The decisions, though narrowly drawn, marked what the *Amsterdam News* called the "beginning of the end of race segregation."

The color lines in America were beginning to break down in the years after World War II. Jackie Robinson signed a contract with the Brooklyn Dodgers in 1947, becoming the first black player in Major League Baseball. President Harry Truman desegregated the armed forces two years later, under pressure from A. Philip Randolph, the African-American labor leader and president of the League for Non-Violent Civil Disobedience Against Military Segregation. That same year, the Supreme Court barred restrictive covenants.

Back at Stuyvesant Town, Metropolitan finally made its move against the Town and Village Committee in June, notifying thirty-five tenant leaders, including Ross, Rabbi Davis, Lorch and the Hendrix family, that their leases would not be renewed. For nearly two years, the tenants fought the evictions in the streets, in the legislature and in the courts, where they were represented by Paul O'Dwyer, the brother of then-mayor William O'Dwyer. Allied with the New York State Committee on Discrimination in Housing, the activists mobilized public support to force Metropolitan to postpone any action.

The August doldrums broke with the news that Metropolitan would allow three "qualified" Negro families into Stuyvesant Town, although the company paradoxically denied any change in basic policy. The insurer simultaneously opposed a bill sponsored by Councilmen Earl Brown and Stanley M. Isaacs compelling Stuyvesant Town to accept Negro tenants by portraying the legislation and integration as Communist inspired. The charge was echoed in the *Daily News* and the *Daily Mirror*.

The Communist Party, which had thousands of members in New York City at the time, vehemently supported the bill and the fight at Stuyvesant Town, much to the embarrassment of some of its allies. Yet, the city council unanimously passed the Brown-Isaacs Law in March 1951, making discrimination a misdemeanor carrying a $500 fine. The Board of Estimate approved it and Mayor Vincent R. Impellitteri signed it into law.[12]

The battle at Stuyvesant Town culminated in a showdown at the complex. The city marshal had given the remaining tenants scheduled for eviction until 9:00 A.M. on January 17, 1952, to pack up and be gone. Instead, nineteen of the families refused to leave, barricading their doors after sending their twenty-six children to stay with relatives. Food was relayed from window to window by rope. That evening, tenants sent aloft a red meteorological balloon bearing a streamer emblazoned with the words "Stop the Evictions." The balloon was positioned so that it was even with the tenth-floor windows of Ecker's apartment at 660 Park Avenue.[13]

In a front-page editorial, *Town & Village* said, "These people are being forcibly ousted because they espoused a cause which the landlord found undesirable and embarrassing." Sixteen organizations, including the American Jewish Congress, American Veterans Committee, Citizens Housing and Planning Council, New York Society for Ethical Culture, Anti-Defamation League, New York Board of Rabbis, NAACP, New York City CIO Council, Commission on Christian Social Relations of the Episcopal Diocese of New York and Social Action Committee of the Community Church, urged Metropolitan to "reconsider its action."

Civic groups and labor unions set up picket lines with hundreds of people at Stuyvesant Town, at city hall and at Metropolitan's headquarters on Madison Avenue, where a nonstop vigil went on for three days. Hours before the deadline, Metropolitan backed down, agreeing to negotiate with the tenant leaders.

Three days of intense talks mediated by city council president Rudolph Halley ensued before a deal was struck. Metropolitan would drop the eviction proceedings on the condition that the Lorch, Kessler and Ross families would voluntarily leave Stuyvesant Town. Finally, the insurer agreed to provide the Hendrixes with an apartment. *Town & Village* reported that persons "close to the negotiations express no doubt that the insurance company felt, in the face of the violent public reaction, that it was in a 'tight spot' and was relieved when the negotiations offered a way out." Early in 1952, Metropolitan told officials that the company was processing the applications of a number of Negro families.

"We left without prejudice, according to the agreement," Lorch recalled fifty-eight years later in the living room of his apartment in Toronto. Lorch's storied career took him to Fisk University in Nashville and to Little Rock, Arkansas, where he and his wife, Grace, played a role in the desegregation of Central High School in 1957. Ultimately, he was blacklisted from teaching and moved to Toronto, where he became a distinguished professor at York University and continued to fight for justice and civil rights. "The Hendrixes were given an apartment in their own name, but they wouldn't let them stay in my apartment. The Stuyvesant Town fight mobilized public opinion against segregation. Because of its prominence, it was given enormous attention. I have no regret over what we did or what it cost us, although I would have much preferred living in my hometown."[14]

Many residents of Stuyvesant Town, and most New Yorkers today, know little of the fiercely waged struggle against discrimination during the birth of the complex. It was led by tenants, who wanted to define for themselves, outside the regimented strictures laid out by Metropolitan, how they would live and interpret the meaning of American ideals like justice and equality after the harrowing experiences of World War II.

The battle of Stuyvesant Town lasted from 1943 to 1952 and gave rise to the open housing movement in the United States, even if integration came very slowly to the sister complexes overlooking the East River. Seven years later, the 1960 census would show that only 47 Negroes lived among the 22,405 residents of Stuyvesant Town. Still, the heated struggle over Metropolitan's discrimination at Stuyvesant Town brought the issue into the public realm and inspired others to take up the cause. The groups involved in the effort to desegregate Stuyvesant

Town formed the New York State Committee on Discrimination in Housing in 1948, which in turn led to the establishment of the National Committee Against Discrimination in Housing in 1950, which campaigned for fair housing laws in cities across the country.

The New York committee helped win adoption of a 1950 law barring racial discrimination in any housing constructed with public funds and both groups supported a 1963 law barring discrimination in private housing. Their efforts culminated in passage of the Fair Housing Act in 1968, which prohibited discrimination in the sale, rental or financing of housing.

For some activists, the fight against discrimination at Stuyvesant Town was bound up with the way they viewed the complexes as a refuge for the middle class, where anyone could live and raise their family in an urban setting while struggling for a better life. Blacks and Latinos would never make up more than 5 percent of the residents. But that tradition of defending the middle class would wind its way through the residents' opposition to exorbitant rent hikes in the 1950s and 1960s. And it would find expression in their anguish over the sale of Stuyvesant Town-Peter Cooper Village during a real estate boom five decades later. If the working-class Gas House District was demolished to make way for a middle-class neighborhood, many of the residents were not going to let Stuyvesant Town be taken from them so that a wealthy elite could capture another corner of Manhattan.

CHAPTER THREE

The Golden Age

One of Al Doyle's fondest memories is Christmastime at Stuyvesant Town. The oaks and London plane trees were bare, having shed their leaves weeks earlier. As a young boy growing up in the 1950s, Doyle, with his brothers and their friends, would watch the maintenance men turn off the water and drain the fountains in Stuyvesant Oval, the geographic and social center of the sprawling complex. The workers would haul in a half-dozen newly cut pine and fir trees and install them in the basins of the fountains. Holiday music would waft through the limbs as workers decorated the towering trees and erected a manger and a menorah. Passing residents paused to watch.

"Stuyvesant Town was almost resortlike," said Doyle, the long-standing tenant union president who has never really lived anywhere else. "In the wintertime, you could sleigh down the embankments. Some kids would play roller hockey on the loop roads."

"MetLife was the best," he added. "They set all the standards and they never really wavered."[1]

Those are some of the memory loops that run through his head and are at the foundation of what he is willing to fight to preserve. The sense of community. Of commonality.

His father, Alvin D. Doyle, came back from the war in the Pacific, where he had served as a combat correspondent for the Third Marine Division. Like most veterans he did not talk much about the war. He got his old job back at the *Daily Mirror,* a newspaper owned by William Randolph Hearst. He and his wife, Therese, had just about given up finding their own apartment when they got a call from Stuyvesant Town, offering something very different from the tenement life they knew in Brooklyn.

"They thought it was wonderful," Doyle said.

Doyle can remember his father coming home for lunch, his big 1953 Chevrolet double-parked on the street outside. A quick hello to his wife and sons—Howard, Al Jr. and Kevin— and then his father was off to Room 9, the press room at city hall. Doyle played touch football and punchball on Playground 1. His mother served as den mother to his Cub Scout troop. He attended Epiphany Catholic School, and later Power Memorial High School, where Lew Alcindor was a star.

Moving day, August 1, 1947.

Martha Bernard and her husband, Peter, were shaking with anticipation as the moving men hauled their belongings into the newly built thirteen-story building at 605 East Fourteenth Street, the first of thirty-five buildings to open at the vast Stuyvesant Town complex on the Lower East Side. Like tens of thousands of other New Yorkers, they had been unable to find a vacant apartment anywhere in Manhattan. The young couple had lived doubled up, first with family and then with a friend in Greenwich Village. And waited, for a place of their own.

"We were the lucky ones," Bernard recalled sixty-four years later. "There were people dying to get in there. People came back from the war to live with relatives. The greatest thing was to be able to move out and find your own space."[2]

Admittedly conditions were rough. The blocks between Fourteenth and Twenty-Third Streets, east of First Avenue, were mostly a moonscape of half-demolished buildings sitting amid piles of brick and other debris while heavy trucks rumbled along rutted streets and gullies. Her building was surrounded by a fence, behind which the rest of Stuyvesant Town and its sister complex, Peter Cooper Village, would take shape over the next two years. That first year there was no phone service.

"It was a mud hole," she said. "There was nothing but mosquitoes, thousands of mosquitoes and no screens. All we did at night was take pillows and make blood marks on the walls."

But that one-bedroom apartment, with its parquet floors polished to a high sheen, spacious living room and a separate kitchen, was "heaven," said Bernard, eighty-eight, who now lives six blocks to the north in Peter Cooper Village. The difference between the two apartments was not insignificant. A one-bedroom unit in Peter Cooper is a spacious 947 square feet, compared with 755 square feet for the average one-bedroom in Stuyvesant Town.

Thousands of other tenants, 98 percent of them veterans, who followed Bernard in the 1940s and in the succeeding decades shared her sense of elation. For decades, Stuyvesant Town had a ten-year waiting list, making an apartment as hard to come by as the most cherished of New York treasures, season tickets for the Knicks, the Giants or the Yankees.

The Bernards' predicament was by no means unique; city officials estimated that 360,000 families in New York City were living doubled up.[3] Other veterans were living with their families in Quonset huts in Brooklyn. Josephine E. Springer, a captain in the Women's Army Corps, entered Columbia University on the GI Bill and applied for an apartment at Stuyvesant Town.

"The price was right," said Springer, ninety-two, one of the rare unmarried tenants at the time. "It was fresh, clean and had nice grounds. Beautifully maintained. It was like living in a small town. You spoke to everyone in the elevator, at least I did."[4]

Nearly half of the working residents at Stuyvesant Town were professionals, managers and entrepreneurs, according to the 1960 census, while most of the rest were police officers, construction workers, skilled tradesmen and sales workers. At the slightly more upscale Peter Cooper, professionals and managers accounted for two-thirds of the employed residents. Many of the women taught school, some were magazine writers, others worked in the home.

The population explosion that occurred shortly after Stuyvesant Town and Peter Cooper Village opened is the reason that some residents referred to the two complexes as Rabbit Town. By 1950, five years after the war ended, there were over 6,000 children under the age of five living in Stuyvesant Town or Peter Cooper Village, accounting for nearly one-fifth of the 31,173 residents.[5]

"Nine months after it opened, almost everybody had a baby," said Bernard.

Current and former residents say that Stuyvesant Town and Peter Cooper Village were places where you knew your neighbors. Their children often attended the same schools, or at least played on the same Little League teams and in the same playground basketball tournaments. Mothers gathered with their toddlers at other playgrounds with swings and jungle gyms. It was a level of intimacy unknown at most other New York apartment buildings. Many of the original Stuyvesant Town tenants eventually took the traditional middle-class path to a home in the suburbs of New Jersey or Long Island. But thousands stayed, and their children, now adults with their own families, comprise a sizable block of residents.

"I married someone from Long Island," said Stacy Mackey Pfeffer, who grew up in Stuyvesant Town, where her father ran the recreation department, and now lives there with her own family. "Everyone was geared up for us to buy a house on Long Island. I had no interest in moving out of the city, or out of Peter Cooper. I love city living. I wanted to pass it on to my children."[6]

Stuyvesant Town is easily the biggest apartment complex in Manhattan, with thirty-five nearly identical buildings arranged in a symmetrical pattern around the Stuyvesant Oval, a two-acre, tree-shrouded grass lawn at the center of the complex that features a gushing fountain. The red brick facades are relentless, save for the green framed casement windows, especially along the outer borders of the complex where they formed a fortress wall against the surrounding neighborhood. As Ecker planned it, there are no stores or schools inside the complex that might attract outsiders.

There were eight apartments to a floor, each with a similar layout, although the number of bedrooms varied. The standard colors were shades of tan: beige walls and beige-colored metal cabinets in the kitchen, sand-colored porcelain fixtures in the tiled bathrooms. Tenants had to pay extra for a different color scheme. Parquet floors in every room, including the twelve-by-eighteen-feet-seven-inch living room, which was larger than those of many Manhattan apartments and some suburban tract homes. There were two elevators in every building whose red, blue and green enamel interiors were shed during renovations in early 2000.

The twenty-one brick buildings at Peter Cooper Village, where rents were higher, were arranged in more of a herring-bone pattern on the blocks between Twentieth and Twenty-Third Streets. But the lobbies were a little nicer and the apartments larger than in Stuyvesant Town. Most important to families was that the apartments had two bathrooms.

In the late 1940s, Hearn's and Gimbels department stores quickly grasped the significance of this new kind of urban middle-class complex and created furniture lines like the Dearborn with beds, dinettes, china cabinets and sofas designed to fit neatly into the apartments. Hearn's went so far as to build a four-room suite in its store at Fourteenth Street and Fifth Avenue to Stuyvesant Town specifications, including modern, postwar furniture and "warm beige for the walls and a deeper beige for the trim." Roving decorators were on hand to assist residents in making fabric choices.[7]

More than half the land at the complexes was given over to pathways, interior roadways, green lawns and fifteen playgrounds at Stuyvesant Town, three at Peter Cooper. Until the last decade, an eighteen-inch post-and-chain fence surrounded the grassy areas, which were off-limits to pedestrians. Metropolitan employed five to six hundred plumbers, painters, maintenance workers (brown uniforms) and security guards (blue uniforms), many of whom lived in Stuyvesant Town, to maintain the property.

The nature of Stuyvesant Town sparked a bitter debate among planners, newspaper columnists and housing experts. The *New York World-Telegram* hailed Stuyvesant Town in 1948 "as an example of private capital's capacity to lick the housing shortage." "Every bathroom and every kitchen are identical," gushed the newspaper. "By including the cost of electricity and gas in the rent, the insurer saved huge sums on metering, clerks and bookkeepers."[8]

But Lewis Mumford, the architecture critic, likened the complexes' rows of featureless brick buildings to "the architecture of the Police State" in a 1948 review published by *The New Yorker*. He deemed the buildings too tall, the apartment foyers too dark and the playgrounds slathered in asphalt, "a caricature of urban rebuilding . . . considering all the benefits it might have derived from beginning at scratch, on a site as large as this." It was a nightmare, he said, "of impersonal regimentation, apparently for people who have no other identity but the serial numbers of their Social Security cards."

Robert Moses, however, was having none of it. He called Mumford's musings "just plain tripe" and defended the vast housing complex as an outstanding accomplishment. He said Stuyvesant Town's buildings housed more tenants than the tenement "rookeries" they replaced, but the structures took up less than 25 percent of the land, leaving most of the property for tree-shaded lawns and playgrounds. As a practical matter, Moses said, neither Metropolitan nor the public housing officials could afford to build quaint two-story cottages housing a hundred people an acre on slum land that cost $8 to $10 a square foot.[9]

The raging debate was met with a shrug by most residents, who forged close bonds over their shared experiences within the uniform confines of Stuyvesant Town and Peter Cooper, be it in the hallways or on the playgrounds. The *New York Herald Tribune* seemed to capture the sentiment with its headline for a December 9, 1956, story about the complex: "We live in a 'barracks'—and like it."

Daniel Garodnick, whose mother moved into Stuyvesant Town in 1968, before he was born, can still recall the names of his neighbors. Seymour Altman, who lived in apartment 13A and worked in the nearby fur district, taught him how to play blackjack over Tetley tea at the kitchen table. Al Chappel, in 13F, spoke several languages and served as Garodnick's Spanish tutor when he was in high school. "I always had a close relationship with the neighbors in our hallway," he said.[10]

The playgrounds proved to be an important nexus for residents, at least the boys. Playgrounds 9 and 11 were where they played highly competitive basketball. A few Jewish residents also recall instances where Catholic boys on Playground 9 hurled anti-Semitic taunts, which led them to confine their basketball to Playground 11. There were also games of punchball and a quieter playground for mothers and their younger children. In the spring, there were Little League games on a field near the East River and the massive Con Edison power plant.

"For guys growing up, sports was very central," Steven Sanders, a former state assemblyman who grew up there, said. "There was always a football game. There were rivalries between the playgrounds. It took on a religious fervor."[11]

MetLife was very careful in its tenant selection, seeking the same uniformity in its residents as it had achieved in the design of the buildings. The company preferred married couples with steady jobs and sent employees to interview every prospective tenant. Elaine T. Haber and her husband Dr. Leonard D. Weinberg, a doctor and army veteran who died in 1950, were living with Haber's parents in a two-bedroom apartment on the Grand Concourse in the Bronx when MetLife came calling.

"They wanted to know if we paid our rent on time," recalled Haber, who lives in Peter Cooper Village. "They wanted to see our bank books, which were practically nil. I guess they felt we had potential, a doctor and a teacher making a pittance."[12]

After her first husband died, Haber remarried and moved from Stuyvesant Town to Peter Cooper, where she chose an apartment overlooking the basketball courts so she could watch her son Eric play ball.

Thirty years later, MetLife was still checking. "Somebody came over to make sure I didn't have any pets lurking around, that I seemed like a good upstanding citizen," said Susan Steinberg, who moved into Stuyvesant Town in 1980, after her Upper East Side apartment building was converted to a cooperative. "In those days you were shown a layout of the apartment but you couldn't go and view it."[13]

At one point, there was a twenty-year waiting list for Peter Cooper Village and a fourteen-year waiting list for Stuyvesant Town, said Mitch Ryan, a MetLife housing director.[14] Of course, there were always exceptions if you knew "someone" at MetLife or Stuyvesant Town. MetLife kept about a hundred apartments for its executives, including those rotating through the New York office. "It was a safe, conservative, employee-friendly institution," said Harry P. Kamen, a MetLife employee for thirty-nine years and chairman of the company from 1993 to 1997. "There was a good pension you could depend on. A lot of people who worked there also lived in Stuyvesant Town-Peter Cooper, so you could walk to work."[15]

Kamen himself lived in Peter Cooper for fifteen years, beginning in 1962.

It was not just MetLife executives who lived in the complexes. Carmela Garcea, seventy-eight, who is retired and living in Peter Cooper Village, worked for many years as a banquet coordinator at MetLife headquarters, only six blocks away on Madison Avenue, between Twenty-Third and Twenty-Fifth Streets. Headquarters was a small city complete with a medical clinic staffed with doctors and nurses, dental offices, a tailor, a commissary and twenty-one underground cafeterias that, Garcea said, "served nineteen thousand five hundred people every day for free."[16]

Mistresses tied to senior executives also shot to the top of the waiting list. It was also good politics to accommodate Police Commissioners Lee P. Brown and Howard Leary and the top FBI official in New York in the 1990s, James Fox. Police officers were given priority, as were FBI agents after MetLife hired a former FBI official to head its security force.

Martha Bernard, eighty-eight, kept the secret about her entry to Stuyvesant Town for more than six decades. Unlike most tenants, neither she nor her husband was a veteran. Her father, Isadore Binswanger, president of Thomson-Porcelite Paint Company in Philadelphia, put in a call to a senior officer at MetLife asking for help. His company supplied all the paint for Stuyvesant Town, Peter Cooper and Parkchester. "You had to be married to a veteran," she said with a giggle. "But we got in surreptitiously because of the pull I've never mentioned publicly before."[17]

It took Richard Toes, a former New York City narcotics detective, a while to find his connection. It turned out that a low-level bookie he knew had a relative working in the administration office. "It was really hard getting in here," said Toes, who has lived in Stuyvesant Town for thirty-three years. "Some people wondered if there really was a list, or was it just a way to keep some people out until they found someone they wanted."[18]

Once tenants got into Stuyvesant Town or Peter Cooper Village, they encountered MetLife's rules of engagement, which were in keeping with the regimented layout of the buildings: No pets. No walking on the grass. Carpets must cover the wood floors to muffle footsteps. No double parking. Bicycles were banned from the footpaths in the 1950s when kids started careening around the complex in packs of forty. And woe to anyone who broke the rules.

"If there was an infraction and security came to your apartment, the world stopped," said John Marsh, a tenant leader who lives in the same Peter Cooper Village apartment once occupied by his father. "There was a deep sense of law and order. Then, it felt oppressive, but now I think about it with a deep sense of melancholy."[19]

"It felt like a military camp at times," said Joseph Strasburg, who lived in Stuyvesant Town from 1977 to 1987, before buying a condominium on Staten Island. "When I moved in you couldn't have an air conditioner because the wiring wasn't up to standards. If you turned on the TV and plugged in a hair dryer at the same time, the electricity went out. They'd confiscate it if they found one."[20]

Denis Delaney, a second-generation resident, said the regulated environment seemed appropriate for a generation coming back from the war. His father, Raymond, he said, went from driving a milk wagon to the Civil Conservation Corps and then the army; he saw combat in Europe. After the war, he landed a job with the city's transit system, as a motorman. "My father's generation followed the rules," he said. "It didn't mean they liked them, but they liked living there."[21]

Delaney himself owned a bar for nearly twenty years in the 1980s and 1990s called First Avenue, across the street from Stuyvesant Town. He wanted to attract patrons interested in a short beer or Dom Perignon, but it was also marketed directly at Stuyvesant Town. First Avenue was known for its meat-locker temperature in the summertime, when the air-conditioner-less apartments were sweltering. He became a keen observer of the Stuyvesant Town culture.

"The identities were Jewish and Irish Catholic," Delaney said. "There were a lot of Protestants, but it divided up almost by schools. The Jewish kids went mainly to the public schools. Catholics almost exclusively to the parochial schools."

Many of the schools were within easy walking distance: Immaculate Conception on Thirteenth Street, just south of Stuyvesant Town; Epiphany, at Second Avenue and Twenty-Second Street; St. Emeric's, on East Twelfth Street at Avenue D; Public School 40 on Twentieth Street, between First and Second Avenues; and Public School 61, on Twelfth Street and Avenue B. If the lives of the Irish and Jewish youngsters revolved around their respective schools, they did mix on Little League teams, or in playground games of dodgeball.

Stuyvesant Town children were often warned not to venture south into the poorer, scrappier neighborhoods of the Lower East Side, where many Puerto Rican families lived. And MetLife's security guards kept a vigilant eye out for intruders. There were no gang wars. But on the rare occasion when Puerto Rican youths did venture onto Stuyvesant Town playgrounds in the 1960s and 1970s, local teenagers were very territorial. Word of the incursion leaped from playground to playground like lightning and suddenly the knots of teenagers were lined up on opposing sides like the Jets and the Sharks.

"The word would go out, 'There's a bunch of Spics on the playground,'" said Gerald O'Neil, fifty-six, a heavyset man with a reddish beard streaked with white, who described the scene sheepishly. His parents, Bill and Patricia, never swore, at least not in front of their four children, or uttered racial epithets. His friends referred to them as Ward and June Cleaver, for their straight-as-an-arrow, *Leave It to Beaver* style. "Kids would grab baseball bats, basketballs, whatever, and sometimes things got out of hand. But I don't recall anyone really getting hurt. It was more about teenage chest-thumping. We had a pretty limited exposure to blacks and Puerto Ricans, until later."[22]

As much as the residents praised Mother Met's paternalism and its management of the development, they went toe-to-toe with the giant insurer right from the beginning over rents, establishing the tenor of tenant-landlord relations that survives today. The often quiescent tenants of the 1950s and 1960s rose up in opposition to every rent hike proposed by Metropolitan, painting each request as a direct assault on the ability of not only Stuyvesant Town residents but also of the entire middle class to live and prosper in Manhattan. For many residents, salaries and wages rose only modestly even as families at Rabbit Town grew larger. Every rent increase put more pressure on the family budget.

Ecker set the rents for Stuyvesant Town in 1947, only months before tenants began moving into the first completed building. When La Guardia and Ecker announced the project in 1943 they said the apartments would rent for $14 a room per month. But the cost of building the development had gone way beyond the original estimate in 1943 of $40 million to $50 million.

Under the terms of the contract with the city and the state's Redevelopment Companies Law, Metropolitan had to get approval from the Board of Estimate, whose members included the mayor, the comptroller and the five borough presidents, for any rent increase needed to cover costs. The agreements also entitled Metropolitan to a 6 percent return on its investment.

With support from Moses, Metropolitan later got the approval and raised the rents to $17 a room per month, or $68 for a four-room apartment. Ecker said that the cost of the complex had doubled to an estimated $90 million, because of higher-than-anticipated construction costs. He got a similar rent increase for Riverton, the complex in Harlem, at the same time.

In 1952, Metropolitan went back to the city asking for an average rent hike of 46 percent to $24.87 a month per room, from $17, or nearly $100 a month for a four-room apartment. The company said the increase was necessary because the final price tag for Stuyvesant Town came to $112.2 million. "Even with the increase requested in our application," Metropolitan said in a letter to tenants, "the residential and commercial rents will yield a return substantially less than the return provided by the statute and the contract with the city."

This time there were tenants in place and they vehemently opposed the increase. Glenn C. Fowler, chairman of the Stuyvesant Town Joint Tenants' Organizations Committee, denounced Metropolitan and called on city officials to reject the request. One tenant, Lotte N. Doverman, framed the issue in a letter published in the *New York Times* as "a dilemma that is of most serious and immediate concern to a good many local members of our 'vanishing middle class.'"[23]

Metropolitan countered with a public relations campaign replete with full-page ads in *Town & Village* and *The Villager*, as well as a series of letters and leaflets placed under residents' doors, on the reasonableness of the company's request. "There Is No 'Profit' in Stuyvesant Town," one ad declared, adding, "At present there is not even a reasonable return on the investment."[24]

At the same time, the company said it was making a 4 percent return on its investment, less than the 6 percent profit that it was entitled to. Yet, Metropolitan argued, the company also had to put aside money for capital improvements, deal with 55,000 requests annually for repairs and stockpile 40,000 light-bulbs a year for upkeep and 20,000 pounds of salt for keeping walkways clear of ice.

Six hundred tenants, many in suits or dresses and cradling infants, packed the city hall hearing room on May 19, 1952, cheering on speaker after speaker who urged members of the Board of Estimate to vote down the rent increase or postpone action. Fowler, the tenant leader, spoke in favor of a bill that would prohibit rent increases at Stuyvesant Town altogether. The board voted fifteen to one to deny Metropolitan's application.[25]

Frank Reavis, counsel for Metropolitan, said afterward that the company would file suit in the state supreme court to reverse the board's action. Two months later, the court sided with Metropolitan, ruling that the company could increase rents by an average of $2.55 per room monthly each year for three years. In the fourth year, the company was permitted to raise the rent by another $3 per room.

The court said: "The correct and proper action by the Board of Estimate on the application presented required the grant to petitioners of the increase of the maximum average rental per room per month to an amount sufficient to provide a six percent return on the investment in accordance with the contract and the statute."[26]

But the pattern was established. MetLife's attempts to raise rents at the complex met with resistance from tenants and elected officials in 1961, 1963 and 1970, when the company wanted to set the average monthly rent at $56.48. Opponents argued that the rent would provide MetLife with a whopping 14 percent return. While MetLife insisted that the average annual family income at Stuyvesant Town was a comfortable $12,500, elected officials testified at one public hearing that 70 percent of the families surveyed at Stuyvesant Town had a take-home pay of less than $8,400 a year, and more than a quarter of the families relied primarily on their pension checks to pay the rent. Moving to cheaper quarters, they said, was not an option given the city's continuing housing shortage.

The insurer argued in turn that the rent hike was necessary to provide an adequate return and to make up for prior years when MetLife failed to make a 6 percent return. It claimed that it had fallen short during those years by $20.4 million and needed to make it up with the rent hike. The Board of Estimate routinely rejected the requests, while the courts ruled again and again in MetLife's favor, but not before the company took a battering in the court of public opinion.

Stuyvesant Town served as the quintessential illustration of the plight of the middle class in an article in the *New York Times*. A two-bedroom apartment rented for $62 to $87 a month when the complex opened in 1947. Seven increases later, in 1967, that same two-bedroom rented for $138 to $173.50 a month. Although some of the increase was offset by rising wages, the *Times* noted, "it costs more than twice as much to live in Stuyvesant Town today than 20 years ago."[27]

The picket lines, petitioning and raging debates at city hall in the battle to desegregate Stuyvesant Town subsided by the mid-1950s. But the issue and Stuyvesant Town's reputation as a no-go zone for African-Americans never went away. In May 1968, the city's Human Rights Commission launched a broadside against MetLife, charging that the company had engaged in "a deliberate, intentional and systemic" exclusion of Negroes and Hispanics from Stuyvesant Town-Peter Cooper Village and Parkchester, in the Bronx. The complaint followed two years of negotiations between the company and the commission, which had combed through MetLife's tenant records. The company routinely discouraged Negro and Puerto Rican tenants from applying to the three complexes, the commissioner said, referring them instead to MetLife's "black property," Riverton, in Harlem.

The commission said that minorities knew that applying to Stuyvesant Town-Peter Cooper Village and Parkchester would be "futile, embarrassing or degrading," because of the company's "open and notorious past exclusion of Negroes and Puerto Ricans from its 'white' properties."[28]

Only twenty-five Negroes and Puerto Ricans had ever rented apartments at Parkchester, the commission said, yet there were four hundred vacancies a year at the Bronx development. At Stuyvesant Town, where the top monthly rent was $213 a month for a three-bedroom apartment, fewer than fifty units were occupied by Negro or Puerto Rican families.

MetLife flatly denied that it discriminated against blacks and Latinos. Weeks later, however, the company held a joint press conference with the commission, promising to bypass its waiting

lists and funnel qualified black applicants to the three complexes. The company was far more interested in burnishing its
image on race relations in 1968, with the civil rights movement
in high gear, than it was in 1947.

As the Human Rights Commission was making headlines,
John "Butch" Purcell III, who had grown up in MetLife's Riverton complex, sought an apartment at Stuyvesant Town. A college graduate and newly married, Purcell called the recreation
director at Stuyvesant Town, Edward W. Mackey. The two men
knew each other well. Purcell, a standout basketball player at
Rice High School, a Catholic prep school, had worked for
Mackey at the recreation department for six months in 1965
and knew many of the young people there and their parents
through the popular basketball league.

Mackey, a broad-shouldered man with red hair, green eyes
and an abundance of charm, had been a minor league pitcher
for the St. Louis Cardinals organization before going to work
at Stuyvesant Town. A legendary figure at the complexes,
Mackey, who died in 2004, had started many of the sports
leagues, from punchball to basketball, as well as the arts-and-
crafts programs.

His response to Purcell's request was immediate. "Where do
you want to live?" he asked. "How much do you want to pay?"[29]

Purcell and his wife, Mary, director of human resources for
the William Randolph Hearst Foundation, moved into a one-
bedroom apartment renting for $129 a month, near Playground
9. "I wanted to be next to the playground with the best court,
the best players," Purcell said.

His good fortune was connected to an accident of timing and
the fact that he, like so many white tenants before him, had an

"in" at MetLife. "I was the fifth black family," Purcell recounted over a beer at Quigley's, a tavern across First Avenue from Stuyvesant Town, where many customers stop by to say hello. "Once I got in, it was a piece of cake. I was close to a few of the Knickerbockers. I got an apartment for Dick Barnett and Dean Meminger. I must've been responsible for fifteen to twenty families in my years here."

Aside from a few uncomfortable encounters, Purcell, still a bull of a man at sixty-seven, said he has loved living in the complex. "My acceptance in Stuyvesant Town, they knew me already," he said. "But it had nothing to do with being black. I was a Catholic and an athlete. So I just went with it."

The color line did become more porous after 1968, although blacks never made up more than 5 percent of the residents. In 1970, Joseph and Lydia Brown, an interracial couple with two daughters at the time, had little trouble getting a two-bedroom apartment on Fourteenth Street. Lydia Brown, who is white, said it was a matter of timing. "Joe was the right color at the time," she said.[30]

They were drawn to the complex by the parklike setting and the affordable rents. But for Joseph Brown, who had grown up ten blocks to the south at the Lillian Wald Projects, there was a measure of irony. As a teenager, he and his friends frequently rode their bicycles up to Stuyvesant Town, only to be turned away by the complex's ever-vigilant security guards.

"It was like another world," said Brown, sixty-six, sitting at the kitchen table underneath the whirling fan of a first-floor apartment where few changes had been made since 1947. "It was literally across the tracks. People didn't even aspire to live here, it was so far removed."[31]

———

Rumors swept through Stuyvesant Town-Peter Cooper Village in the fall of 1972 that MetLife had signed a contract to sell the two complexes to Harry B. Helmsley, one of the city's biggest real estate tycoons. Residents feared that a new owner would jack up the rents to prohibitive levels, forcing them out of their homes.[32] MetLife seemed to be tiring of its role as landlord to thirty-four thousand families and Helmsley, who controlled the Empire State Building and Plaza Hotel as well as dozens of other properties, was an eager buyer.

Helmsley had bought MetLife's 12,271-unit Parkchester complex in 1968, for $90 million. Two year later, he picked up Parkmerced, the insurance company's sprawling complex of apartment towers and garden apartments near Lake Merced in San Francisco, for $40 million. Helmsley's plan was to convert the complexes to condominiums and make a fortune selling them off unit by unit. MetLife had also unloaded Parkfairfax, the 202-acre complex with a mix of town houses and apartments outside of Washington, DC, selling it for $9.8 million to Arlen Realty.

Stuyvesant Town's valuable property tax exemption was due to expire in 1974 and tenants feared their apartments were next on the hit list. The complex's assessment had been frozen at $13.5 million since 1949 under MetLife's original tax exemption from the city. By 1974, MetLife valued the property at $89.35 million. It had paid just under $1 million in taxes a year earlier, but would have had to pay over $6 million without the exemption.[33] Instead of watching the exemption expire, MetLife could reap a high sale price and get out of the landlord business, the thinking went. Nearly half a century later, the complexes would sell for $5.4 billion.

"Almost every year, especially in the seventies, there was talk about three things, none of which ever came to fruition," recalled Sanders, a lifelong resident of Stuyvesant Town and Peter Cooper Village. "MetLife would sell. Maybe there'd be a co-op or condominium conversion."[34]

The company itself seemed to be of two minds, denying rumors of sale, but at the same time acknowledging that the old place just didn't generate the returns it once did. "The bottom line is net profit," Charles T. Cunneen, MetLife's senior vice president for housing investments and real estate financing, said at one point. "In the beginning, the landlord role fit quite nicely into our image. It filled a social need and it was an opportunity for long-term investment with an adequate return."[35]

In May 1973, MetLife sent a letter to tenants announcing that it was considering a sale. But even if the development was not sold, the company warned, the end of the tax abatement in June 1974 would "require a substantial increase in Stuyvesant Town rentals." It anticipated that its property tax bill would jump by $5.2 million a year. By August, *Town & Village* reported that some residents did not want to wait for a new buyer to emerge. Instead, they were investigating a plan in which the tenants themselves would buy Stuyvesant Town and convert the complex to a cooperative.

"It dawned on people that when the tax abatement ended, Stuyvesant Town would become free market—rents at the whim of the owner," said Steven Sanders, a second-generation resident who was then vice president of the tenants' association. "The rents would immediately go up just because it would now include all these taxes."[36]

State senator Roy Goodman, who represented the East Side, including Stuyvesant Town and Peter Cooper, and Assemblyman

Andrew Stein worked closely with the tenant association exploring whether the tax abatement could be extended. They also
sought to persuade MetLife to take the property off the auction
block. But at least initially, the insurance company was unenthu-
siastic. The city, in its view, had reneged so many times on its
agreement, forcing them to go to court to get rent increases. The
company was tired of being portrayed as the evil landlord in the
periodic scrums with elected officials and tenants.

Goodman and Stein, however, kept at it. They drummed up
support in Albany, where the state legislature met, and continued talking to MetLife on behalf of the tenants. The residents
of Stuyvesant Town and Peter Cooper Village always had an
outsize political voice that elected officials keenly heeded. The
reasoning was simple. There was the sheer number of people
who lived there and their propensity to vote. Since the end of
World War II, the district had been represented by a mix of
Democratic and Republican politicians, several of whom went
on to become mayor. They included Congressmen Edward I.
Koch and John V. Lindsay, as well as Goodman and Stein, all of
whom paid close attention to complaints and political trends at
the complexes. By the late 1970s, the tenants elected one of
their neighbors to office.

"I was the first public official representing Stuyvesant Town-
Peter Cooper Village to actually live there," said Sanders, who
was elected in 1978 to the state assembly, where he represented
the district until 2005. "There was the sheer size of it. Stuyvesant Town-Peter Cooper Village comprised at least a quarter of
my assembly district. If you calculated the voting population, it
was thirty percent of the district."

For two years, the fate of Stuyvesant Town and Peter Cooper
seemed to hang on the diplomacy of the elected officials and the

conflicting views of the upper echelons at MetLife. Despite the prior rent battles, the tenants were ready to stick with the devil they knew.

"Since Metropolitan Life will have recovered their initial capital investment and will own the property free and clear, it seems to us that their continued ownership, with or without a tax abatement, would be a profitable investment for them, while maintaining moderate income residences for families," Charles Lyman, president of the tenants association said at the time. "We hope that they will reconsider and decide to continue ownership of the property. Aside from questions and disputes regarding rent increases, we can only commend Metropolitan Life for their general excellence as landlords."[37]

"The tenants of Stuyvesant Town do not want any outside investors taking over Stuyvesant Town," he added. "Since we are all captives of the housing market, we know that these investors will exploit tenants unmercifully."

Dismayed by the negative press surrounding the affair, MetLife president Richard R. Shinn met Goodman at an unprecedented "summit meeting" where he denied that the company was involved in any sale negotiations. He acknowledged the importance of retaining lower-middle and middle-class people in New York and assured the state senator that "Met does care about the tenants and is genuinely desirous of being cooperative." But, he cautioned, the company was still trying to determine whether it could, or even wanted to, retain ownership of the development.

"Metropolitan has 48 million policyholders," Shinn said, "and the company must get an adequate return on its investments for them."[38]

Shinn said that the company had fallen $23 million short of

recouping a 6 percent return in 1972 and still needed to invest another $25 million to upgrade the electrical wiring at Stuyvesant Town so that tenants could use air conditioners without causing a blackout.

Still, in December 1973, the tenants and their elected officials seemed to be suffering whiplash. Shinn told Stein and Goodman that "Met now has a policy not to continue to own Stuyvesant Town," and he revealed that Peter Cooper was also on the block. Nevertheless, Shinn, who acknowledged that many Stuyvesant Town tenants were Met employees, said that the company realized that it was important to keep lower-middle and middle-income residents in the city. A shocked Stein, besieged by calls from panicky tenants, said, MetLife is throwing Stuyvesant Town to the "real estate wolves of the city."[39]

But the following month, Frank M. Lieher, the resident manager at Stuyvesant Town, seemed to take a step backward in a letter to tenants. He said that the company was not in negotiations to sell the property to a private investor or the tenants. "It is our intention," he said, "to offer Stuyvesant Town for sale at an appropriate time." He also stated a willingness to at least consider some form of tax abatement.[40]

MetLife also let it be known that the expiration of the twenty-five-year tax abatement in 1974 would be followed by rent hikes of as much as 50 percent to cover the increased taxes, operating expenses and new capital investments.

The tenants' association ultimately decided against pursuing a plan to convert the property to a cooperative, in which existing tenants would be able to essentially buy their apartment at a discount from market prices. There were residents who favored the idea, mainly the Ad Hoc Committee for Self-

Ownership of Stuyvesant Town. "MetLife wants to sell," explained Rubin Singer, a member of the ad hoc committee who rented his first apartment in 1948. "We residents want to be prepared with a plan to buy. Why should we let some outside speculator take over?"[41]

But many older tenants, now living on small pensions and social security, wanted to remain as rent-regulated tenants. Four out of every ten residents of Rabbit Town were now fifty-five and older; the baby boom had petered out. Goodman's proposal to convert Stuyvesant Town into a nonprofit rental housing development also failed to gain any traction.

At Parkchester, Harry Helmsley had met with stiff resistance from tenants as he converted the rental complex to condominiums. The drama at Stuyvesant Town was also playing out as the city teetered at the edge of bankruptcy amid the worst economic and fiscal crisis in New York history. Manufacturers were heading south and many of the city's corporate headquarters were relocating to the suburbs.

"Does N.Y. realize it will lose a large percent of its middle class—which it can ill afford to lose," asked one tenant responding to a poll by *Town & Village*. "This is the only plan that would keep us in Stuyvesant Town," said another, C. Anzel. "I am one of the original tenants."[42]

"Our toughest fight is ahead," Lyman, the tenant association president, told a meeting of a thousand tenants and a long list of elected officials, including Stein, Koch, Goodman and council members Miriam Friedlander and Henry Stern, at Stuyvesant High School. "We must convince the city of New York to take a tax abatement, even though there is a huge city budget deficit.

"We must also convince Met. Met has gotten back all of the

money they invested in Stuyvesant Town to build it, and more than 50 percent of the annual rent is pure profit. And that's plenty of profit."[43]

Convince they did. Only days before the tax exemption was due to expire in June 1974, the state legislature approved a bill sponsored by Goodman that provided a ten-year extension of the tax abatement at Stuyvesant Town, Riverton and fourteen other complexes built by redevelopment companies, included under the state's moderate-and-middle-income housing program, known as Mitchell-Lama. The abatement would decrease by 10 percent a year until it was entirely phased out. The apartments would also come under the rent stabilization laws, which regulate the percent increase a landlord can raise the rent.

The legislation cited the "undue hardship and dislocation" if the tax exemption was allowed to expire. "Stuyvesant Town has a wealthy image because of some judges and commissioners who live there," said Assemblyman Stein. "In fact, a large percentage of the tenants are elderly people on fixed incomes."

A spokesman for MetLife seemed resigned. "Some tenants think that because we are a large company, we need not be too concerned about yields," he told the *New York Times*. "They expect more from us than other landlords. We are more susceptible to public relations problems than private landlords . . . However, we recognize that you can't please everybody."[44]

To this day, Sanders said, he was puzzled by MetLife's decision to accept the tenant-supported deal in Albany. The company was "reasonably acquiescent" to the proposal, which might have fallen apart, he said, if MetLife had opposed the extension vociferously. Ironically, the legislation brought the development under the rent stabilization laws and the Rent Guidelines Board, which restricted rent increases, usually, to 3 or 4 percent a year. For most landlords, rent stabilization is the bane of their existence.

"I'm not sure I fully understand it," Sanders said, "in the context of tenant-landlord relations today. Years later, MetLife may have come to rue what they did."[45]

Stuyvesant Town-Peter Cooper Village regained its footing in the 1980s, after suffering through a recession, the city's fiscal crisis and the loss of both manufacturing and headquarters jobs during the prior decade. State and city government eliminated one hundred thousand jobs. Crime and drugs had become a preoccupation in the 1960s and early 1970s in these once-impregnable complexes, much as they had in the rest of the city. Tenants complained of drug sales on the periphery of the playgrounds and called on MetLife to hire doormen for each building after a twenty-nine-year-old woman was raped and robbed in the lobby of her building. The company initially rebuffed the demands, but in 1967 it did install locks on the front doors of Peter Cooper Village buildings and a lobby-to-apartment intercom system. Stuyvesant Town's turn came three years later.

In response to a sharp rise in crime in 1972, state senator Roy Goodman called on MetLife to increase the size of its security force by 20 percent. He told a meeting of MetLife executives and the Town and Village Civic Association that serious violent crimes had climbed 327 percent over the past three years with no increase in either security guards or patrol officers. Raymond Ringler, the vice president of housing, told the group that the complexes were not immune to what was happening throughout the city. "However," he added, "it is the government's responsibility to provide adequate protection and safeguards for its citizens and not primarily ours." Goodman marched over to the Thirteenth Precinct house and within hours, "11 tough members of the Tactical Police Force were assigned exclusively to the community," *Town & Village* reported.[46]

By 1981, Stuyvesant Town was rated the safest neighborhood in New York, followed by Roosevelt Island, TriBeCa and Little Italy, according to a survey by *New York* magazine. "Manhattan's Stuyvesant Town-Peter Cooper Village, for one, recorded less crime last year than many upstate hamlets—less than one burglary and one robbery per thousand residents." That record stood in stark contrast to New York City as a whole, which averaged thirty burglaries and fourteen robberies per thousand.[47]

The kudos kept coming. A year later, the *Daily News* Sunday magazine ranked MetLife among the city's best landlords. It was quite a coup in a city where citizens generally regard landlords like the archvillain Snidely Whiplash. "A leaky pipe at midnight on a weekend is no problem in Peter Cooper," Mary T. Donahue told the magazine. "Efficient, courteous help is on the way in 10 minutes."[48]

The long-suffering tenants of Stuyvesant Town finally got airconditioning in 1991, when MetLife invested $100 million in rewiring the thirty-five buildings and replacing fifty-seven thousand leaky, steel-framed windows. Peter Cooper had had air-conditioning since the 1960s. But this being Stuyvesant Town, change did not come easily. The $70 million rewiring effort took a series of delicate negotiations between Mitchell E. Ryan, then MetLife's director of housing investments; Assemblyman Steve Sanders; the state housing agency; the tenants' association; and Con Edison.

Even MetLife executives seemed to be in a more optimistic frame of mind when it came to their Stuyvesant Town asset, compared with their approach during the tax-exemption battle in 1974, when the company expressed a desire to unload the cash-strapped property. They clearly did not like being hampered by the city's rent-stabilization law, which limited the size of rent increases for one- and two-year leases.

"We have never offered the property for sale," Charles T. Cunneen, a MetLife senior vice president said in 1984. "There may come a day when the bottom line forces us to do it. But while stabilization is a bad thing for housing stock, we are making a profit."

CHAPTER FOUR

Who Would Drive the Last Dollar?

Eleven minutes after the closing bell at the New York Stock Exchange on July 18, 2006, MetLife issued a brief, five-paragraph press release announcing that it was considering the sale of Stuyvesant Town-Peter Cooper Village. "We believe current market conditions are very favorable, and we have decided to test the market to gauge buyer interest in these properties," said the release, quoting Robert R. Merck, the company's head of real estate investments. "MetLife believes there is a lot of capital seeking high-quality real estate of this caliber and anticipates that it will see excellent market pricing for these properties."

But Merck, who labored in MetLife's real estate office in Morristown, New Jersey, thirty-two miles west of Manhattan, sounded one note of caution: "Should market pricing not reflect our expectations, we will not sell the properties at this time."

He needn't have bothered. The real estate market was in a frenzy with billions upon billions of dollars from sovereign funds, foreign and domestic pension funds and private investors chasing real estate deals across the country. It was also easy to obtain loans from the Wall Street banks, no matter what the size of the mortgage. The volume of deals in excess of $5 million for real estate—be it residential complexes, office buildings, hotels, malls or industrial property—more than tripled to $314.9 billion by the end of 2005, from $82.7 billion in 2001, according to Real Capital Analytics. And it showed no signs of abating.

The MetLife announcement was a lot like a silent alarm going off at a bank for real estate investors. They scrambled like the police for a possible siege, while the public went about its business oblivious to the unfolding drama. In this case, Merck's pronouncement dominated discussions in the offices of real estate tycoons, speculators and bankers, who immediately started thumbing through their mental Rolodexes for bankers and investment partners for what was surely going to be a heated auction.

"This was the mama of all residential offerings and you knew it was selling into a piping-hot climate for large deals," said Doug Harmon, a top national sales broker based in New York.[1] With debt and equity in plentiful supply, the number of multifamily property sales nationally soared in 2005 to 4,317, worth $89.8 billion, from 1,397 transactions in 2002 worth $23.7 billion. In Manhattan alone, 292 apartment complexes changed hands in 2005 for a total of $8.23 billion, up from 36 deals in 2002 worth $1 billion.[2]

In 2005, Harmon had overseen the sale of Parkmerced in San Francisco, a 3,483-unit complex on 150 acres that MetLife had sold off in 1968. He sold Parkmerced to Stellar Management and the Rockpoint Group for almost $700 million in one of the largest apartment deals ever done on the West Coast.

With prices skyrocketing, these were heady days for brokers.

A sales commission for prime commercial property might be half a percentage point of the sale price, or $4.5 million on a $900 million transaction. But for the biggest deals, the commission was just another negotiating point. Sellers were loath to hand over so much money to the broker. Instead, they offered a smaller percentage of the price, assuring the broker that a rival company would accept the sum. Still, the broker was confident of making millions of dollars upon closing. Rarely, however, would a broker discuss a commission with anyone outside of the industry.

Over the July 4 holiday weekend, Harmon had completed the sale of 1211 Avenue of the Americas, a forty-five-story modernist office tower in Manhattan that had drawn a raft of bidders for a relatively nondescript building between Forty-Seventh and Forty-Eighth Streets. It was where Rupert Murdoch and News America made their home. But in yet another sign of an overheated market, a half dozen bidders, including Rob Speyer of Tishman Speyer, offered $1.5 billion for the property. That was more than double the $600 million that the owner, the German investment group Jamestown, had paid for the building only six years earlier. Beacon Capital edged out the competition with an offer of $1.52 billion. The sale came in second only to the $1.72 billion sale of the MetLife Building as the highest price paid for an American office building.

Hours before the announcement on July 18, C. Robert Henrikson, MetLife's new chairman and chief executive, introduced himself to Mayor Michael R. Bloomberg at city hall. Not wanting the city's top official to be caught unaware, Henrikson told Bloomberg that the company was putting Stuyvesant Town-Peter Cooper Village on the auction block.

Meanwhile, the Stuyvesant Town-Peter Cooper Village

tenants remained largely oblivious to the behind-the-scenes maneuvering over the fate of their homes for nearly two months.

Just prior to the announcement, Merck telephoned the top real estate brokers at four firms—CB Richard Ellis, Cushman & Wakefield, Eastdil Secured and Goldman Sachs—inviting them to compete in what is known in the business as a "beauty contest" to run the sale of Stuyvesant Town-Peter Cooper Village. He did not have to explain the enormity of what was at stake: 110 buildings, 11,232 apartments on 80 acres in one of the most lucrative real estate markets in the country. It would almost certainly fetch the highest price ever for a single asset at a time when the appetite for real estate, especially New York real estate, appeared insatiable. The fees could be substantial, but more important, a deal this big could be a career maker, one that generated fame and a roster of new clients.

Merck, a twenty-four-year veteran of MetLife, was all business when he reached Darcy Stacom, the top sales broker at CB Richard Ellis, who was outside Grand Central Terminal on Forty-Second Street. "We're announcing the sale of Stuyvesant Town and Peter Cooper Village," Merck said. "We're issuing an RFP [request for proposals] to four firms. You've got a week to prepare a presentation and we expect full underwriting."[3]

Around the same time, Harry E. Giannoulis, president of the Parkside Group and a longtime lobbyist for MetLife, placed a courtesy call to Daniel Garodnick, the city councilman who represented Stuyvesant Town and a lifelong resident of the complexes. "I just want to let you know," Giannoulis said, "MetLife is putting Stuyvesant Town and Peter Cooper Village up for sale."[4]

Garodnick, who had been elected to the council in November, dropped back into a chair in his council office at 250

Broadway, across the street from city hall. He brought the staff meeting he was holding to an abrupt end. Now what? he asked his aides.

"It's not every day that twenty percent of your district goes up for sale," he thought. "This is going to be a mess. People are going to be very scared about the future."[5] A new owner paying top dollar for the complexes would almost certainly seek to eject longtime residents from their homes to make way for tenants willing to pay far higher rents. The thirty-seven-year-old lawyer and councilman spent hours sitting by himself trying to puzzle out what to do next. Could he try to block the sale through some regulatory mechanism, providing that one even existed? Or could the tenants themselves try to compete for the complexes in the rarified world of billion-dollar real estate deals?

But even as Garodnick struggled to digest the shocking news, many real estate moguls took the announcement in stride, jotting down back-of-the-envelope calculations of the property's potential worth. Clearly, it was worth billions and a competitive auction would drive the number higher.

Several companies had approached MetLife over the years to talk about buying Stuyvesant Town and Peter Cooper Village. After all, MetLife had sold off every other major residential property—Riverton and Parkchester in New York; Parkfairfax in Alexandria, Virginia; Parkmerced in San Francisco; and Park La Brea in Los Angeles—decades earlier.

As far back as 1994, Richard Ravitch, a former developer who had turned around the city's subway system in the 1980s while serving as chairman of the Metropolitan Transportation Authority, had put a proposal before MetLife's chairman at the time, Harry P. Kamen. Ravitch and Harold S. Jensen, a

successful Chicago developer who had ties to MetLife, wanted
to convert Peter Cooper Village, the more upscale of the two
East Side complexes, into condominiums. But Mitchell E. Ryan,
the MetLife housing director at the time, persuaded Kamen
and the MetLife board to oppose the idea. "We were kind of
Mother Met, a benevolent mother," said Ryan, who left the company in 2004. "We were really about trying to do the best for
tenants and keep it an affordable place to live. We weren't trying
to squeeze every last nickel out of the place. We certainly weren't
trying to work the rent roll."[6]

Ravitch was puzzled by their lack of interest. "We met with
MetLife," Ravitch recalled. "They were never really interested.
I always had the impression it was because half their executive
officers lived there."[7]

MetLife executives also did not have the pressure of shareholders and quarterly earnings reports; it was a mutual company run for the benefit of policyholders.

In 2001, Lloyd Goldman, a billionaire and second-generation
developer, had determined that MetLife's real estate assets in
New York and elsewhere were worth more than the company
itself, at least according to the company's share price at the
time. Goldman and his partners, Jeff Feil and Stanley Chera,
discovered that MetLife's then-chairman, Robert H. Benmosche, liked to eat at Prime, a kosher restaurant in Manhattan. Goldman and Chera arranged to get a table near Benmosche
and then struck up a conversation. Gradually, Goldman proposed buying a stake in the insurer's entire real estate portfolio,
including Stuyvesant Town and the MetLife Building in New
York and the Sears Tower in Chicago. Benmosche was friendly
but noncommittal.

"Bob was very guarded," said Goldman. "But Stanley convinced him I knew a little bit about real estate. I said, 'I'd like to buy a forty-nine percent interest and manage your real estate.'"[8]

Ultimately, MetLife declined Goldman's offer. But a year later, Goldman, Chera and several other partners did buy two of sixteen buildings the insurer put on the market, paying $259.4 million for the Fred French Building at 551 Fifth Avenue in New York and the Otis Building at 10 South LaSalle in Chicago.

Goldman was far from the only real estate executive chasing MetLife's real estate assets. Four months prior to the Stuyvesant Town-Peter Cooper Village announcement in 2006, William P. Dickey, the founder of the Dermot Company, a residential real estate company that owned property in New York and Colorado, took a run at buying the two adjoining complexes. Dickey and other real estate operators had started buying residential buildings in working- and middle-class neighborhoods with the expectation that rents would continue marching upward. Better management and renovations could bring higher profits, they gambled.

Stuyvesant Town-Peter Cooper Village was the biggest prize of all, with 11,232 apartments, many of them renting for below-market levels to longtime residents. Dickey and his then-son-in-law, Andrew MacArthur, calculated the property was worth $4 billion, or roughly 11 percent of MetLife's $35 billion market capitalization. "It dawned on me that this property was going to get sold," Dickey said during an interview in his office fifteen floors above Times Square. "It was going to be the biggest residential sale of its kind."

Dickey decided his company was too "small potatoes" to do the deal alone so he started talking about a partnership with Richard J. Mack, chief executive officer of what was then known as Apollo Real Estate Advisors, a global real estate investment and management firm. In the past, private equity firms had had little interest in anything other than trophy office buildings in Manhattan and other major business districts, glass condominiums, hotels and high-end retail. But with rents for housing sailing northward, Apollo and others saw an as-yet-underappreciated opportunity. Earlier in the year, Apollo, in partnership with Neil Rubler of Vantage Properties, had begun buying rent-regulated complexes such as Delano Village in Harlem, where they believed rents were 20 to 30 percent below market.

As the alliance with Apollo gelled, Dickey and MacArthur worked up a proposal and an "investment memorandum" for Stuyvesant Town and Peter Cooper Village entitled "Project X." The two men culled data about the two complexes from MetLife's website, public documents and newspaper articles and combined it with a market analysis of what the property was worth under "aggressive management." "Aggressive management" meant a thoroughgoing effort to weed out what they thought were hundreds of tenants who did not qualify for rent-regulated apartments. The rent for those apartments, in turn, could be raised by $1,000 or more after a significant renovation.

Their analysis projected a 13.1 percent internal rate of return over a fifteen-year investment horizon. They proposed a hybrid model in which Stuyvesant Town-Peter Cooper Village would be run as a rental property, but the owners would convert and sell one hundred units a year as condominiums. MetLife, which would retain a 25 percent equity interest valued at $500 million, would get $3.5 billion at closing and $1.5 billion over the next fifteen years under the proposal.

"We were prepared to offer them $4 billion for the property," recalled Dickey, who was hoping to preempt a possible auction by MetLife. His price was "aggressive," but, he thought, doable.

In March 2006, Dickey and MacArthur followed what was becoming a well-worn path to Robert Merck and MetLife's real estate offices in Morristown, New Jersey. Dickey and Mac-Arthur spent ninety minutes laying out their presentation and the financial analysis for Merck and a group of MetLife executives. Merck, forty-seven, had joined MetLife in 1982, not long after getting his master's in business administration from Georgia State University. Smart and loyal, he rose steadily up the ranks. Polite as he is, no one mistook him for a pushover. His customary stance was to get the maximum possible price for MetLife, whether he was negotiating with buyers or brokers.

By 2006, he was a senior managing director and head of real estate and agricultural investments, overseeing a staff of 250, in the U.S. and overseas. Courteous but never gregarious, he was not about to disclose the internal deliberations of Mother Met.

"It's not for sale," Merck said after they'd finished their spiel. "We have no intention of selling, and if we do sell, we think we can get more."[9]

Afterward, Dickey said he left the meeting with a "sick feeling." He suspected that MetLife would hire a broker and put the property out to bid, which would push pricing to the way beyond. "Merck was all eyes and ears," Dickey said. "Why not? I was giving him all this information. Maybe he knew all this, but he did not indicate he knew it. I don't think they had a clue as to what it was worth."[10]

Unbeknownst to Dickey, MetLife had secretly engaged Stephen Jones, Scott Latham and John Feeney, top executives at Cushman & Wakefield, in 2005 to advise them on the fate of Stuyvesant Town-Peter Cooper Village, strategies for boosting revenues and alternatively, the value of the property if it was sold in the current market and the potential political fallout from such a move. They would eventually estimate the property's value at $4.8 billion to $5.1 billion. Like Dickey and others, their estimate was based in part on a rollicking market and the belief that big lumbering MetLife had been a soft landlord, often missing opportunities to evict "illegal tenants" and push rents closer to market levels.

By July 2006, real estate executives were buzzing with talk of a sale and MetLife's beauty contest for a broker to handle the auction.

Metropolitan Life was a far different company by 2006 than it had been in the days when employees and tenants referred to the insurer as Mother Met. The company changed its corporate signature to MetLife in 1990 and spent much of the decade refocusing on its life insurance business amid growing competition from other financial institutions and health maintenance organizations. In 1995, it acquired New England Mutual in the largest merger in the history of United States life insurers, providing access to higher-income clients and a better data-processing system. During the same period, MetLife shed its health care and health insurance businesses and sold its home mortgage division and the Century 21 real estate brokerage.

MetLife itself was a shrinking presence in New York, where it once had a payroll of over 20,000 employees. The widespread use of computers reduced the need for thousands of clerks to input policy data at the home office. Over three years, the company cut its staff by 15 percent, from 28,000 to 23,700. That enabled MetLife to clear out its landmark limestone building at

11 Madison Avenue and lease much of the space to an invest-ment bank, Credit Suisse First Boston.

These actions set the stage for MetLife's decision to convert to a stock company after eighty-five years of being owned by policyholders. Mutual companies were designed to provide in-surance to people at the lowest possible price. And MetLife had grown to be the largest issuer of life insurance policies by selling coverage to low- and middle-income families ignored by other companies. But with the industry rattled by rapid consolidation, MetLife and other mutuals, like Prudential Insurance Company of America in Newark, New Jersey, and John Hancock Mutual Life Insurance in Boston, sought to tap into capital markets for cash to acquire competitors, banks and other financial services in order to compete in the global markets. Under the conver-sion, which required approval by policyholders and the New York State Insurance Department, the company's stock would be distributed to more than nine million policyholders and sold to the public.

The conversion plan was led by MetLife's chairman, Robert H. Benmosche, who had not come up through the company ranks. He had been brought in by the board from Wall Street, via Paine Webber. On April 5, 2000, MetLife held its initial stock offering, raising $2.88 billion. A huge MetLife banner was stretched across the front of the New York Stock Exchange, while a thirty-five-foot version of the MetLife blimp floated nearby proclaiming that MetLife had "landed" on Wall Street.

The conversion also marked a distinct shift in the corporate culture that reverberated from MetLife's boardroom on Madi-son Avenue to Stuyvesant Town and Peter Cooper Village. The dining rooms, where the company served free meals to nineteen thousand employees on white china, were gone. The company offered policies through third-party distributors, reducing the need for a large sales staff. It also started selling its most valuable real estate and boosting income at its remaining housing complex. Executives now had a keen interest in containing costs and increasing profits.

"Certain changes occur with demutualization," said Suneet Kamath, a senior analyst at Sanford C. Bernstein & Co. who follows the insurance industry. "There is a lot more focus on earnings and a return on equity, because those are the drivers of share price. They're much more focused on bottom-line profitability. When you're a mutual company, you don't have that daily report card, the stock price."

The resulting changes came swiftly at Stuyvesant Town-Peter Cooper Village. MetLife tore up the reputed ten-year waiting lists for rent-regulated apartments and, for the first time in fifty-four years, brought in an outside firm—Douglas Elliman—to manage the two complexes. Instead of simply re-leasing the rent-regulated apartments, the company renovated the units and raised the rent by hundreds of dollars to free-market levels.

"You can date the day things changed to the day MetLife went public," said Soni Fink, whose living room window at Peter Cooper offers a mesmerizing view of the East River, Brooklyn and Queens. "They went from an altruistic approach to a profit center."[11]

As always, MetLife was extremely sensitive as to how the company was perceived by the public. It did not want any negative publicity that would hurt the company's ability to sell policies to working- and middle-class families. But MetLife's decision to cut services and hike rents at a complex built for the middle class put them on a collision course with the tenant association, which battled the company at every turn.

"They wanted to convert a lot of apartments to free-market rents," said Steve Stadmeyer, who was brought in as the first outsider to manage the complex in 2001. "And they wanted a political buffer, to have a management company take the brunt of the negative publicity that they might get."[12]

MetLife told its managers it wanted an improvement in revenues from Stuyvesant Town-Peter Cooper Village, where the average monthly rent was less than $1,000. Ordinarily, a landlord can only raise rent-regulated rents by a percentage mandated by the Rent Guidelines Board, usually 2 to 4 percent a year.

But under rent regulations in effect since 1997 an apartment can be decontrolled after it becomes vacant, or if the legal rent reaches $2,000 a month and the existing tenant's household income rises above $175,000 for two consecutive years. Owners can also pass on to tenants part of the cost of capital improvements, which can help push rents toward the $2,000 level.

At the time, MetLife said it was spending $30,000 to $40,000 per vacant apartment on upgrades, including new wood cabinets, stone countertops and fixtures in the kitchen, remodeled bathrooms and new lighting fixtures. The landlord could then increase the rent by one-fortieth of the cost of the improvements, or $1,000 a month for a $40,000 renovation. So the rent on an apartment that previously rented for, say, $1,500 could jump to $2,500. Once an apartment was deregulated, the owner could charge whatever the market would bear.[13]

There were fewer than one hundred market-rate apartments at Stuyvesant Town-Peter Cooper Village in 2001, but the rents were substantially higher, ranging between $2,100 and $2,500 a month for one-bedrooms and $2,600 to $3,200 a month for two-bedrooms, the company said at the time. At Peter Cooper Village, the comparable rents were $2,800 to $3,200 for one-bedrooms and $3,600 to $4,200 for two-bedrooms.

To increase vacancies, MetLife ousted tenants who illegally subletted an apartment without company approval and residents whose apartments were not their primary residence, although, at least in the beginning, an exception was carved out for MetLife executives who had a pied-à-terre at Stuyvesant Town. "A lot of senior MetLife executives had apartments there," Stadmeyer said. In a move that shocked many longtime tenants, Stadmeyer also took down the post-and-chain fences that surrounded every patch of grass and invited tenants to enjoy lounging on the lawn.[14]

Tenants, however, complained about cutbacks at the complexes and MetLife's lack of commitment to preserving Stuyvesant Town as a middle-class sanctuary. Tenants who could recount stories of a maintenance worker knocking on their door on Christmas Day only an hour after they'd called the administration office now had to wait days for a response. "On a New Year's Day my toilet flooded and within half an hour someone came to fix it," said Elaine Haber, who raised two boys in Peter Cooper, where she still lives today. "That doesn't happen now."[15]

Al Doyle said that when he first got involved with the tenants association in 1997 residents were reluctant to bother MetLife, which they viewed as a benign landlord despite the constant rounds of rent increases. "That feeling disappeared," Doyle said. "They seemed to cut back on maintenance and security. They didn't seem to be as helpful and, I guess, benevolent."

Like any volunteer organization, there was an ebb and flow

to the life of the tenants association in relation to the severity of the issues—straight rent hikes or the installation of new electric lines, air-conditioning and other capital improvements that also triggered rent increases—at any one time. When Doyle first got involved, the dedicated core group was down to less than a dozen. But their numbers started to swell with the flow of complaints about MetLife's cutbacks at the complexes.

Retirees living on a small pension and social security, who accounted for a substantial number of tenants, were acutely sensitive to any increase in housing costs. Many of them were union members, particularly teachers, who were accustomed to group action. Elected officials also paid attention, because Stuyvesant Town-Peter Cooper Village's twenty-five thousand residents represented a concentrated block of voters.

State senator Roy Goodman, a longtime advocate for the tenants, was also taken aback by MetLife's approach. "I consider MetLife to be one of the best landlords I know of," Goodman said, "but lately with the demand for more revenue they seem to have changed their emphasis."[16]

But Doyle was also upset about the broader trends as landlords like MetLife converted onetime bastions of the working and middle classes into luxury rentals. "It's a shame," Doyle said. "The same opportunities I had and my mother and father had are not available to people today. My father was an original tenant, a marine who came back from the war. When we grew up, my friends had fathers who were police officers and firemen. They made the city work and made this neighborhood desirable."[17]

There was one other change that some longtime residents noticed. MetLife removed the stone marker from the Stuyvesant Oval that had been erected in 1947 to commemorate

Ecker's eightieth birthday. The inscription on the bronze plate reminded all who read it of Ecker's vision for the Stuyvesant project, which had been created so "that families of moderate means might live in health, comfort and dignity in parklike communities, and that a pattern might be set of private enterprise productively devoted to public service." Stadmeyer, the general manager at the time, said the marker floated around the property for a while as first one area and then another was renovated. "Then they decided not to put it back."[18]

Although many analysts and tenants believe that MetLife's decision to sell can be traced back to demutualization in 2000, the company initially made no overt moves in that direction. In late 2003, the insurer did sell its historic twenty-nine-story headquarters on Madison Avenue for $675 million. The following year, it auctioned the Sears Tower for $840 million. In a sign of the times, the new owners, a group led by New York investors Joseph Chetrit and Joseph Moinian, slapped an $825 million mortgage on the property, 98 percent of the sale price.

Merck, the MetLife real estate executive, said in 2006 that the company had made a decision to diversify its real estate portfolio, which was concentrated in several large-scale office buildings in a handful of cities. "Diversification and high property values were the two driving forces behind our selling some of these really large assets," he said.[19]

In January 2005, MetLife announced that it was buying Citigroup's Travelers Life and Annuity and substantially all of Citigroup's international insurance business, a deal that made MetLife the largest individual life insurer in North America.

The $11.8 billion price tag prompted MetLife to tap into unrealized gains in the value of its trophy real estate assets in order to pay for the transaction. The company put 11 Madison Avenue, the forty-one-story building and clock tower at Twenty-Third Street, and the fifty-eight-story MetLife Building that sat astride Park Avenue up for sale.

The timing was propitious. Commercial property sales in the United States, and Manhattan in particular, had been climbing steadily since the slump after the 2001 terrorist attack on the World Trade Center in New York. In 2004, 2,745 U.S. office buildings sold for a total of $75.4 billion, more than twice the 1,237 properties that sold in 2001 for a combined $32.4 billion, according to Real Capital Analytics, a real estate research firm. The demand by investors for office towers was evident in the sale of the Bank of America Center, San Francisco's premier financial-district skyscraper. An investment group led by Mark Karasick and David Werner bought the fifty-two-story complex in 2004 for $870 million and then put it back on the market in 2005, eventually selling it to a Hong Kong consortium for a record $1.05 billion and a quick 21 percent profit.

Prices were the highest in New York, which attracted not only pension funds and insurance companies, but also foreign investors and sovereign funds who viewed it as one of the safest and most stable real estate markets in the world. The commercial vacancy rate was down throughout Manhattan and rents were up, with the best space leasing for more than $100 a square foot.

One hundred and twenty-five office buildings in Manhattan changed hands in 2004 for a collective $11.2 billion, an average of $291 per square foot. That compares with a national average of $165, or $126 less than New York City. As prices soared, buyers were willing to accept initial returns of 5 percent or less, primarily because there were few investment alternatives.

"It's probably the most competitive environment we've seen in a long time," Dan Fasulo, director of market analysis at Real Capital Analytics, said in the spring of 2006. "Whereas in the past you might have had two to four bids on a property, now it's not uncommon to have double-digit bids for the most desirable properties. For some unique assets here in Manhattan, I've actually heard of up to 30 bids, which blows my mind."

The broker's job is to sell the property. With both the volume and the size of deals escalating, there were numerous six-figure and even seven-figure commissions for the victor. Brokers' memories only go back as far as the last deal. They don't spend a lot of time worrying about real estate busts that happened years ago. Despite the euphoria surrounding the boom, a few brokers were worried, although they kept their misgivings to themselves. "Every deal exceeded expectations because the buyer knew they could get more debt," said one broker who competed to sell Stuyvesant Town. "Every new transaction was a record. We kept scratching our heads. It was this whole concept of negative leverage."

MetLife's property sales generated more than a dozen offers. Stacom, the broker from CB Richard Ellis, sold 1 Madison Avenue, whose relatively small floors with numerous columns were not well suited for modern office tenants, on behalf of MetLife for $918 million to SL Green, a publicly traded real estate investment trust that planned to convert the stately tower to condominiums.

The sale of 200 Park was handled by a separate group from Cushman & Wakefield, Stephen Jones, Richard Baxter, Scott

Latham, Jon Caplan and Ron Cohen. Rob Speyer of Tishman Speyer Properties emerged from a hotly contested auction as the winning bidder for the MetLife Building at 200 Park Avenue, with a record offer of $1.72 billion, the most money ever paid for an office building. The 2.8-million-square-foot tower was an enormous prize, offering more rentable office space than the Empire State Building.

Speyer was giddy as he drove out to MetLife's Morristown offices with a group of executives for his first all-night negotiating session on the evening of March 31, 2005, to hammer out the details of the contract. His partners, the New York City Employees' Retirement System and the Teachers' Retirement System of the City of New York, were putting up most of the money for the 2.8-million-square-foot tower. Lehman Brothers provided the financing.

Knowing that there was little or no food available at Met Life's offices, Speyer pulled up to the take-out window of a nearby Friendly's for dinner. As they waited for their food, a departing patron passed their car with his daughter in tow. "See, honey," the man said to the little girl as he eyed the five executives in their business suits crammed into the car, "that's why you never want to be a lawyer."[20]

Ultimately, Speyer made it through a night of relatively easygoing discussions fueled by cans of Red Bull. MetLife insisted that its corporate logo remain atop the skyscraper. The insurer also leased the penthouse floor at the top of the tower for its 112-year-old boardroom, which oozed old-world money. The forty-five-foot-long room featured hand-tooled leather walls, custom carved woodwork, a ceiling of ornamental plaster covered in three shades of gold leaf and a massive fireplace modeled after one in the Château de Villeroi in France. At the center of the room was a twenty-five-foot-long mahogany table surrounded by the directors' hand-carved chairs with green leather saddle seats. [21]

Built in 1893 for the company's home office on Madison Avenue, it was dismantled and reassembled in 1958 when MetLife renovated 1 Madison Avenue. The company painstakingly dismantled the boardroom again in 2005 and moved it to the fifty-seventh floor of the MetLife Building. The costly decision to move the ornate boardroom contrasted with Benmosche's simultaneous decision to send most of MetLife's executives into exile, at a converted factory in Long Island City, far from the company's historic home on Madison Avenue.

"Think about it," Speyer said the next day. "It's the opportunity of a lifetime. To buy one of New York City's iconic properties is an opportunity we just leapt at."

With the sale of the MetLife Building behind him, Merck and Steven A. Kandarian, the company's new chief investment officer, turned their attention to Stuyvesant Town-Peter Cooper Village. Prior to joining MetLife in 2005, Kandarian was executive director of the federally sponsored Pension Benefit Guaranty Corporation, which oversees retirement income for forty-four million American workers. He did not have the same sentimentality about the complexes as perhaps the MetLifers. "I didn't predict the day the bubble would burst, but I knew things had gotten overheated," Kandarian said during an interview in 2011. "The market was frothy. We were having a hard time finding things to buy in New York and elsewhere. We had a difficult time making the numbers work. It made sense to sell."

Kandarian and Merck concluded that the value of Stuyvesant Town-Peter Cooper had soared during the boom to the point where the complexes accounted for half the value of the company's entire worldwide real estate portfolio, up from 12 percent in 2001. There was little affection left in the executive suite for MetLife's greatest housing complex. The company needed to diversify; its portfolio was overly concentrated in New York and in a select group of trophy properties. Their recommendation to sell was endorsed first by Henrikson, then MetLife's chief executive, and later the company's senior management team.

"It was the last remaining extremely large asset," Merck said. "From a diversification standpoint it made sense. It also made sense to unlock the capital value in the property. Another reason was that the market was so strong, not only in real estate generally, but in Manhattan especially. We were also concerned that those market conditions would change."[22]

Darcy Stacom, her partner William M. Shanahan, and other members of her team, Eric Negrin, Paul Liebowitz and Robert Garrish, drove out to 10 Park Avenue in Morristown, New Jersey, on July 27, 2005, from their offices in the MetLife Building at 200 Park Avenue. They were early for the appointment with Merck at MetLife's real estate offices. Every broker competing for the job knew it would be a career-making or career-changing assignment.

"I knew it was likely to be a record-setting deal in New York," Stacom recalled. "I had a sense there was nothing bigger anywhere else. This was one assignment we wanted to win. It was so unique, so different than anything we'd done."

The team from Goldman Sachs had been out a day earlier. Unlike the other firms in the competition, Goldman had never sold a property for MetLife and the bank was not a major force when it came to investment sales. More important, the Gold-man executives did not share MetLife's optimism about the price. As far as Merck and Kandarian were concerned, the Goldman executives were a scratch before their car hit the highway back to Manhattan.

Eastdil, which two years earlier had sold the Sears Tower in Chicago for $835 million, had made their presentation that morning. Merck, a straightforward executive whose soft Southern accent betrayed his roots in Georgia, had made it clear to the four broker teams that any one of them could do a good job. Merck liked to spread the work between the major firms, rather than favor one broker who might become complacent. The question in his mind was, Who would drive the last dollar? He made it clear that MetLife wanted the highest possible price for the asset, somewhere in the neighborhood of $5 billion.

Doug Harmon and Jean Celestin, who were part of the East-dil team, had been involved in converting rental properties to cooperatives in the 1980s. Increasingly prices were predicated on a rapid conversion of rent-regulated apartments to market rents, which could be 20 to 30 percent higher. But a landlord could not simply evict rent-regulated tenants in New York, where tenant rights were still pretty strong and housing court was a nightmare for landlords. The conversion process had to balance the push to increase revenues against the possibility of antagonizing existing tenants and elected officials, creating a political quagmire that could make conversion nearly impossible.

They also evaluated some of the environmental issues associated with the site, where the long-demolished manufactured gas plants that gave the Gas House District its name had contaminated the underground soil. Con Edison, which owned the gas plants, had taken responsibility for the cleanup, but every property owner had a potential liability. Given the size of the property, they also outlined the possible difficulties in financing a sale that would presumably require the biggest mortgage of all time.

The Eastdil executives set a baseline value for the property at about $3.5 billion, with a series of steps and assumptions that, if met, would bring the number higher, but nowhere close to $5 billion. Investors had to buy into the idea that residential rents would continue to rise in the coming years and that rent-regulated apartments could be converted to market rents at a more rapid pace than customarily happened in New York. Privately, Harmon and Celestin were skeptical. From their own experience they knew how hard it was to dislodge rent-regulated tenants. But they wanted MetLife's business, so they offered a wide range of values. If everything went right, they said, the bids might come in at more than $4.5 billion.

But as they got up to leave, Celestin and Harmon, a street dragster of a real estate executive who jealously vied with Stacom for the crown of top sales broker in the country, could tell that their cautious approach did not match the expectations of the MetLife executives sitting across the table.

"We were very aware of the growing political storm in New York and the desire to keep housing more affordable," Harmon told me. "We reflected that in our pro forma and in our thought process to a higher degree than others."[23]

The Cushman & Wakefield group was just pulling into the parking lot when the brokers from Eastdil were leaving the building. They felt outnumbered by Eastdil's twelve-man coterie. Stephen Jones, who managed the company's relationship with MetLife, had brought along three brokers, Richard Baxter, Scott Latham and Ron Cohen, and a top appraiser of multifamily properties, John Feeney.

Jones had developed a close working relationship with Merck and other MetLife executives dating to 2002, when he and a colleague, Arthur Mirante, had sold a package of sixteen office buildings in New York, Houston, Boston, Chicago and Denver for about $1.75 billion.

It was not unusual for these brokers to bump into each other while they competed for a top assignment. They had been in the business for more than a decade and were arguably the most successful brokers in New York. Despite the friendly greetings, it was hard to tell who wanted the deal more.

As they started their presentation, Baxter, Latham and the others handicapped their chances. They had an advantage over the other firms in that they had been secretly evaluating Stuyvesant Town-Peter Cooper Village on MetLife's behalf for nearly a year. But hiring an adviser could also be perceived as a conflict of interest. And Jones and Latham had sold the MetLife Building at 200 Park Avenue for a record-setting price, so maybe it was another firm's turn. All in all, the Cushman guys felt like the underdogs in this fight.

Like the other teams, the Cushman executives ticked off the price-driving options for a new buyer, including the possibility of building new senior housing on all that green space at Stuyvesant Town. But over the course of the allotted hour, they focused on illegal tenants and the yawning delta between the rents for regulated apartments versus those for deregulated units. The Cushman team confidently predicted that a sale could yield as much as $5.1 billion.

As Stacom and her team sat in an anteroom, they could hear

the murmurs from the boardroom where the team from Cushman & Wakefield were making their presentation. A burst of loud laughter from inside the boardroom made Stacom's heart sink. Jones was scoring points. The door to the boardroom suddenly opened and out strode Jones, Latham and the others. There were friendly nods all around, but it was clear that Jones felt confident about whatever had happened inside.

Stacom led her team into the boardroom, where Merck; Steven A. Kandarian, then MetLife's chief investment officer; David V. Politano, a regional director in the real estate investment group; and Kevin Wenzel, the complex's manager, waited. She made a quick and calculated decision to start the presentation with a video instead of a long presentation about the underwriting for the property sale. They had spent $15,000 of their own money preparing the presentation. They rented a helicopter and flew north from the Battery to midtown, as a video camera recorded the vastness of Stuyvesant Town in the midst of Manhattan, an establishing sequence for any foreign investors who might not be familiar with the complex. There were also stills of the apartments and the grounds at Stuyvesant Town-Peter Cooper Village. As the video finished, the sound of Billy Joel's hit song "New York State of Mind" filled the room.

Merck looked quickly over at Kandarian and smiled. "Yes," Stacom thought to herself, "Billy Joel fans." Merck was actually more partial to a Southern blues band from his hometown of Macon, Georgia—the Allman Brothers. But the aerial shots, the music and the video were indicative, he thought, of a competitive spirit that could serve them well.

After that, the presentation flew by. The brokers laid out the cash-flow projections for the 12.7-million-square-foot complex, and the kind of revenue generation a buyer could expect by converting rent-stabilized apartments to higher, market rents, and the price it could sell for. Based on a vigorous conversion program and a steady increase in market rents, the annual rent stream at Peter Cooper Village could top $100 million by 2011, up from $67 million in 2007. Rental income at Stuyvesant Town could jump to over $320 million in 2011 from almost $208 million four years earlier, under the same conditions. Times were good; no sense figuring out what might happen in a recession.

There was a zoning study and data on the tightening rental market and comparisons with similar apartment buildings. The presentation also looked at other sources of income, including the six parking garages on the property, 100,000 square feet of storefronts, the laundry rooms and unused development rights. An estimated $1 million could be generated by offering 275 special parking permits for spaces along the inner roadways of the complexes, where parking had not previously been permitted. Electricity was currently included in the rent, but the brokers suggested that a buyer could reap substantial cost-savings from the installation of electric meters for individual apartments.

The brokers described the complex as Manhattan's only city within a city, combining serene pastoral living with convenient urban access. They predicted that the property could bring offers of well over $4.5 billion, a stunningly large number. But this was eighty acres on one of the most valuable islands in the world. If there was a selling theme it was simple: "We believe ongoing deregulation will continue to allow new ownership to fully leverage the unparalleled competitive advantages of the complex and take advantage of the soaring rental market."

As she was leaving, Merck asked whether she had plans for a

summer vacation. Yes, she replied. "My husband plans to swim the English Channel and we're going to spend some time in Wales. But I know I may have to cancel."

"Good answer," Merck said.

Stacom and the CB Richard Ellis team left the meeting in high spirits. But as she got back to Manhattan and the car pulled onto the East River Drive, her cell phone rang. It was an executive from TMW, a German investment firm that owned 666 Fifth Avenue and the Chrysler Building in a joint venture with Tishman Speyer Properties, with unexpected news. Stacom had been working with TMW to value 666 Fifth, a forty-one-story office tower clad in embossed aluminum panels between Fifty-Second and Fifty-Third Streets, in preparation for a sale. The tower, with the numerals 666 at the top, was a recognizable part of the Manhattan skyline, even if the elite Top of the Sixes club had been replaced by a cigar bar, the Grand Havana Room.

Now TMW told her that a different firm, Cushman & Wakefield, would be handling the assignment. The news hit hard. "I felt drop-kicked to the center of the earth," she said. "Based on the size of the building and the retail component, I knew it would be a record-setting sale." Brokers, particularly those operating at the stratospheric levels that Stacom did, want a piece of every deal that comes along. Stacom and her team had sold $7.1 billion worth of commercial property in 2005 alone. She wanted to top that number in 2006.

She and her sister, Tara, a vice chairman at Cushman & Wakefield who is currently overseeing the leasing at One World Trade Center in Lower Manhattan, are second-generation real estate executives. Their father, Matthew J. Stacom, was a top broker at Cushman & Wakefield who was involved in developing the Sears Tower. Even their late mother, Claire, was a broker.

Her father encouraged Darcy and her siblings to get a real estate license while they were still in high school. Stacom, whose corner office is crowded with pictures of her two daughters, established her career at Cushman & Wakefield, but later jumped to CB Richard Ellis.

After losing the 666 Fifth Avenue deal, Stacom would have to wait five days before Politano at MetLife called with the verdict on the Stuyvesant Town-Peter Cooper Village beauty contest. The deal was hers, he said. But the elation over her victory was tempered by a piece of business.

Merck set a hard line on the commission. Just because the deal was going to involve a record-busting price, it did not mean that the broker should get a windfall. Brokers at Darcy's firm had rarely if ever seen a commission fall below 35 basis points, or 0.0035 percent of the sale price. That amounts to $3.5 million on a billion-dollar sale. But a $5 billion sale was beyond anyone's experience.

Merck named an unusually low, but not insubstantial, number for a property whose price tag was so enormous. Stacom could have refused, but the deal would almost certainly have gone to Cushman & Wakefield. The tradeoff, of course, was that the sale would bring her team the biggest trophy of all, bragging rights, lots of publicity and a new round of clients.

Over the years, Stacom and Merck steadfastly refused to disclose the number to reporters. But it was known by many within her firm, and even outside the firm, to be $5 million. It is more money than many New Yorkers see in a lifetime.

Stacom and her team began to obsessively craft their approach to selling this deal. They took three-quarters of their winning presentation to MetLife and incorporated it into a full-color sales book for prospective bidders. They also designed a website that registered bidders could access with a special password that would provide even more detailed financial information about the complex and its history. The timeline was extremely tight: marketing was set to begin after Labor Day, with first bids due on October 5, and a second and final round set for October 16.

CHAPTER FIVE

Let's Make a Deal

In late July 2006, Rob Speyer and his father, Jerry I. Speyer, were sitting in a meeting with top executives from Black-Rock, one of the world's largest investment management firms, at its headquarters in a forty-four-story glass tower on Fifty-Third Street between Madison and Park Avenues in Manhattan. As the meeting ended, the conversation around the conference table turned to the pending sale of Stuyvesant Town-Peter Cooper Village. The temperature in the room went up as they debated the potential price for what everyone described as a unique asset, an eighty-acre complex on the East Side of Manhattan, overlooking the East River.

"This is going to be a rather large transaction," Laurence D. Fink, BlackRock's chairman and chief executive officer, said as he turned to Rob Speyer. "Why don't we do it together?"[1]

Speyer responded enthusiastically. Tishman Speyer and BlackRock were comfortable as partners. In January of 2006 the two companies had joined forces to buy a partial stake in a pair of suburban Chicago office buildings, paying $106.6 million.

A year earlier, Tishman Speyer and BlackRock Realty bought the Mellon Bank Center in Los Angeles for $245.6 million, while Tishman Speyer sold BlackRock a thirty-two-story office building in Burbank for $167 million. In a bit of serendipity, Fred Lieblich, the head of BlackRock Realty Advisors, was a former MetLife executive who had actually lived in Peter Cooper Village at one point. He and Rob Speyer started working on the project that afternoon.

"We at BlackRock have always preferred to be less visible," Fink said in 2006. "Tishman Speyer had a wonderful relationship with New York City, great visibility. It was obvious to me, with our desire to keep a lower profile, and our ability to raise equity, and our history of dealing with each other, that we should do it together."

BlackRock, which managed about $20 billion in real estate equity assets for public and private pension funds, endowments and private investors, and Tishman Speyer had similar reasons for chasing the deal, much of it resting on their belief that income from rental apartments would grow quickly, while the complexes themselves required far less capital for periodic modernization than office buildings, hotels and shopping malls. The demand for rental apartments would continue to grow, especially in New York City, where fewer and fewer buyers could afford the sky-high prices. But those frustrated buyers still needed somewhere to live and the only alternative was the rental market.

Dale Gruen, a managing director at BlackRock Realty who was heavily involved in the Stuyvesant Town bid, described the market at the time in a couple of breathless, jam-packed sentences.

New York City's housing market has yet to experience a significant slowdown. Prices are high and continue to rise, which is depressing affordability. In fact, housing affordability, which takes into account home prices, incomes and mortgage rates, recently dropped to a record low. Above average job growth, favorable demographics and a record-low for-own housing affordability are driving strong demand for rental units. Against the backdrop of limited supply of new rental units, vacancy rates are extremely low and rent growth is strong. These strong trends are expected to persist, and we currently rank New York as one of the nation's best apartment markets for investors.[2]

Even before the property officially went on the auction block, dealmakers were building their teams and casting about for financing. Jeffrey A. Barclay, head of acquisitions for ING Clarion Partners, the real estate arm for a giant Dutch asset manager, was driving north on I-95 in late July 2006 to visit his kids at camp in Maine when Lee S. Neibart, a cofounder of Apollo Real Estate, called to tell him that MetLife had hired Darcy Stacom to sell Stuyvesant Town-Peter Cooper Village. Just as Dickey at Dermot had gone to Apollo with the Stuyvesant Town deal, Apollo, in turn, had brought Barclay and ING Clarion to the bidding partnership. The whole notion of a preemptive bid for the two complexes was dead, the two men concluded. "It's showtime," Barclay told Neibart.[3]

ING Clarion had just completed the $2.8 billion acquisition of the publicly traded Gables Residential Trust in partnership with Lehman Brothers. The sale included the assumption and refinancing of about $1.2 billion in debt and preferred shares. ING Clarion invested $400 million, with the remaining money coming from equity investors brought in through Lehman. The deal quintupled ING Clarion's multifamily real estate holdings. Gables, a publicly traded real estate company based in Florida, managed 41,750 units at 162 complexes in Atlanta; Houston; South Florida; Austin; Dallas; Washington, DC; and San Diego. ING already had 10,000 units in its vast real estate portfolio.[4]

Over at the Time Warner Center complex at Columbus Circle in Manhattan, Bruce A. Beal Jr., an executive vice president of the Related Companies whose internal motor always seemed to be revving at a higher RPM than anyone else's, called one of his closest friends, Michael Barr, then a senior vice president at Lehman Brothers, to see if the bank was interested in the Stuyvesant Town deal.

Beal joined Related in 1995, a couple of years out of Harvard University. As a teenager, he had immersed himself in the world of Jacques Cousteau, working during the summers in a fish market on Nantucket and at a dolphin laboratory in Hawaii. But his father was a prominent developer in Boston, chairman of the Beal Companies, so real estate held a certain allure.

His responsibilities grew as Related became one of the most prolific developers in New York. He eventually took over responsibility for Related's residential portfolio, as well as day-to-day oversight of development projects throughout the country. He was known to be amiable, blunt, facile with numbers and caustic. Occasionally, his booming voice could be heard rumbling down the hallway from his office at the Time Warner Center as he excoriated a colleague for some unimaginable offense.

Beal had gotten an early tip about the pending Stuyvesant Town sale from a real estate broker who had competed unsuccessfully to run the sale for MetLife. How many real estate companies had the experience and the ability to manage more than eleven thousand units, Beal wondered.

"I'm hearing about Stuyvesant Town," Beal said to Barr. "Why don't we work on it together?"[5]

"Funny," replied Barr. "I was going to ask you the same thing."

Related, which is based in New York and is also active in Miami, Boston, Chicago, Las Vegas and Los Angeles, as well as China and the Middle East, owns and operates $12 billion worth of real estate, including nineteen luxury apartment buildings, thirteen thousand subsidized housing units, office complexes and retail space. It also manages real estate investments for the State Teachers Retirement System of Ohio, the California Public Employees' Retirement System and others.

Related, which made a remarkable comeback after nearly capsizing during the recession in the early 1990s, is led by the tall, trim billionaire Stephen M. Ross, who also owns the Miami Dolphins football team. Intensely competitive, Ross, in partnership with the Mack family and Apollo Real Estate Advisors, built the first new commercial complex after the 2001 terrorist attack on the World Trade Center: the $1.7 billion Time Warner Center, a two-towered mixed-use complex at Columbus Circle that includes the headquarters for Time Warner, condominiums, high-end restaurants and shops, a Mandarin Oriental hotel, CNN Studios and Jazz at Lincoln Center. The glassy, fifty-five-story towers are a highly visible addition to the New York skyline.

The alliances were forming against a backdrop of unprecedented real estate deal making. Every day seemed to bring another record-breaker: the most money ever paid for any real estate asset; the most money paid for an office tower on a per-square-foot basis; or the most money paid per "key," or room, for a hotel. The volume of hotel deals alone jumped from $574.8 million in 2002 to a staggering $28.4 billion in 2005. Midway through 2006, multifamily and commercial property sales were headed for another record-setting year.[6] Very often, buyers and sellers were juggling multiple deals at the same time.

The real estate boom had started amid the economic slump after the terrorist attack on the World Trade Center in September 2001. Alan Greenspan, the economist who served as the chairman of the Federal Reserve from 1987 to 2006, sought to reinvigorate the economy by initiating a series of interest-rate cuts that brought the federal funds rate—the rate banks charge each other for loans—down to one percent in 2004. The economy responded; employment numbers went up and credit was easily available.

The low cost of borrowing was a boon for both commercial and residential real estate, heating up an already boiling real estate market. With Treasury rates falling to record lows, real estate, which was offering 8 or 9 percent returns, suddenly became a more attractive option for pension funds, endowments, private equity firms and other investors. The California State Teachers' Retirement System, the nation's second-largest pension fund with $144 billion in assets, announced in the summer of 2006 that it would nearly double its target portfolio allocation for real estate assets to 11 percent from 6 percent.[7]

Pension funds were expanding their high-risk investments in real estate in order to make up for lower returns or losses elsewhere in their portfolios. With Treasury bonds providing a yield in the lower single digits, speculative real estate with its double-digit returns looked so much more attractive.

With more money pushing its way into the system, investment banks and real estate companies raised money from wealthy private investors, pension funds and foreign firms for funds designed to focus on office buildings in emerging international markets, or apartment complexes in major metropolitan cities, or hotels. Morgan Stanley Real Estate completed raising $1.75 billion for its fifth U.S. real estate fund and Shorenstein Properties, a well-regarded San Francisco–based real estate fund, closed its eighth private equity real estate fund, this one totaling $1.1 billion.[8]

There was just so much money chasing deals. So private equity firms, pension funds and other investors looked for new trends, new sectors in which to make their bets on the real estate market. In the spring of 2006, they suspected that the rental market would be the next hot real estate sector. Consumers, they figured, who could not afford to pay the escalating cost of buying a house or condominium would still need shelter, creating additional demand for multifamily housing. Blackstone, ING Clarion and other private equity firms also saw an opportunity in buying publicly traded real estate investment trusts, whose individual assets were thought to be worth far more than the company's share price would reflect.

But the continuing boom in the real estate market was also fueled by a financing mechanism popular on Wall Street called commercial mortgage-backed securities, or CMBS. The idea with CMBS was to turn commercial mortgages into securities. Lenders had learned a lot from the collapse of the last big real estate boom in the 1980s, when commercial banks and savings-and-loan institutions stumbled—and in some cases died—under the weight of billions of dollars in bad real estate loans. For a good part of the 1990s, it was nearly impossible to get a commercial real estate mortgage from suddenly gun-shy commercial banks.

Lehman Brothers, Credit Suisse, Nomura Securities and other Wall Street firms stepped into the breach. The Wall Street banks provided the loans, but instead of letting them linger on their own balance sheets, they pooled the loans and divided the pools into classes with ratings from triple-A on down, just like municipal bonds, and then sold the loans to institutions, including pension funds, hedge funds and mutual funds. The bankers in turn made money underwriting the loans and by turning the loans into securities. The annual volume of CMBS loans surged 227 percent over five years, rising to $172.6 billion in 2006 from $52.8 billion in 2002, according to Trepp, a research firm that tracks securitized debt.

Scott J. Lawlor, chief executive of Broadway Partners and a relative newcomer to the real estate business, made news in 2006 when he paid $3.4 billion for ten office buildings in major cities across the United States, including the landmark John Hancock Tower, a sixty-two-story glass skyscraper in Boston's Back Bay. Lawlor was part of neither a multigenerational real estate family nor a publicly traded real estate investment trust.

He was not at all sentimental about the buildings he bought and sold like pork bellies. He was not interested in accumulating an empire. Lawlor was a trader, or flipper, who bought and sold heavily debt-laden property for quick profits for his investors and himself. In 2006, he boasted of delivering 38 percent returns for his investors, while he earned hefty fees as the general partner. By then, he had made it to the promised land, lavish offices in the Seagram Building on Park Avenue.

"We have a very strict discipline we try to bring to bear about sales," Lawlor said at the time. "Once the building's income has increased, the company's job is done. We never track assets under management as a measure of growth."

The high-flying Lawlor, son of a Queens, New York, cab driver, had worked for a couple years in the financial industry after earning an MBA at Columbia University in 1993. He opened his own company in the relative backwater of tony Greenwich, Connecticut, in 2000. His first deal was appropriately small, buying a former school building in Hartsdale, New York, for $4.8 million and converting it into an office building. He sold it three years later for $5.1 million and a modest 6 percent return. That same year he bought a retail and condominium complex in Washington, DC, for $185 million, a $30 million premium over what the seller had paid in 2001. Some analysts at the time said Lawlor had overpaid and predicted that he would soon be in trouble. But he quickly spruced up the retail space, signed new leases and sold the complex less than two years later for $220 million to Prudential Real Estate Investors.[9]

Lawlor's deals represented just a fraction of the commercial property deals nationally in excess of $5 million. According to Real Capital Analytics, 3,770 office complexes traded hands in 2006 for a combined $136.9 billion, up from 1,237 transactions in 2001 totaling $32.4 billion.

By the time Lawlor bought the John Hancock Tower, he was

playing in real estate's major leagues. The skyscraper had been owned and operated by John Hancock Insurance until 2003 when the insurer sold the building and three related properties for $926.8 million to Alan M. Leventhal, the founder of Beacon Capital Partners. In a transaction typical of that period, Leventhal put up $304 million in cash, or roughly one-third of the purchase price, and took on a $623 million mortgage for all four buildings. Beacon valued the Hancock Tower and a nearby garage at about $639 million.

But by 2006, real estate financing had changed dramatically. The Wall Street banks were willing to provide a larger and larger chunk of credit toward the purchase price. Why not? The market was booming and the mortgages could be pooled, securitized and sold to investors. Once sacrosanct loan-to-value ratios went out the window. If Beacon's mortgage was a relatively safe 66 percent of the purchase price for Hancock Tower, Lawlor was upping the ante. His deal valued the Hancock Tower and the garage at $1.35 billion, more than double the price in 2003. And he loaded down the property with a mortgage and secondary loans totaling 82 percent of the purchase price.

The deal left little margin for error. Rents and property values had to continue to rise. He ran the risk of defaulting on his loan if he failed to replace a departing tenant with one paying a higher rent.

"This is a significant group of marquee properties in highly desirable markets that we are confident will deliver strong risk-adjusted returns to our investors," Lawlor said in 2006, three years before he lost the tower to lenders.[10]

No real estate sector was immune from the deal mania.

In March 2006, Blackstone Group, the giant asset management and financial services firm, announced its latest megadeal: it was buying CarrAmerica Realty, a publicly traded real estate company with a national portfolio containing 26.3 million square feet of office space, for $5.6 billion. But Blackstone, a standout in the takeover field, had not quenched its thirst for commercial real estate. The company, in partnership with Brookfield Properties, agreed in June to pay $4.8 billion for Trizec Properties, which owned 40 million square feet of office buildings in Canada and the United States, including 1 New York Plaza in Lower Manhattan and the swooping white Grace Building in midtown.

Although rents and prices for commercial buildings had been rising steadily for five years, Blackstone and other buyers of commercial real estate remained optimistic about the future. The economy was strong and commercial markets in major American cities were doing well, with employment up, vacancies declining and only a handful of new buildings under construction in any one central business district.

That spring, Blackstone Group continued its high-stakes shopping spree, buying MeriStar Hospitality, a real estate investment trust based in Bethesda, Maryland, that owned 57 high-end hotels with a combined 14,404 rooms, including the Ritz-Carlton Pentagon City and the Hilton Washington Embassy Row Hotel. Blackstone, which already owned the La Quinta and Wyndham International chains, had its eye on the hotel sector's rising profit rate, up 13.1 percent in the first half of 2006 from a year earlier.

In both the CarrAmerica and MeriStar deals, Blackstone paid a 20 percent premium above the respective companies' closing stock price the day before the deals were announced on the presumption that the stock price undervalued the individual assets. Therefore, the parts were worth more than the whole.

Laurence Gluck, a founder of Stellar Management, acted with the same kind of exuberance in the residential market in New York when he paid $132 million in 2005 for the Riverton Houses in Harlem, the black middle-class complex of seven buildings that was built by MetLife in the late 1940s. "Getting into Riverton was a coup," Stephanie Tolbert, a retired library clerk who has lived in Riverton for more than forty years, explained. "At one time, you wouldn't dare go into the playground if you didn't live here. They didn't want outsiders sitting on the benches."[11]

But Riverton was a very different kind of deal than ING Clarion's acquisition of Gables Residential in that the Riverton apartments were rent regulated. Big-time landlords had rarely ventured above 125th Street in Manhattan or into scrappy neighborhoods in the Bronx or Brooklyn. But the demand for housing was cutting across all class and racial lines. New York is one of the few cities in the country with tens of thousands of apartments whose rents are regulated and kept below market levels by law.

Prospectors like Gluck realized that there was money to be made, even with pedestrian tenements. Under state law, there were a variety of ways to deregulate those apartments. Gluck had focused in recent years on buying sixteen rental complexes built under New York's middle-class Mitchell-Lama housing program. After twenty or twenty-five years, owners were allowed under certain conditions to buy their way out of the program and escape rent regulation.

Gluck and his financial partner, the Rockpoint Group, got a $105 million mortgage for Riverton from North Fork Bank to pay for the deal. A year later, the partners refinanced Riverton, more than doubling the debt on the property to $250 million, a $225 million CMBS mortgage from Deutsche Bank and a $25 million loan. The refinancing enabled them to take out about $60 million for themselves, after paying off the original loan, recouping their investment and establishing a $53 million reserve fund for renovations. Gluck, a shambling real estate investor who favors khakis rather than bespoke suits, renovated the lobbies, which dated to the 1940s; installed new elevators; and landscaped the seven-hundred-foot-long mall.[12]

But the rental income from the property covered less than half the debt service and turnover was slow. Mr. Gluck expected to refurbish vacant apartments and rapidly replace rent-regulated residents with market-rate tenants willing to pay a higher rent. It was a simple business plan that required lenders to buy into his projections for higher rental income in the years ahead. The lenders did require him to set up a separate reserve to cover the shortfall between the debt payments and income from the property, at least for a while.

In the end, the rating agencies, who are paid by the banks underwriting the loans, gave the mortgages an investment-grade rating. They bought into the speculative predictions of ever-rising demand and the upward march of rents. The rating agencies thought that the substantial reserve funds, established with borrowed money, would mitigate the risk. Critics would later say that the rating agencies were only too willing to go along rather than risk losing their fees.

In one of the largest multifamily real estate deals ever on the West Coast, Gluck and Rockpoint also bought another former MetLife project in San Francisco, Parkmerced, which had 1,683 middle-income rental apartments in 11 towers and 1,538 two-story town houses sprawled across 112 acres near Lake Merced. The partners paid about $700 million, with a $550 million CMBS mortgage and a $28 million secondary loan.[13] The secondary or junior loans are also called mezzanine loans, a cute catchphrase to denote that it is subordinate to the mortgage. In other words, the mezzanine lenders stand in line; their loan is paid each month with what is left over after the mortgage or senior loan is paid in full.

San Francisco, like New York, was one of the few cities that still had rent regulation. Annual rent increases for existing tenants at Parkmerced were governed by the San Francisco Rent Board. But leases for new tenants were subject to market conditions. Gluck's strategy at Parkmerced, however, was different than at Riverton. In San Francisco, he wanted to demolish nearly half the apartments at the rent-regulated, middle-class complex in order to erect a larger, high-density luxury complex. San Francisco State University and several neighborhoods had grown up around the once-remote complex in the southwest corner of San Francisco. Gluck and his partners pitched their project as an eco-friendly, transit-oriented development. Critics described the plan as a land grab designed to eliminate affordable housing, although the developer promised that the total number of rent-regulated units, 3,200, would remain the same.

Still, the partners' debt load accounted for roughly 83 percent of the purchase price. Parkmerced appeared to generate enough income to pay the debt service, but the partners were also spending money on architects, engineers, publicists and other consultants to develop a plan that they hoped would be approved by San Francisco.

Gluck, with his deals for Riverton and Parkmerced, triggered a new fashion trend. Another New York apartment operator, Neil L. Rubler, formed Vantage Properties in 2006 intent on following Gluck's lead in borrowing money to buy property while putting up very little of his own money. Rubler, who had married into the Olnick real estate family, rising to become chief executive of the Olnick Organization, went off on his own when the Olnicks declined to adopt his more aggressive approach to investing. He took note of Mr. Gluck's strategy of buying rent-regulated, working- and middle-class complexes with securitized debt and plans to upgrade the buildings and bring in market-rate tenants. Mr. Rubler's first purchase in what would become a $2 billion buying spree in 2006 and 2007 was Delano Village, a nest of seven buildings with 1,800 apartments sitting across Fifth Avenue from Riverton in Harlem. Rubler, backed by Apollo Real Estate Advisors and the Dutch ABP pension fund, paid $175 million, using a $128.7 million mortgage.[14]

A year later Rubler nearly tripled the debt on the property to $367.5 million with an interest-only CMBS mortgage. The new financing allowed him to recoup the original investment, repay the initial mortgage and establish $87 million in reserve funds, leaving the partners with a cool $100 million for themselves. The annual cash flow at the complex was only $4.3 million, yet the loans were underwritten for an ultimate cash flow of $19.1 million. But Rubler money was not at risk. The lenders bought Rubler's business plan: to rapidly replace rent-regulated residents with tenants paying higher rents.[15]

The hefty debt load also created enormous pressure to increase revenues swiftly. The lenders required Vantage to establish a $30 million interest reserve fund to cover the gap between the monthly mortgage payment and the income from the property. But the reserve would not last forever.

In regulatory filings, Vantage laid out its "recapturing" strategy, in which the company expected to convert 20 to 30 percent of the units in its properties from rent-regulated to market-rate rents during its first year of ownership. Vantage was setting a blistering pace considering that the average turnover at rent-regulated buildings in New York was less than 6 percent. In order to accelerate the departure of rent-regulated tenants, Rubler issued eviction notices to fully one-fifth of the residents, claiming that under state housing laws they were not entitled to a rent-regulated apartment since it was not their primary residence. Tenants had to vacate or hire lawyers to defend themselves against the charges. No doubt some rent-regulated tenants were there illegally. But the tenant association, and later the state attorney general's office, viewed the shower of eviction notices as a "systemic pattern of harassment" designed to prod illegal and legal tenants to move.

These deals emerged in a time when investors stopped looking at complexes like Riverton, Parkmerced and Delano Village "as housing and started looking at them as commodities," such as oil or tin, said Harold Schultz, a senior fellow at the Citizens Housing and Planning Council and a former city housing commissioner. Very often, he said, they did not make economic sense because the rents in those neighborhoods were already at or near market levels, regardless of whether the units were rent regulated.

As Rob and Jerry I. Speyer began working on a bid for Stuyvesant Town-Peter Cooper Village with Fred Lieblich of BlackRock, Rob and Lehman Brothers were bidding for CarrAmerica's Washington, DC, portfolio, more than two dozen office buildings totaling 6.3 million square feet. In effect, Blackstone bought CarrAmerica at a wholesale price, added a larger mortgage and was now unloading pieces of the portfolio at higher, retail prices to buyers in the local markets. Blackstone used the money it borrowed against the portfolio for its next deal and for executive bonuses. Whoever acquired the buildings would immediately become a major player in Washington.

The Speyers ultimately won the bidding with an offer of $2.8 billion. Their company invested $250 million for a 5 percent ownership stake and cobbled together a dozen investors, including Lehman and SITQ, a subsidiary of the Canadian pension fund manager Caisse de Dépôt et Placement du Québec, for an additional $350 million. That brought the equity total to $600 million. They also obtained $1.6 billion in senior loans and $570 million in mezzanine loans. The deal was put together by Rob Speyer, whose eleven-year apprenticeship would soon come to an end. Increasingly, Rob was speaking on behalf of the company, but his father was still the public face of Tishman Speyer. The plan, Jerry Speyer told the *Washington Post* at the time, was to renovate the building facades, refurbish the lobbies and install new elevator systems. "I'm thrilled our company was able to buy the portfolio," he said, "and we'll try to continue to do all the things the Carrs have done in the past and establish the name of Tishman Speyer as a first-rate landlord."[16]

But Rob Speyer, thirty-seven, was not just an eager buyer in 2006. He and his partner, the German investment firm TMW, also sold the forty-one-story skyscraper at 666 Fifth Avenue for $1.8 billion, deciding to use Cushman & Wakefield for the sale instead of Darcy Stacom and CB Richard Ellis, setting a new record for the highest price paid for a North American office building. But 666 Fifth was not just another generic Manhattan skyscraper; it was deeply woven into the family history. His grandfather Robert V. Tishman had built the tower. Robert was part of the third generation of a real estate family whose New York roots trace to the 1890s. He led the publicly traded Tishman Realty and Construction in 1958 when the firm built the tower with the distinctive embossed aluminum-paneled skin at 666 Fifth.

Robert Tishman, who died at ninety-four in 2010, extended the firm's operations well beyond New York, building the one-hundred-story John Hancock Tower in Chicago, the Renaissance Center in Detroit and Alcoa's twin-tower Century City complex in Los Angeles. "We package everything," Robert Tishman told *Business Week* in 1968. "We locate land, design the building, select the architect, work out interim and permanent financing, do the leasing, build and manage the building."

Jerry Speyer, son of a family of German-Jewish builders who fled Hitler in the 1930s, married Robert's daughter Lynne Tishman shortly after graduating from Columbia Business School in 1964 and joining Tishman Realty. Lynne's great-grandfather Julius Tishman had founded the company in 1898. Jerry Speyer, who graduated from Columbia with an MBA, had worked briefly as an assistant to the vice president and treasurer of

Madison Square Garden. Speyer tells friends that he wanted to work on real estate deals but found himself consumed with the Rangers and the Knicks. Tishman, a kindred soul who, like Speyer, was soft-spoken, polite and very smart, offered him unparalleled resources. Jerry quickly established himself as the heir apparent. "I believe in nepotism," Robert Tishman once told reporters, "so long as the son-in-law you're bringing in is smart."

But the public company, the largest builder-owner of high-rise office buildings in the country, ran into financial problems during the recession in the mid-1970s and dissolved in 1976, when the skyscraper at 666 Fifth was sold for $80 million. Three firms emerged from the demise: Robert's cousin John formed a construction company (Tishman Realty and Construction) and his brother Alan became a major force in leasing and building management (Tishman Management and Leasing). Robert Tishman and Jerry Speyer formed Tishman Speyer Properties. The two men were a physical contrast—Robert was tall and slim compared with Jerry's compact physique—but great partners, quickly establishing themselves as a force to be reckoned with. They developed the Equitable Center in New York and the NBC Tower in Chicago and the one-million-square-foot building at 520 Madison Avenue and the Saatchi Building at 375 Hudson in Manhattan.[17]

Speyer and Lynne Tishman separated in 1987 and eventually divorced. The breakup, however, had no effect on the partnership between Jerry and Robert. "It was about the most decent divorce I've ever heard of," Bob Tishman told the *New York Times* in 1998. "There was no reason in the world to destroy what we built up over 20-something years."[18]

As the Manhattan real estate boom lost air in the late 1980s, Speyer made a key decision to move to Germany rather than wait for the market to recover. Speyer, who speaks fluent German, built the seventy-story Messeturm, then the tallest tower on the European continent. The success of that project led to a larger development, a two-million-square-foot complex in Berlin that became the European headquarters for Sony.

Over the next decade, Speyer transformed the company from a mom-and-pop operation, albeit a lucrative one, into an international player when he tied up with a real estate fund and acquired his biggest trophy of all, a New York icon and an international symbol of capitalism, Rockefeller Center. Tishman Speyer had long relied on a small coterie of investors for its projects, including one of the world's richest families, the Lester Crown family of Chicago. But in 1997, Speyer and the Travelers Group put together an $800 million investment fund that allowed him to get involved simultaneously with a broader range of development projects.

A year earlier, Speyer and Goldman Sachs had led a group that bought Rockefeller Center and its ten landmark buildings, which sit between Forty-Eighth and Fifty-First Streets, from Fifth Avenue to the Avenue of the Americas. The Rockefeller family had sold the twenty-two-acre complex in 1989 to a Japanese company, Mitsubishi Real Estate. But the center fell into receivership in 1995 when Mitsubishi failed to make its mortgage payments. Speyer, with David Rockefeller's blessing, saw an opportunity to revive the complex, which had lost some of its luster. Mitsubishi initially accepted his $200 million offer for the property but then pulled out, creating a financial crisis for the trust that held the mortgage. The trust was led by Goldman Sachs and included the Rockefeller family.

Goldman Sachs, whose co-chairman Hank Paulson was a friend of Speyer's, soon forged a partnership to buy the famed

complex that linked the bank, David Rockefeller, Gianni
Agnelli of Italy, Stavros Niarchos of Greece and Tishman
Speyer, which took a 5 percent stake in what was a $900 mil-
lion deal. "Every project has one big idea," an elated Speyer said
at the time. "The one big idea here was to bring Rockefeller
Center back to having the majesty it had when it was first built."

In short order, Tishman Speyer gave the limestone surfaces
of Rockefeller Center a facelift and boosted revenues. The company replaced the candy stands and shoe stores in the underground mall with national retailers such as Banana Republic,
Sephora and Dean & DeLuca and installed the prestigious
Christie's auction house in a once dowdy space used for a parking garage. It leased Radio City Music Hall to Cablevision for
about $13 million a year and the Rainbow Room at the top of
30 Rock to Cipriani International, pushing the annual rent up
by 25 percent to $4 million a year.

In 2000, Speyer and the Crown family bought out their
partners in a $1.85 billion deal for Rockefeller Center, once
again outmaneuvering other bidders, including Mortimer B.
Zuckerman, chairman of Boston Properties; Steven Roth, chairman of Vornado Realty Trust; and Sam Zell, then chairman of
Equity Office Properties Trust.[19] Speyer acquired not only a
famed office complex but also international cachet that would
soon have him doing projects in Brazil, India and China.

Jerry Speyer, whose ever-present Mickey Mouse wristwatch
lends a dash of whimsy to an otherwise sober, buttoned-down
mien, travels in rarefied political, social and corporate circles
even for a New York real estate mogul. He is chairman emeritus
of Columbia University; a minority owner of the Yankees; a
member of the Council on Foreign Relations, an influential,
nonpartisan think tank; vice chairman of the Museum of

Modern Art; and the only real estate executive to have served on the board of the Federal Reserve Bank of New York, much of the time with his good friend Richard S. Fuld, the former chairman of Lehman Brothers.

Indeed, Speyer has carefully established an image for himself as someone who rises above the craven self-interest of your typical real estate developer. He has been chairman of both the Real Estate Board of New York, the industry's powerful lobbying arm, and the Partnership for New York City, a not-for-profit comprised of the top two hundred corporate leaders that was created by David Rockefeller in 1979, in part as a counterweight to the real estate industry. When the Real Estate Board opposed Mayor Michael R. Bloomberg's property tax increase to close the city's budget gaps in 2003, Speyer and the Partnership supported it. The following year Speyer and the Partnership favored the mayor's plan to give middle-class homeowners a $400 tax rebate, much to the chagrin of the Real Estate Board.

"He's the only real estate executive who the corporate CEOs think of as one of them," said Kathryn S. Wylde, president of the Partnership. "He's truly unique in the real estate world as somebody who is a man for all seasons, much the way David Rockefeller has been."[20]

To a degree, Speyer modeled himself after Rockefeller, the patriarch of the famous family and the only surviving grandchild of oil tycoon John D. Rockefeller. David Rockefeller, an influential figure in banking, foreign affairs and philanthropic circles, rose to become chairman of Chase Manhattan Bank and oversaw construction of One Chase Manhattan Plaza, an office tower that is credited with reviving New York's downtown business district. Rockefeller was close to presidents and foreign leaders; intimately involved in influential think tanks, from the

Council on Foreign Relations to the Trilateral Commission; and a generous patron of both Rockefeller University and the Museum of Modern Art.

"Jerry loves the image of being a very important man in New York without necessarily cultivating that the way a Donald Trump does," said Burt Lehman, a corporate lawyer and a friend of Speyer's since college. "There is a kind of exalted standing that comes of not being seen to seek any standing at all."[21]

Shortly after joining the Modern in 1982, Speyer, whose substantial collection of contemporary art adorns his Rockefeller Center offices as well as his home, sought out Rockefeller, a founder of the museum. "He made it clear that he wanted to be in the inner circle of the museum," Rockefeller recalled in 1998. Several years later, Speyer endeared himself to the museum's elite board when he haggled with the family that owned a property next door to the museum. Speyer knocked their sale price down by a third to $50 million, allowing the Modern to buy the land and expand. "I'm not sure anyone else could have done that," Rockefeller concluded.[22]

Although Speyer acknowledges to friends that he "doesn't do warm and cuddly well," he is painstaking in nurturing his relationships with prominent figures in business, social and political circles. He is always discreet, offering judicious advice or a brief note of congratulations on a birthday. "He understood the entire business, and better than anyone else," said Geoffrey P. Wharton, a top executive at Tishman Speyer who left the company in 2001. "He was a master at creating relationships and transmitting a tremendous confidence in what the company could do."[23]

Just as he drew on those connections in acquiring Rockefeller Center, Speyer pulled all the philanthropic and social levers he could manage during the hotly contested bidding for the Chrysler Building in 1997. The negotiations involved a tricky two-part process of buying the building from a bank and working out a new lease with the Cooper Union for the Advancement of Science and Art, which owned the land underneath the Art Deco landmark on Forty-Second Street. The school was emphatic that it would not accept less than $4.5 million.

Speyer outmaneuvered seven other bidders with a phone call to the chairman of Cooper Union, Robert A. Bernhard, a longtime friend of the Tishman family. The two men shared an interest in the arts and memberships at the Century Country Club in Purchase, New York. "Speyer called me up and said, 'If we guarantee you $5.5 million will you give us an exclusive for sixty days?'" Mr. Bernhard told me. "He did, and he now manages the building. Another bidder was very irritated with me. But Jerry took an aggressive point of view, and nobody else came forward with anything like that."[24]

Speyer married Katherine G. Farley, an architect by training and a top executive at Tishman Speyer, in 1991. The couple, who live in a mansion on the Upper East Side that Speyer built, have a daughter, as well as three children from Speyer's first marriage. She, too, is actively involved in New York's cultural institutions, currently the chairwoman of Lincoln Center for the Performing Arts and, until recently, a trustee at Brown University and a board member at the Alvin Ailey American Dance Theater.

In 2000, the Speyers repurchased 666 Fifth, the tower where Jerry Speyer had started his career with the Tishmans thirty-four years earlier, for $540 million. The company's partner in the deal was the Crown family from Chicago, the same billionaire family that had been a partner in building the tower. By then, Tishman Speyer controlled a $10 billion international portfolio of mainly office buildings totaling 36.4 million square feet.

Rob, who joined Tishman Speyer in 1995 at twenty-six, put his own stamp on the building in 2002. He recalls as a young boy spying the deep-red numerals "666" atop the building from the living room of his grandfather's apartment, 1.5 miles to the north at Eighty-Sixth and Madison Avenue. Twenty years later, he was looking for ways to enhance revenues from the building and he viewed the signage as "an untapped asset." In 2002, Rob struck a deal with Citibank to put the bank's name at the top of 666 Fifth and to lease Citibank space on the fifth floor that had been vacant for three years. Real estate executives said the sign alone was worth $1.5 million a year. "It was ironic," Rob said with a laugh. "It was our 666 sign. I was proud of that sign. On the other hand, it was this red 666, definitely an oddity given the symbolism."[25]

Rob had few qualms about putting 666 Fifth up for sale in 2006, when the company's partner, TMW, pushed to sell the property. Prices for prime commercial towers had jumped to unimaginable levels. The Kushner real estate family, eager to make a mark in New York after selling its vast residential holdings in New Jersey, won the auction with a breathtaking bid of $1.8 billion, more than three times what Tishman Speyer paid for the building six years earlier and the highest price ever paid for a single office building in the United States. The previous record had been set by Rob in 2005 when he bought the MetLife Building for $1.72 billion. The Kushners in turn arranged for a massive interest-only, $1.215 billion CMBS mortgage from a group of lenders led by Barclays Capital that would haunt them for years. The existing cash flow from the building covered only two-thirds of the debt service for the first mortgage, let alone the payments on a set of junior loans. There was a $100 million reserve fund to cover the $5-million-a-month shortfall, until, theoretically, a rising market yielded higher rents.

But by Labor Day of 2006, Rob Speyer and Fred Lieblich and Rob Friedberg from BlackRock Realty were focusing on what promised to be an even bigger, record-breaking deal, Stuyvesant Town-Peter Cooper Village. Their rivals at the Related Companies had already paired up with one of Tishman Speyer's favorite banking partners, Lehman Brothers. So Tishman Speyer turned to a banker at Wachovia, Robert A. Verrone, the number one underwriter of CMBS in the country. He only did deals of $50 million or more. Rob wanted him to work his magic. BlackRock brought in a second lender, Merrill Lynch, which owned just under 50 percent of the capital stock in BlackRock.

Verrone's meteoric rise in the rarefied world of high finance was something of a rags-to-riches story. He had grown up in the late 1970s in Paterson, New Jersey, a crumbling, working-class city west of Manhattan whose proud days as the Silk Capital of America were sixty years gone. His parents were Italian immigrants; his father labored in the cutting room of a garment factory. A brash, funny man with a shaved head and raspy voice, Verrone attended Don Bosco Prep and Moravian College before heading for Wall Street and an apprenticeship at Bear Stearns.

He moved in 1995 to First Union, which merged with Wachovia, an upstart bank based in Charlotte, North Carolina, with aspirations to be a major player. With a keen interest in deal financing he made his way up the ranks until in 2003, top executives at Wachovia finally gave in to his constant pleadings and dispatched him back to New York to build a large loan department from scratch. The bank had made a decision to challenge the venerable Lehman Brothers, which seemed to be financing most of the biggest, most important real estate deals in the country.

Verrone, his tie always a little askew, his shirttail habitually escaping his pants, offered slightly better interest rates and slightly better terms to outmaneuver the competition. He set up a lavish office in the Seagram Building on Park Avenue and wooed borrowers at the city's power spots, the Four Seasons and San Pietro restaurants. Everyone wanted an invitation to his parties on the rooftop of the Hudson Hotel. Soon, Verrone was financing Donald Trump's seventy-story office tower at 40 Wall Street, the former Metropolitan Life Building at 11 Madison Avenue, the Insurance Exchange Building in Chicago and the Ritz-Carlton in New Orleans.

On his watch, the value of Wachovia's loan originations soared from $3 billion in 2003 to $10 billion in 2005. It was quite a coup for Verrone and for a bank whose name many potential clients did not even know how to pronounce. He pulled it off by being the most aggressive bidder for the financing deals.

The following year, *Institutional Investor* magazine named him to its 2006 "20 Rising Stars of Real Estate" list. "The biggest challenge is to find creative ways to finance deals with a low debt service coverage or high [loan to value] ratios so that you can get to a loan amount and spread that works for the borrower, while creating a loan that can be sold to investors, and all the while making money for your institution," he told the magazine. "The biggest reward is the opportunity to work with the most sophisticated borrowers in the world while competing against the most creative lenders in the world to try and win business."

It was a high-wire act, juggling a buyer's demand for bigger, interest-only loans at lower costs, while fending off siren calls from rival lenders with possibly sweeter deals, all the while making hundreds of millions for the bank. With the Stuyvesant Town deal, he planned to beat Lehman Brothers at its own game.

Daniel R. Garodnick, the newly elected city councilman who lived in Peter Cooper Village, had none of the business connections to Wall Street enjoyed by the tycoons lining up to buy Stuyvesant Town-Peter Cooper Village. After learning of the pending sale, Garodnick spent days talking to former colleagues at his old law firm, Paul, Weiss, Rifkind, Wharton & Garrison; city council speaker Christine Quinn; and anyone else he could think of who might be able to advise him on how tenants could intervene in a sale that he sensed could be disastrous for residents. He also talked to Alvin D. Doyle, president of the Stuyvesant Town-Peter Cooper Village Tenants Association. "It was kind of jaw dropping," Doyle said of the sale. "We were concerned that an unscrupulous landlord would purchase Stuyvesant Town-Peter Cooper and try to kick everyone out."[26]

Garodnick quickly discovered that they had some allies who could also give him a short course in the intricacies of real estate finance. He got a call from Kevin Gallagher, a real estate financing veteran, who had been relaxing on a Long Island beach in July when a friend from the banking industry told him about the pending sale of Stuyvesant Town-Peter Cooper Village.

Gallagher's interest was immediately piqued, but not because he saw a way to make a quick buck. Four years earlier, Gallagher had decided that there was more to life than money. He signed on as the director of housing for the New York City Central Labor Council, a coalition of four hundred union organizations with 1.3 million members. Gallagher immediately created a low-cost mortgage program for union members using pension funds. But affordable housing was a nagging problem in a city where the "average" condominium cost over $1.2 million. Union members in increasing numbers were moving as far as the Pocono Mountains of Pennsylvania, one hundred miles west of Manhattan, to find a house they could afford.

Gallagher was confident they could devise a way for the tenants to make a credible bid for the property so that this bastion of affordable housing could be preserved. Perhaps some kind of cooperative in which longtime tenants could buy their apartments while other units would remain as rent-regulated rentals. He estimated that 40 percent of the Stuyvesant Town-Peter Cooper Village residents were union members, including nine hundred current or retired teachers. He made an appointment to see Garodnick and then rushed downtown to see Ed Ott, executive director of the Central Labor Council, who happened to have lived in Stuyvesant Town for a dozen years.

"He comes barreling into my office," Ott recalled, "saying, 'They're trying to sell Stuyvesant Town!'

"I said, 'Oh yeah; we should buy it.'

"I understood how important it was on the affordability side," Ott continued. "Our goal was to get the CLC behind fighting for affordable housing in the city. It was a no-brainer."[27]

When Gallagher met with Garodnick at the councilman's office near city hall, he brought along John A. Crotty, a lifelong

Stuyvesant Town resident and executive vice president of the
Housing Development Corporation, the city agency that issued
bonds on behalf of affordable housing projects in the five boroughs. Gallagher suggested that the AFL-CIO's $5 billion
housing investment trust could back a tenant bid, while Crotty
outlined various city housing programs and tax breaks that
might be available. Gallagher told Garodnick that the trust had
been used to finance twelve thousand units of low-price housing over the past four years in New York City alone.

"We're interested in coming up with a solution that works
for tenants," Gallagher told Garodnick. "Raising the money
won't be difficult. We'll use pension funds as the anchor investor and we'll go to the opportunity funds that would provide
credibility with MetLife."[28]

Garodnick blinked. "What do you mean, 'Don't worry about
the money,'" he demanded. "This is a multibillion-dollar bid."

The three men batted around various possibilities, including
whether the city could provide property tax breaks and even
cash for a tenant-led purchase. Gallagher recommended that
Garodnick and the tenants talk to a lawyer by the name of
Leonard Grunstein, a partner at Troutman Sanders who headed
the firm's real estate investment and capitalization practice.
They were far from putting together a formal offer, but Garodnick decided to take the concept to the upcoming meeting of
the directors of the tenants association on August 2.

Garodnick, who saw himself as a "deputy for the tenant
leadership," was very careful in handling his relationship with
the tenants association. He spoke to Doyle before every meeting he had dealing with Stuyvesant Town-Peter Cooper Village.
Early on, Garodnick, a high achiever, had learned the importance of grooming his political relationships. At Trinity, the

private school he attended, students were required to do some kind of community work. It was his mother who first suggested that he try the nearby Jefferson Democratic Club, where he met elected officials and political operatives. When Garodnick ran for office in 2005 his opponent for the Democratic nomination was Jack Lester, a lawyer for the tenants association. But the fresh-faced Garodnick diligently knocked on every door at Stuyvesant and Peter Cooper Village, impressing residents and securing the election.

"He was a natural," his mother, Barbara Garodnick, said proudly. "He was president of his class from eighth grade at Trinity, all the way through Trinity High School and Dartmouth. At U Penn, he was editor in chief of the law review."[29]

A few days later, Garodnick met with a half dozen directors of the tenants association near his apartment in Peter Cooper Village. The association had come off a hard-fought but ultimately unsuccessful campaign opposing MetLife's decision to replace building keys with electronic key cards emblazoned with tenants' photographs. Doyle and other tenants viewed the cards as an invasion of privacy, a sneaky attempt to gather data on residents. Still, the tenant leaders felt energized. Garodnick was the second item on the agenda that evening. He told them that they could not afford to sit on the sidelines while the complex was sold out from under them. He said they should begin work immediately on mounting their own bid for the complexes; it was the only way to preserve the community they loved at Stuyvesant Town and Peter Cooper Village. His enthusiasm was infectious. But there was a nagging feeling that a multibillion-dollar auction was well beyond the ken of their little tenants association.

"What're we going to do, pass the hat?" cracked Helen

Thompson, a white-haired, seventy-seven-year-old widow with a keen sense of humor. "It was the most ridiculous thought, that we could ever buy something like this."[30]

John H. Marsh III, the third generation of his family to live in Peter Cooper Village, said little, but he was intrigued by the idea. He wondered to himself, "How do we get twenty-five thousand tenants to agree?"[31]

"We were astonished," said Susan Steinberg, then the association's executive vice president, "although we were beginning to think there was nothing that MetLife could do to surprise us. They'd gone from a paternalistic Mother Met to a more bottom-line-oriented company. It became very mercenary."[32]

Still, the group decided to explore a bid. Quinn, the city council's speaker and a likely mayoral candidate in the next election, promised help. "It required a leap of faith," Garodnick said, "that we could structure something with a partner that would deliver good results, without us having to collect spare change on the corner of Twentieth Street."

Five days later, Quinn attended a cocktail party for Andrew M. Cuomo, the Democratic candidate for state attorney general, in the Chrysler Building on Forty-Second Street, near Grand Central Terminal. The affair was sponsored by Troutman Sanders and held at the law firm's offices. Not long after she arrived at 5:45 P.M., Quinn was locked into a discussion with Cuomo about the pending sale of Stuyvesant Town-Peter Cooper Village. Cuomo pointed to a bearded, heavyset man in a three-piece suit as he told Quinn, "Well, you've got to talk to Len Grunstein."[33]

Cuomo, the eldest son of former governor Mario Cuomo, had served as secretary of the Department of Housing and Urban Development in the Clinton administration, and had met

Grunstein years earlier in the midst of another affordable-housing battle. In 2002, Cuomo worked for Island Capital, a real estate company that had announced plans to take the West Village Houses out of the state's Mitchell-Lama moderate-income housing program. The tenants fought the plan, fearing that Island Capital would triple the rent and force them from their homes.

The West Village Houses, 420 apartments in 42 low-rise buildings on the far west side of Greenwich Village in Manhattan, were built with a set of tax breaks and low-cost financing. But after 20 years, landlords could withdraw from the program by paying off their government mortgages, if they met certain conditions, and then raise rents to market levels. The acrimonious dispute dragged on for nearly two years before Cuomo was able to reach a settlement with the tenants association and city officials. Under the agreement, tenants were able to purchase their apartments at a 20 percent discount, while the city forgave $19 million in accumulated mortgage interest and extended an existing property tax exemption.

The tenants association hired Grunstein to help design a tenant-sponsored, noneviction conversion to a housing cooperative. Existing tenants who did not buy their apartments were allowed to remain in place. The conversion was completed in March 2006, with tenants buying 250 of the 420 units.

"We didn't know where we were going to live," said Kathryn Bordenaro, the former president of the West Village Houses Tenants Association, who also attended the cocktail party at Troutman Sanders. "Len was very reassuring. He could bring experience and resources to bear on our behalf."[34]

When Al Doyle subsequently called to inquire about Grunstein, Bordenaro was emphatic: "If you're going to buy

Stuyvesant Town and you want to figure out how to get people to buy their apartments, these are the people who know how to do it." It wasn't as if they had many choices. It was hard to find a high-level real estate lawyer in Manhattan whose firm did not have a conflict of interest or wasn't already engaged by another bidder. Despite his role at the West Village Houses, Grunstein did not typically represent tenant organizations. He was a bit of an operator, serving as counsel for some of his wheeler-dealer clients and taking an equity stake in the same deal. But no one disputed his credentials.

Grunstein met first with Garodnick and then Doyle and the tenants association. "I tried to explain that they had nothing to fear," Grunstein said. "There was going to be an opportunity for some tenants to buy their homes. But the rent-regulated tenants had nothing to fear.

"I believe," Grunstein continued, "that in order to have a strong economy in the city there has to be housing available for people who work in the city. You're undermining the economy if all your firemen, construction workers and nurses have to commute in from Bucks County [in Pennsylvania.]"[35]

Doyle, for one, was impressed. "He had quick and authoritative answers to every question we asked," Doyle said of Grunstein. "He exuded knowledge." The tenants association gave Grunstein a $10,000 retainer.

"We had our lawyer and our strategist," Garodnick said.

It is perhaps fitting that Stuyvesant Town-Peter Cooper Village, an oasis for the middle class in Manhattan, is the perfect place to play six degrees of separation, even for the high-powered players who wanted to own it. Robert V. Garrish, a young broker on Stacom's team at CB Richard Ellis, had grown up there. Fred Lieblich of BlackRock had lived there for a year when he was a rising executive at MetLife. John Crotty, then a city housing official, is a lifelong resident. Robert Wertheimer, a lawyer at Paul Hastings who worked on the deal for the Apollo–ING Clarion–Dermot group, is married to Lynn Schackman, who grew up in Stuyvesant Town. Garodnick is a lifelong resident. Ed Ott lived there for twelve years and Doug Eisenberg of Urban American dated a woman who lived there. Finally, Richard Mack's grandfather H. Bert Mack owned Wreckers and Excavators, the company MetLife hired to demolish the five hundred buildings in the Gas House District to make way for Stuyvesant Town-Peter Cooper Village.

Now they and others were each ready to take a chair at a high-stakes poker game for numbers that were out of sync with the safe, stable, middle-class ambiance of Stuyvesant Town. It was all about how much risk the participants were willing to take, because the betting was about to go beyond all reason.

CHAPTER SIX

For Sale

For many New Yorkers, the headline on the front page of the *New York Times* on August 30, 2006, was the first they heard that Manhattan's largest residential development was on the auction block: "Housing Complex of 110 Buildings for Sale in City." The target price was $5 billion and the article identified a long list of potential buyers, including privately owned real estate companies like Tishman Speyer Properties and the Related Companies; publicly traded investment trusts like Archstone-Smith and Vornado Realty Trust; the ruling family of Dubai; and New York's multigenerational real estate families the Rudins, LeFraks and Dursts. "This is the ego dream of the world," Darcy Stacom, the broker handling the sale, confided to a reporter.

Almost immediately, the telephone in Stacom's corner office at the MetLife Building next to Grand Central Terminal rang and rang with calls from high-powered investors, global pension funds, Middle Eastern sovereigns and storied banking families from Europe like the Rothschilds and the Safras. She told potential buyers they had to register and sign a confidentiality agreement in order to get the 117-page sales book and a special password enabling them to access a website with the complex's financial history and tenant data.

The article sent a shock wave through Stuyvesant Town-Peter Cooper Village, where residents had a starkly different reaction from the clamoring buyers. They feared that their beloved complex was about to be turned into a yuppie enclave. Marilyn Phillips, fifty-two, a nurse who had lived in Stuyvesant Town for fourteen years, was bereft. She and her husband, a social worker, were paying $1,700 a month for a rent-stabilized two-bedroom apartment. "It may mean we may no longer be able to live here," she told the *Times*. "The management is intent on making this luxury apartments and driving the working class out."[1]

An agitated Al Doyle called Garodnick, the city councilman, at six o'clock that morning to say that the sale had hit the papers. Garodnick had just gotten a news alert on his cell phone. "Al," Garodnick replied calmly, "we knew this."[2] Now it was time to go public, drumming up political support as well as unifying and activating the tenants. Consumed with worry about what the future would bring, Garodnick had not been able to sleep well for a week. The next day, a Thursday, Garodnick's aides and tenant activists slipped a letter underneath all 11,232 apartment doors at Stuyvesant Town-Peter Cooper Village.

"As a lifelong tenant, I am concerned that a new owner, motivated exclusively by profit, will make decisions that could be unfavorable to all of us. That is precisely why we need to actively involve ourselves in this sale, and not sit passively by.

"Accordingly," the letter continued, "I am exploring the possibility of assembling an investor group to assist tenants by purchasing the property on terms that are favorable to us. The purpose of doing this would be to protect the rights of all tenants—both rent stabilized and market rate—to stay in their homes as renters, to maintain the current layout of the property, and if tenants so desire, to purchase their apartments themselves."

The tenants association issued a "fact sheet" outlining the public benefits MetLife received to build Stuyvesant Town and why this public resource should be preserved for middle-class families. On its www.preservestuytown.org website, the association listed answers to frequently asked questions. Finally, on September 1, as Stacom's marketing plan went into effect, Garodnick wrote to MetLife's chairman, C. Robert Henrikson, saying that he was encouraging tenants to explore assembling an investor group to make a competitive bid for the property, consistent with the founding principles of the property—"namely, to be a sustainable community for middle-class residents."[3] Finally, he demanded that MetLife make available all the documents being given to other bidders, ranging from audited financial statements to information regarding pending litigation.

Neither Stacom nor Merck believed that the tenants association could mount a credible multibillion-dollar bid. The notion seemed laughable. Yet, the tenants did represent trouble, if they were able to drum up the kind of political support and garner headlines that might scare off credible bidders.

If MetLife or any bidder believed that the sale of Stuyvesant Town-Peter Cooper Village would be treated as just another in a long line of blockbuster transactions, they scrapped that notion on September 5, when Garodnick, the freshman councilman, held his first public rally and press conference, under a copse of oak trees at Stuyvesant Town. Not only did Christine

Quinn, the council speaker, and Ed Ott from the Central Labor Council show up, but so did U.S. senator Charles E. Schumer, Congresswoman Carolyn Maloney, City Comptroller William Thompson, Manhattan borough president Scott Stringer and state senators Tom Duane and Liz Krueger, all pledging to support a tenant bid.

Schumer characteristically issued his own press release highlighting his support for the tenants and six types of federal aid that might help the tenant bid. "When MetLife hung the 'For Sale' sign on the door of Peter Cooper Village and Stuyvesant Town last week, all New Yorkers, particularly those in the middle class, should have been troubled by the news," the senator told the crowd. "It is getting more and more difficult for firefighters, police officers, teachers, nurses and other working folks to call New York City home and that is why we need to do everything we can to preserve this vital stock of affordable housing."

A *Daily News* headline the next day questioned whether it was a "Pie-in-Stuy-Plan." That was pretty much the view of city hall and most executives in the real estate industry; a tenant bid seemed fanciful when you got into multiple billions. But no one doubted that politics might play a role in the outcome. Garodnick and Doyle were buoyed by their gathering support. "We knew the deck was going to be stacked against us," Garodnick said. "But it felt like we were onto something big and important."[4]

Immediately more than 140 prospective bidders, financiers and real estate executives registered for the sale. The password-protected website contained, in the words of one bidder, "everything you could possibly want to know about the property." The idea was that prospective buyers would be able to conduct their due diligence on the property well before the bidding started, so the winner would sign a contract in October and close in

November. The proposed sale had the kind of highly condensed timeline that had become de rigueur during the boom. No one wanted a winning bidder to bail out before the closing, because of a rise in interest rates or a change in market conditions.

Stacom then organized what turned out to be nearly sixty eighty-minute tours of the sprawling property that fall for bidders, bankers, engineers and management executives. A seven-story banner hung down the side of a Stuyvesant Town building on Fourteenth Street heralding, "Luxury rentals." Dealmakers who rarely spared the time for property tours showed up, including Stephen Ross of the Related Companies, Richard S. Fuld of Lehman Brothers and Steven L. Cantor, head of leveraged finance and real estate at Credit Suisse First Boston. Richard LeFrak, who unlike other bidders already owned thousands of rent-regulated apartments, asked specifically to see the boilers for the buildings. Ofer Yardeni, the Israeli investor who cofounded the real estate company Stonehenge Partners, visited several times, once bringing his wife and children. The billionaire Simon Glick, who paid a publicist to keep his name out of the papers, also took the tour, as did Rob Speyer, Fred Lieblich, Rob Friedberg and Dale Gruen of BlackRock Realty. Richard Mack, a third-generation developer and the chief operating officer for Apollo Real Estate Advisors, toured the complexes several times.

"I did a lot of explaining about the property," said Steve Stadmeyer, Stuyvesant Town's general manager, who accompanied Stacom on many of the tours. "The most common question was about how much it cost us to renovate apartments." Stadmeyer told them he was spending $40,000 to $50,000 renovating vacant apartments. "Depending on the people," he added, "they thought it was too high."[5]

Stacom was broker lucky. There was little rain that fall and the property looked spectacular underneath vivid blue skies and the changing colors of the pin oak, sycamore and London plane trees. The tours meandered from lobbies and apartments recently renovated by MetLife as part of a $320 million upgrade, to the playgrounds and Stuyvesant Oval, before ending at the storefronts along First Avenue, the western boundary of the complexes. "It's magnificent," Douglas Eisenberg, chief operating officer of Urban American Management Corporation, said to himself as he looked out the window of a renovated two-bedroom apartment during one tour. "You could walk through the gate at Twenty-Second Street and stroll down a private tree-lined street with no cars. Not bad for Manhattan living, although it did have an institutional feel. I could do wonderful things here."[6]

"It was eighty acres in midtown," said James Simmons, a partner at Apollo." You can't replace that. They're not building any new land on the isle of Manhattan."[7]

By the time C. Robert Henrikson, MetLife's chief executive, arrived in San Francisco on September 19 for a real estate conference, he was ebullient about how the sale was proceeding. "There's been a terrific amount of interest in the properties," Henrikson told investors at the conference sponsored by Bank of America. "We're very pleased at the reception."[8]

Douglas Durst and other members of New York's real estate aristocracy—families that had been building office towers and apartment buildings in New York for several generations— picked up a copy of the sales book but blanched at the price tag. Having been through the highs and lows of the real estate cycle over the decades, he and the other aristocrats tended to avoid inordinate risk and oversize mortgages, even if their caution prompted modern deal-makers to refer to them derisively as lumbering dinosaurs. Durst discussed a possible joint venture with Richard LeFrak, but he had a difficult time with the new math that seemed to govern real estate.

The real estate investment trusts, publicly traded companies like Vornado Realty Trust, were also wary of taking part in a deal that required blind faith in future projections and a potentially unhealthy amount of debt. But there were plenty of others who were willing to pick up an auction paddle enthusiastically.

Yet, Henrikson wasn't only getting calls from wealthy buyers eager to pay top dollar for his apartment complex. Senator Schumer, Congresswoman Maloney and city council speaker Christine Quinn had each called Henrikson's office demanding a meeting to discuss the sale. Maloney and fourteen other members of Congress—mostly New Yorkers, but also Representatives Barney Frank of Massachusetts and Maxine Waters of California—sent the chief executive a letter urging MetLife "to not only identify a purchaser committed to maintaining long-term affordability of the units but also to try to secure financing to facilitate the sale and acquisitions of the buildings."

"Government helped MetLife build Stuy Town and Peter Cooper and it can help keep the developments affordable in the years to come," Maloney said.

Quinn was sitting in the back of her black Suburban outside the Moonstruck diner at Twenty-Third Street and Ninth Avenue when she finally got Henrikson on her cell phone. "He could not have been ruder and less helpful," Quinn said, her voice rising with the memory. "He said, 'I don't have to talk to you; I barely have to talk to Chuck Schumer.' He was unwilling to have a dialogue, unwilling to slow down the process. A furious exchange ensued. I got off the phone and my driver asked, 'Who was that?'"[9]

Schumer did not have better luck, although he did meet with Henrikson on September 25 at the Crowne Plaza hotel in White Plains, thirty minutes north of Manhattan, and the conversation was more civil. "I begged him not to do it," Schumer said, "but it was clear that they were going to maximize profits. It was home to nurses, life insurance clerks, the middle class. There's plenty of profit to be made in putting up new buildings. There seemed to be no justification for converting Stuyvesant Town into a luxury complex."[10]

The cover of Stacom's 117-page sales book featured an aerial view of a forest of red brick Stuyvesant Town-Peter Cooper Village buildings across the broad middle of the island of Manhattan, with the Empire State Building in the background and the East River in the foreground.[11] Inside was a playbook for potential buyers seeking higher revenues to justify the highest price ever for a single real estate asset in the United States. It was, as the brochure stated, a "once in a lifetime opportunity." It was maybe a hundred pages thicker than the typical sales brochure from a longtime landlord, which tended to sketch out some vital statistics about the number of units in the building and the current rent roll. The pro forma is almost always rosy, but not so rosy that it would discourage the buyer from thinking that he or she could do better.

Stacom's starting point was the sheer size of the sister complexes: 12.7 million square feet—the equivalent of nearly five Empire State Buildings—with 11,232 apartments, 100,000 square feet of convenience-oriented shops, 17,000 square feet of professional office space, 15 playgrounds and a total of 2,260 parking spaces in six separate garages. The book suggested a new owner could pull a variety of levers to boost the income stream, ranging from combining apartments for larger families and creating "senior friendly" buildings to filling the retail space with deluxe stores paying higher rents. The parking garages could be opened to the public at higher rates than those currently charged to tenants. In addition, the loop roadways in the complexes could be reserved for monthly parkers "with revenue potential approaching $1 million."

Although the rather spartan apartments at Stuyvesant Town-Peter Cooper never had a "luxury" image in the minds of most New Yorkers, the book suggested that "importing doormen" and adding "health club amenities" and "an elite private school" would establish a compelling ambiance for "the discerning tastes of Manhattan's market-rate apartment community." Finally, there were potential "development rights" on the eighty-acre site that might enable a new owner to erect a more typical brass-and-glass high-rise condominium building.

"New ownership has infinite opportunities to personalize, improve and transform the complex into the city's most prominent market-rate master community," the book from CB Richard Ellis stated.

But the sales pitch indicated that the primary way to increase revenues and, presumably, profits was to deregulate apartments and hike rents. If all went according to plan, the book estimated that rents could more than double by 2018 to nearly $519 million at Stuyvesant Town and to $170 million at Peter Cooper. Approximately 72 percent of the complex's 11,232 apartments were rent stabilized under New York law, meaning rent increases were restricted by the city's Rent Guidelines Board, usually to 2, 3 or 4 percent per year.

The disparity in rent and income between regulated and

market-rate rents was striking. At Stuyvesant Town, where few apartments have more than one bathroom, residents of rent-regulated apartments paid an average of $1,351 for a two-bedroom unit, while the average rent for a deregulated apartment was 134 percent higher, at $3,167.

At Peter Cooper Village, where the apartments are some-what larger, the average rent for regulated units was $1,178 for a one-bedroom to $1,581 for a three-bedroom. The average rent for deregulated apartments, which routinely underwent a $50,000 upgrade at Peter Cooper with new kitchen cabinets, stone counters and a refurbished bathroom, ranged from $2,662 to $5,842. The yawning gap between rent-stabilized rents and market rates is what made so many buyers willing to, essentially, overpay. The question in their minds was, how fast can we bring apartments to market rents?

A landlord cannot simply evict a tenant and start charging higher rents. The New York rent-stabilization laws protect more than one million apartments from steep rent increases. However, under a byzantine set of regulations, once an apartment becomes vacant, it can be deregulated under certain conditions. Landlords are permitted to pass on to tenants a portion of the cost of certain capital improvements, which helps them in getting above the $2,000-a-month threshold. So for instance, MetLife said it usually spent $40,000 renovating vacant apartments at Stuyvesant Town. Under the law in 2006, the landlord would be permitted to increase the rent by one-fortieth of the cost, or $1,000 per month. Therefore, a vacant apartment that had rented for $1,100 or more per month would automatically be deregulated.

At the same time, MetLife and its managing agent, Rose Associates, sought to weed out tenants who did not qualify for a stabilized unit, either because the tenant had illegally subleased the apartment, or because the apartment was not the tenant's primary residence. Between the eviction of so-called illegal tenants and the renovation of vacant apartments, known as "vacancy decontrol," MetLife had deregulated roughly three thousand apartments in Stuyvesant Town and Peter Cooper since 2000. In other words, the MetLife executive, or anyone else, who lived in New Jersey but kept an apartment in Stuyvesant Town for the occasional weekend visit to Manhattan was now out of luck.

The sales book suggested that a new owner could more quickly deregulate apartments by adopting a more aggressive approach to eliminating those "illegal" tenants. And the turnover rate, the number of apartments that could be brought to market rents in any given year, became critical to any buyer's calculations. According to the projections in the book, the number of market-rate apartments in Stuyvesant Town-Peter Cooper Village would rise to 6,307, or more than half the total units, by the end of 2011, from 3,247 in 2006. That kind of rapid turnover—an average of 612 apartments per year, and nearly 100 units more than what MetLife had done in the prior two years—would result in a tripling of the net operating income to $316.7 million in 2011, and $437.6 million in 2015. That upside potential was what had captivated so many bidders. Of course, it all depended on rents and demand continuing to rise at a steady clip. And it meant they would have to evict many people and raise rents by 25 percent or more.

But in the first couple of years, the new owner would have to plug the shortfall between the income from the property and the mortgage payments or debt service. The CB Richard Ellis sales book estimated that the net income in 2007 would be

$167.4 million, meaning the initial return for an investor paying the target price of more than $4 billion would be less than the roughly 5 percent return on a Treasury bill. In the feverish market for apartment buildings in New York City, buyers had been willing to accept smaller and smaller returns, in part because of the ready availability of credit from Wall Street and equity from investors. Bidders had their pick of banks and pension funds for the Stuyvesant Town-Peter Cooper sale.

"There's a lot of interest in this asset because of the fact it's a one-of-a-kind purchase," LeFrak said at the time. "On the other hand, however they try to cast it, it's not a trophy. It's meat and potatoes."[12]

"There was a lot of buzz," said Fred Lieblich of BlackRock, who was working with Rob Speyer. "Capital sources came out of the woodwork."[13]

"The lenders weren't exclusive," added James Simmons, a partner at Apollo. "Every single lending institution wanted to be aligned with what it thought were the leading bidders."[14]

As giddy as the bidders and their lenders were, tenants and housing activists were appalled by Stacom's book. For Garodnick, Doyle and their supporters it sounded like the death knell for Stuyvesant Town-Peter Cooper Village as Manhattan's unpretentious bastion for middle-class families. "Stuyvesant Town is a middle-class community, and we do not want to lose that identity to the highest bidder," said Garodnick. "The tenants are not going to sit by and watch it become a place of pieds-a-terre. This is a place where people live and work in New York City."

The tenants association and their lawyer-strategist Len Grunstein said Stacom and MetLife had initially refused to recognize them as a legitimate bidder and provide the sale book and other pertinent financial information. That prompted another rally at city hall with Garodnick, Quinn and other elected officials chastising MetLife's arrogant posture. MetLife insisted that it never tried to exclude the tenants. Stacom subsequently called Garodnick saying there must have been a misunderstanding and quickly relinquished the documents. If MetLife hesitated, they may have wanted to avoid conferring any legitimacy on the tenants by providing the book.

Inside Stuyvesant Town-Peter Cooper Village, Doyle; John H. Marsh III, a computer programmer; and other tenant leaders began circulating resolutions and petitions throughout the complex, as a way of informing both rent-regulated and market-rate residents about the issues and building a united front in favor of retaining their middle-class community. Marsh set up forums on the tenant union website and organized a network of volunteers in every building in Stuyvesant Town and Peter Cooper to relay the concerns of residents and to disburse literature. Often, Marsh said, the most diligent volunteers, easily identifiable in their official yellow T-shirts, were former MetLife employees and retired teachers living on their pensions.

"I saw it as a way of building a stronger, more self-sustaining tenant association," said Marsh, an intensely private man in his forties. "I kind of saw each building as its own village and the board as the unifying federal government."[15]

Senators Schumer and Hillary Clinton, Congresswoman Maloney, the city's public advocate Betsy Gotbaum and other elected officials publicly endorsed the tenant-led bid. By the end of September, the New York City Central Labor Council had also signed on. The council sent a September 29, 2006, letter to Mayor Bloomberg asking him to call for a meeting between MetLife and the tenants "in order to mediate a positive outcome for the residents of Stuyvesant Town-Peter Cooper Village."

"We have secured the sources of capital to join in purchasing this property," the letter also said. "We have an economically viable plan for MetLife to preserve their profit so we can save this working middle-class neighborhood."

Broadly speaking, Grunstein and Doyle wanted to create a condominium or cooperative in which at least 20 percent of the units would remain at affordable rents in perpetuity and another block of apartments would be sold to existing tenants at a discount to the market. There would be restrictions on the resale of those units so that they would remain affordable in the future. Another chunk of apartments would be sold to outsiders, with the proceeds used to pay down the debt and subsidize the rental units. "We're trying to maintain affordability and the same opportunities we and our parents had when they first moved here," Doyle said at the time.[16]

Stuyvesant Town-Peter Cooper Village was becoming a cause célèbre for housing activists in a city where even 750-square-foot, one-room studio apartments rent for more than $2,000 a month. "We have a housing crisis," said Rosie Mendez, city councilwoman for the Lower East Side, who submitted a bill designed to hobble MetLife's sale. "The city really needs to take a look at this. It alarmed me how much affordable housing we might be losing."[17]

The city's inventory of affordable housing for low- and moderate-income tenants had fallen sharply in recent years as private investors with deep pockets had purchased tens of thousands of tenement apartments in the poor and working-class neighborhoods of Harlem, Washington Heights, East New York,

Brooklyn and parts of Queens. Increasingly, not only poor people were finding it difficult to find housing that fit their budget, but now many middle-class New Yorkers saw prices and rents soar beyond their grasp. In 2005, Mayor Bloomberg announced an expanded $7.5 billion program to build 92,000 units of affordable housing and to preserve 73,000 units that were in state and city programs due to expire by 2013. But activists complained that the city was losing affordable housing units faster than new apartments were being built.

"This sale is the perfect illustration of the hole in the bottom of the bucket in the Bloomberg housing plan," Michael McKee, treasurer of the Tenants Political Action Committee, told the *New York Sun*, a weekly newspaper. "The plan deals only with production. They will never build as much as we're losing."

Grunstein and Gallagher, just like the other bidders, set up "war rooms" at their respective offices stocked with data about the two complexes and an elaborate financial model and tapped into New York's financial networks for partners capable of investing or financing the tenant bid. Gallagher talked to bankers at Deutsche Bank and JPMorgan Chase, as well as RREEF (Rosenberg Real Estate Equity Fund, named after founder Claude Rosenberg) and SL Green, a publicly traded real estate investment trust. He also talked to Colony Capital, a private real estate investment firm based in Los Angeles that controlled $36 billion worth of real estate around the globe, about becoming involved in the deal. It was an unusual transaction for Colony, a clear-eyed investor. But the company thought that the tenant group might emerge from the crowded field as a contender, if only because of the increasingly political atmosphere.

"It was not, when you think about who we are, the most natural fit for us," recalled Richard B. Saltzman, Colony's president, who was involved in the negotiations. "That's why we ended up playing it with a different angle, dealing directly with the tenants. We thought, 'Maybe there's an opportunity for us to buy on a much more cost-effective basis, versus any of the other groups.' It was going to be a fairly visible hot potato and there was a chance that the seller might bite and deal directly with the tenants."[18]

Grunstein approached Ziel Feldman and Kevin P. Maloney of the Property Markets Group, a New York real estate firm with $3 billion in assets. He also turned to a client and onetime friend who owned the landmark Woolworth Building near city hall in Lower Manhattan, Ruby Schron. A billionaire, Schron ran a real estate company with holdings in fourteen states that managed over thirty thousand apartments. Despite the size of his empire, he was not well-known because he rarely if ever talked to the press. But he did operate a complex similar to Stuyvesant Town, Fresh Meadows in Queens, which was originally built by another insurance company, New York Life. Schron considered investing as much as $300 million and managing the two complexes.

As the October 5 deadline for the first round of bids neared, Grunstein and Gallagher hopped from one meeting to another with bankers, investors, the tenants association and Garodnick in an effort to formalize the offer. With the help of Quinn's office, Garodnick also met with many of the other bidders, who were interested at least in hearing the concerns of the tenants and at most in forming a partnership. He also met with city officials, including Shaun Donovan, then the city's housing commissioner, about enhancing the value of the tenant bid. Would the city provide subsidies for the units that would be rent stabilized and, perhaps, provide tax-free financing? Could the city also provide a property tax exemption to keep the complex affordable in perpetuity? Grunstein was already talking about creating a nonprofit corporation to own the property.

Early on, city officials had seemed receptive. Emily A. Youssouf, president of the city's Housing Development Corporation, which encourages private investment in low- and moderately priced housing through low-interest mortgages and tax-free bonds, told reporters that her agency could use its reserves to make a loan to a buyer that would enable them to offer the apartments to current residents at a price they could afford. "Clearly, the potential sale of Stuyvesant Town-Peter Cooper Village is of significant concern to the administration and the mayor would very much want to work with any potential buyer to preserve affordable housing in these properties," said Donovan, the housing commissioner.[19]

But as the weeks wore on and it became clear that the sale price would be well above $4 billion, two opposing views surfaced within the Bloomberg administration. Shaun Donovan, the housing commissioner, and Rafael E. Cestero, a deputy commissioner, began analyzing the sale book and the potential cost of subsidizing the tenant bid. City hall had gotten a heads-up from Henrikson about the pending sale, so it was no surprise. Separately, Emily Youssouf at the Housing Development Corporation conducted a similar analysis. In August, Deputy Mayor Daniel L. Doctoroff, Donovan and Cestero met with Stacom at city hall to discuss the sale process, the real estate market and the underwriting for the sale. They knew it was "going to create a lot of noise."

Cestero set up what he referred to as a SWAT team at the Department of Housing. The officials recognized that the sale did not have to go through a regulatory review, which somewhat limited the city's ability to intervene. But Cestero also knew that the loss of rent-regulated housing at Stuyvesant Town-Peter Cooper Village could knock a big hole in the mayor's much-heralded housing plan. He and his team spent weeks digging through Stacom's sale book and analyzing different financial structures in which the city could use its standard tools for creating affordable housing—low-cost financing, a property tax break and cash subsidies—on a $5 billion deal.

Doctoroff met at city hall on September 7 with MetLife's general counsel James L. Lipscomb and its senior vice president in charge of government relations, Michael A. Zarcone, in an effort to gauge the insurance company's reaction if the city were to intervene on behalf of the tenants. Was there a way for the city to preserve a block of units as affordable housing that would not impair MetLife's ability to make a profit? For their part, the executives were absolute: The sale of the property was a private transaction. MetLife was furious that the Stuyvesant Town sale was being cast as a blow to "affordable housing." They had kept true to the bargain struck with Mayor La Guardia by keeping rents low for thirty-five years. Moreover, John Calagna, a MetLife vice president, said, "This is not a middle-class oasis. The median income at Peter Cooper is $80,000 and the average is $120,000."[20]

Whether or not they qualify as middle class by MetLife's definition, a two-income family earning $100,000 finds it hard to raise children in Manhattan given the high rents and sale prices. According to census figures, 15 percent of the Stuyvesant Town-Peter Cooper residents were sixty-five or older and presumably living on social security and pension payments. Cestero came up with a plan and presented it to Doctoroff, a former investment banker, who poked holes in the proposal, questioned some of the assumptions and asked him to run the numbers again. By the third week of September, Cestero had revised his analysis and was questioning the economic viability of a $5 billion price tag for the two complexes. His judgment was that the sales book assumed a turnover rate that was far too aggressive.

He surmised that the size of the mortgage would be prohibitive and the revenue assumptions, based on the rapid conversion of rent-regulated units to market rents, were unlikely to be achieved. Therefore he concluded that it would be a poor use of scarce city resources to intervene in such an overheated market on behalf of tenants, a move that could cost as much as $700 million in cash, incentives and tax breaks, the equivalent of the capital budget for the city's housing agency for two and a half years.[21] In any event, his report said that 20 percent of the apartments would remain rent regulated for twenty-five years under the current laws. Cestero said he sent his conclusions to Donovan, who passed it on to Doctoroff, who concurred.

"Even after making a number of aggressive assumptions about what would happen at the property in terms of turnover, we couldn't figure out how to get to more than $4.5 billion in value, and that was at the far end of our projections," said Donovan, who was later appointed U.S. secretary of housing and urban development by President Barack Obama. "And $4.5 billion would've been a very high price to pay for that amount of affordable housing."[22]

Doctoroff, Cestero and Donovan met privately at city hall with what they viewed as the leading contenders for the property, including Rob Speyer, Jim Simmons of Apollo, and William P. Dickey of Dermot. All three men said that while city officials mainly asked questions, they left the meeting with the clear sense that the city would remain on the sidelines. "They said," Dickey recalled, " 'We haven't seen a reason to intervene and we don't know what we'd do if there was one.' "[23]

Stephen Ross and Bruce Beal of Related also met with Donovan, Youssouf and Doctoroff, who had a long-term friendship with Ross. Ross and Beal had been hoping that Donovan or Doctoroff would make a public statement urging MetLife to ensure that one-fifth of the apartments at Stuyvesant Town remained under rent stabilization forever. They owned and managed subsidized housing in the city, as well as luxury buildings. Beal told them he would bid for the property and he wanted the city to pledge to freeze property taxes and provide incentives for affordable housing. But his plea was met with silence.

"They wanted the city to put in a ridiculous amount of money," Youssouf scoffed.[24]

Meanwhile, Youssouf, who continued meeting with Garodnick, was more sympathetic to a tenant-led bid. She had told the *Times* early on that MetLife had "built the properties with the help of the city" and the tenant today could make a winning bid with a city-assisted deal. Youssouf and her deputy John Crotty, a lifelong resident of Stuyvesant Town, devised a non-eviction plan to turn Stuyvesant Town and Peter Cooper into a co-op with city bonds and a cap on property taxes for ten years. William Thompson, the city comptroller, said he was willing to invest pension funds in support of the tenant bid, and Quinn offered enthusiastic political support.

It was nowhere near as expensive as her colleagues from the housing agency indicated, Youssouf insisted. Renters could remain in place, while the proceeds from the sale of thousands of other apartments could be used to pay down the initial debt. She sent her own report to Doctoroff and lobbied for its adoption by phone while attending a housing conference in San Francisco on September 19.

But Mayor Bloomberg had already assured MetLife executives at their first meeting at city hall that he had no intention of interfering in a private transaction. He had made public statements to that effect. His deputies were well aware of Bloomberg's views.

For those who said the city should not intervene in a free-market deal, Youssouf countered that MetLife was given free land in the 1940s to build the complexes and had since made a fortune on the property. She argued that the city should act to preserve this middle-class enclave in Manhattan. "This was a way to create a large amount of affordable housing," Youssouf said. "We tried to counter every argument to make it the least costly alternative. I was frankly devastated they didn't do this."[25]

Her relationship with Donovan, an equally strong personality, was stormy and she was unable to convince Doctoroff, who subsequently ordered her to fall into line. "You're off the reservation," Doctoroff told her, according to housing officials. "You've got to get on the same team."

Publicly, Doctoroff would only say that the city "continued to monitor the situation," but he warned reporters privately that he did not want to leave the impression that intervention by the city was likely.

CHAPTER SEVEN

"The More You Spend, the More We Can Lend Against It"

On October 5, thirteen bidders submitted their offers to Stacom in what was essentially the qualifying round for the sale. All the bidders knew that the second round would be the showdown. Like elite runners in a marathon, the question for the bidders was whether to come out strong and try to scare off the competition, or draft behind the front-runner until the last mile, then spring to the finish line with a blockbuster number. All of the bidders signed confidentiality agreements prohibiting them from disclosing information about the bidding, the sales book and the finances of Stuyvesant Town-Peter Cooper Village. But there are few secrets in the clubby world of real estate.

Rob Speyer and BlackRock were the highest, with a $5.1 billion offer, according to key figures in the sales process. Simon Glick, who owned a major stake in the Canary Wharf office complex in London, was not far behind. His partner was the Morgan Stanley Real Estate Fund and he had a $5 billion line of credit from Barclays. The Apollo–ING Clarion–Dermot group was also ranked near the front.

Garodnick, Doyle and the tenant association submitted a surprisingly high offer, $4.5 billion, in partnership with Colony Capital, Ruby Schron and JPMorgan Chase. Yet, it was a very tenuous alliance that threatened to unravel at any moment. The tenant group wanted to stay in the game. Even if it was not the highest offer, they hoped that a respectable bid might prompt MetLife to strike a deal with them, if only to avoid the political fallout from ignoring the residents.

The Related Companies and Lehman Brothers were in the same neighborhood, as was Steve Roth of Vornado Realty Trust, who had picked up the royal family of Qatar as a partner. Ofer Yardeni, the Israeli cofounder of Stonehenge Partners, offered $4.6 billion. He was backed by Cadim, a division of the giant Canadian pension fund manager Caisse de Dépôt et Placement du Quebec. Yardeni planned to move his headquarters to Stuyvesant Town if he won so that he could oversee what he saw as a long-term project, providing high-end renovations and better amenity packages. He said he would dedicate several buildings for "elderly people," hoping to move long-term residents, whose children had gone, from two- and three-bedroom apartments to smaller units.

Many of the city's wealthy real estate families decided to stay on the sidelines. In their minds, the risks were too great. The Rudins never made an offer. Douglas Durst, the patriarch of the Durst real estate family, which owned ten skyscrapers in Manhattan, had been talking about joining Richard LeFrak, who also dropped out, saying, "It was just too expensive."[1]

Durst had taken a chance in the late 1990s when he started building the first speculative office tower in Times Square in more than a decade, the forty-eight-story tower at 4 Times Square, on Forty-Second Street. As it turned out, the building was fully leased by the time it opened in 2000 and helped lead the revival of Times Square. At Stuyvesant Town, he was interested in erecting new buildings on the green spaces while LeFrak ran the existing housing. But the bidding made it riskier than Times Square. "When it got north of four billion dollars, it was just too ridiculous," Durst said. "It was too much of a hope and a prayer that all these things would happen. We just stopped."[2]

Douglas Eisenberg of Urban American also went to the sidelines. Residential buildings were his business, he said, but in the last year, he had been outbid for the Riverton complex in Harlem in 2005 and the nearby Delano Village complex in early 2006. To him, the prices were based on highly speculative assumptions about where rents and revenues would be in the coming years. "We got up to about $4.4 billion," Eisenberg recalled. "Darcy said, 'Guys, this is going for a lot higher than that.' But there was no way you could promise a reasonable return to your investors and make it work. A week before the bids were due, we came to the conclusion that this was really silly."[3]

Stacom's job, at this point, was to keep as many players in the game as possible while coaxing each of them to sweeten their offer, sometimes substantially. Stacom, bidders said, was very effective at leaving each bidder with the impression that she was telling them, and them alone, some piece of vital information that would help them gauge the unfolding battle. Discreetly, she would signal the bidders that they had to raise their offer to stay in the game.

"Nobody manages a complex, intensely competitive bid process better than Darcy," said Marty Edelman, a shrewd real estate lawyer who was working for the Apollo–ING Clarion–Dermot group. "She is like the best auctioneer at Christie's:

Every deal is priceless and she will help you understand why you must move your bid to the winner's circle."[4]

Dan Neidich, a partner at Dune Capital who was working with LeFrak, was more blunt: "What Darcy did well was pit people against each other who all wanted the same thing."[5]

Garodnick, Doyle, Grunstein and the unions had been hoping that they could catapult ahead of the other bidders with the political and financial support of the city. But a day after the first bids were submitted, Mayor Bloomberg expressed no willingness to jump into the middle of what he called a private transaction during his regular Friday radio broadcast. He assured listeners that regardless of the sale, the city would continue to build low-, moderate- and middle-income housing.

"MetLife owns it and they have a right to sell it," Bloomberg said of Stuyvesant Town-Peter Cooper Village. Moreover, Bloomberg played down the consequences of the sale for the ability of the middle class to live in Manhattan. "A lot of people want to live there," he told listeners. "That's part of the problem. When people want to live somewhere prices go up. When they don't, prices go down. The character of this community will change, but it will change slowly, over time. And it would change whether this is sold or not."[6]

Bloomberg's insistence that he would not interfere with a private transaction was somewhat disingenuous. The Bloomberg administration had played a critical financial role in supporting a tenant-led cooperative conversion plan at the West Village Houses. And in the late 1990s, the city and state had provided tax abatements that enabled an organization called CPC Resources to take over Parkchester, the 12,200-unit complex built and once owned by MetLife in the Bronx, where a condominium conversion had failed and the property had begun to crumble. In a partnership with a private developer, CPC was able to rescue the complex, restructure its finances and ensure that the apartments remained affordable. But it is also true that the scale of a Stuyvesant Town–Peter Cooper Village intervention would have been well beyond the $19 million in interest payments the Bloomberg administration forgave the owner of the West Village Houses.

Garodnick, of course, saw the situation far differently than Mayor Bloomberg. Just as Mayor Fiorello La Guardia and Robert Moses had encouraged MetLife to build Stuyvesant Town as a way of anchoring the middle class to the urban center, Garodnick argued that it was important for the city to ensure that the middle class could live in Manhattan. "The city cannot survive and attract new businesses if teachers, firefighters, municipal clerks and nurses are priced out of the market," he said.

"It's very important for the city's economy to do so," Garodnick told the *New York Times*. "That's why it's generated so much interest, not just locally, but nationally. We expect to make a competitive bid here, one that will allow MetLife to make a profit and also honor the tradition of affordability."

Stephen M. Ross and Bruce Beal of Related made a similar argument, even if city officials deemed their subsidy demand to be ridiculously large.

More than three-fifths of the fifty-one-member city council signed a resolution backing the tenant bid. Community Board Six, a city-sponsored advisory group whose district included Stuyvesant Town–Peter Cooper Village, also voted to support the tenants. Playing defense, Garodnick and Councilwoman Rosie Mendez proposed legislation that, in light of the loss of thousands of rent-stabilized units every year, would require large residential property owners to provide 120-day notification of their intention to sell if more than half the units were rent regulated. Sponsors said the proposed law was not meant to restrict an owner's right to sell, but rather to give the city time to assess the potential impact of a transaction on the city's housing crisis.

Bloomberg seemed to stake out an ideological position that government should not interfere with private transactions, even if government routinely mediates between business interests and the public good through environmental regulations, zoning, licensing and the bully pulpit. But it also would have been fiscally irresponsible for the city to feed the speculative fires by subsidizing a bid that housing officials believed would collapse from unrealistic assumptions and oversize debts.

However, many critics suggested that Bloomberg could have mounted the bully pulpit, much as he has to advocate for gun control, green buildings, bike lanes and banning supersize sugary sodas. He could have urged MetLife and prospective bidders to preserve some percentage of the apartments as permanently rent-regulated housing, ensuring that middle-class families could make their homes at Stuyvesant Town. After all, Stuyvesant Town was built jointly by the private sector and the city, which provided tax breaks, land and zoning to ensure its success. That kind of stance by one of the nation's most prominent mayors might have achieved a public good and tamped down the extravagant bidding that ensued. But that is exactly what MetLife wanted to avoid when it made its case to Bloomberg at city hall.

The trajectory of Richard S. LeFrak's bid illuminates the seasoned approach of a real estate veteran and the effect of a casino-like atmosphere on Wall Street that was driving prices higher and higher. Unlike all but a handful of bidders, LeFrak actually owned rent-regulated apartments in New York, more than ten thousand of them. Rent-regulated, or -stabilized, apartments were a distinct subset of residential housing, with their own culture, laws and tenant history. They couldn't be confused with luxury, market-rate housing. A landlord who failed to grasp the difference could end up subsumed in bitter courtroom battles with tenants, regulatory sanctions and political attacks from elected officials.

LeFrak, a third-generation developer with deep pockets, jumped at the opportunity to buy Stuyvesant Town–Peter Cooper Village. He figured few companies would be willing to risk entering the sometimes-treacherous terrain of rent-regulated housing in New York City. The LeFrak empire, which was all about large scale, was founded by Harry LeFrak, a glazier who moved to New York in the early 1900s. Harry made enough money to buy a 120-acre farm in Brooklyn, which he subdivided and then built small houses and apartment buildings on the subdivisions.

But it was his son Sam, a blustery, oversize personality with unbridled ambition, who took great chances on large-scale real estate development. Everything about Sam was big, even his business card, which was embossed with honorary degrees and knighthoods. Although Sam consistently denied craving acceptance by the Manhattan elite, he donated $10 million to the Guggenheim Museum, but only after they agreed to inscribe his name prominently on the fifth-floor gallery of the Fifth Avenue building.

Starting in 1959, Sam built LeFrak City, a vast network of twenty eighteen-story towers, comprising five thousand apartments and fifteen thousand residents, as well as two million square feet of retail space, atop a former swamp in Queens. It was far larger than most projects built by private developers. He was focused on the expanding working and middle class who lived outside of Manhattan, rather than building glass and brass towers for the wealthy. In those days, Sam, whose empire included a stable of fifty-five horses and oil wells in Louisiana, was fond of saying, "We serve the mass, not the class."

But many observers thought Sam had lost his touch in the 1970s when he bought a six-hundred-acre defunct railroad yard on the Hudson River waterfront in Jersey City, a declining industrial city. For years, the land sat fallow. He and his son Richard, however, typically bought property for the long term, rather than a quick killing. Over thirty years, they were instrumental in creating a modern skyline with more than twenty-five residential and commercial towers in Jersey City, one mile across the Hudson River from downtown Manhattan. Richard and his sons, Harrison and Jamie, now preside over twenty-two million square feet of residential property, the equivalent of about twenty-five thousand apartments, and twelve million square feet of office space.

Richard has none of the noisy flamboyance of his father but all the family's work ethic and aversion to high-risk financing. The LeFraks are wealthy enough to finance their own projects. "Our normal modus operandi," he said, "is to use our own capital. But that approach wasn't applicable" at Stuyvesant Town. Unlike many developers, he usually says what he means, regardless of whether it offends mayors or community groups.

LeFrak envisioned putting up perhaps a billion dollars of his own money to buy Stuyvesant Town-Peter Cooper Village and getting a $2 billion mortgage. He was largely unfamiliar with the exotic financing methods that had come into vogue on Wall

Street, be it mezzanine loans or "bridge financing," which are short-term loans designed to give a buyer time to line up equity partners to fill in any gaps.

Stacom's sale book indicated that MetLife had converted 525 rent-regulated apartments annually to market rates, or 4.7 percent of the total number of units, in recent years. Her projections indicated that a new owner could push the conversion number to 600 units in 2007 and 1,000 units in 2008. This was important information for any bidder trying to understand future cash flows.

"I didn't pay much attention to Darcy's projections," said LeFrak, then sixty-one, "only because I had my own statistics." Based on the history of his own apartment buildings, he knew that tenants in rent-regulated apartments tend to stay in place far longer than market-rate tenants, a critical point for anyone trying to calculate the value of the property. "The longer they stay the more likely it is that they'll never leave," LeFrak said. "So the remaining stabilized tenants at Stuyvesant Town-Peter Cooper Village are going to be much stickier than the first twenty-eight percent."[7]

Based on his experience with 13,000 stabilized apartments between 1996 and 2005, the turnover rate was likely to be 2.9 percent to 3.6 percent, which would translate into a far more modest increase in net income in the coming years than Stacom or most other bidders projected. By contrast, a quarter of all market-rate tenants turn over every year. He figured that there might be some "illegal" tenants, although MetLife had been weeding them out for six years. So in September, LeFrak ran his numbers and estimated that Stuyvesant Town-Peter Cooper was worth about $3 billion as a rental complex. He did not think that a co-op conversion was feasible.

But he knew that $3 billion would not win the day. So he ran his numbers a second time, adjusted his return expectations and raised his projections for rents on the commercial space at the complex. But that only got him to $3.35 billion. LeFrak was working with Steven T. Mnuchin and Daniel Neidich of Dune Capital Management, which invests in entertainment and real estate projects. Coincidentally, Neidich, a former investment banker at Goldman Sachs, had overseen the investment bank's purchase of Rockefeller Center in partnership with the Speyers. LeFrak and Mnuchin were also working with the bankers at Credit Suisse First Boston, Citicorp and UBS. The bankers, however, did not share LeFrak's sense of caution. "They kept saying, 'Don't worry about the money,'" LeFrak said. "In those days, nobody worried about the money. We always did.

"Our colleagues were encouraged by Darcy and the unbridled optimism of the debt community," LeFrak continued. "We were told, 'The more you spend, the more we can lend against it.' Our good judgment was cast aside. We finally came up with a bid of $4.5 billion in the first round."[8]

At that price, LeFrak figured there'd be "no cash flow for the first three to five years. You had to capitalize the negative cash flow until you could turn over more apartments." But LeFrak, by his own description, was like a man teetering on the ledge of a high-rise building. He felt sweaty and disoriented by the yawning gap between his revenue estimates and the sale price. Then, Stacom called him about the second round of bidding, saying, "If you come up to $5 billion you can keep playing," LeFrak recalled. "I thought it was ridiculous when it got beyond $3 billion."[9] Instead, the billionaire stepped down off the ledge and quit playing.

After the initial flurry of activity leading up to the first round, there were still nearly ten groups scrambling to refine their bids, locate partners and lock down lenders. The second, and presumably final, round was only days away, on October 17. With so much money at stake, Tishman Speyer, the Apollo–ING Clarion–Dermot group, the Related Companies and the others were meeting on a daily basis. How much higher could they go? The real estate industry is notoriously incestuous in New York and the grapevine was rife with information, however inaccurate, about each bid. The industry rumors put the Apollo–ING Clarion–Dermot group among the front-runners, along with Related. But Steven Roth, the chairman of Vornado Realty Trust, which owned mainly commercial, industrial and retail property, was still in the game, along with Ofer Yardeni, the Israeli commando turned real estate investor, who had nicknamed his bid Project Snoopy, in reference to MetLife's mascot. And even if few people in the real estate industry knew who he was, Simon Glick had the wherewithal and assets to buy the prize. But Tishman Speyer and the gigantic BlackRock firm were the team to beat. They had the connections and they both usually got what they wanted.

After a decade of on-the-job training, Rob Speyer was in command. Sure, his father's imprint was on every Tishman Speyer project. Jerry also had the long-standing personal relationships with Richard S. Fuld, chairman of Lehman Brothers; Sandy Weill, who merged Travelers into Citicorp; and Lester Crown, patriarch of one of the country's most wealthy families and Tishman Speyer's largest, most consistent partner. The Crowns owned hefty stakes in General Dynamics, Maytag, Hilton Hotels, Alitel, Rockefeller Center and the Chicago Bulls basketball team. Like Jerry Speyer, Lester Crown was also a minority partner in the New York Yankees.

But Rob had been running deals for his father's company for several years now, even if it was largely outside the media spotlight. He had proven to be a fast, if impatient, learner during his apprenticeship. Rob had been a latecomer to real estate, not having shown the slightest interest in the field until he was well into his twenties. He grew up in Manhattan, attending Dalton, the elite private school on the Upper East Side, where he was a top student and competed on the wrestling team. He went to Harvard, where he was a research assistant for Graham T. Allison, dean of Harvard's John F. Kennedy School of Government and an expert in foreign policy and nuclear deterrence. But not long after arriving in Cambridge, Massachusetts, Rob realized "it was the wrong place for [him]."

He stuck it out at Harvard through his second year, before dropping out of school. He moved back to New York, where his parents were in the middle of a divorce. Feeling adrift, Rob went to work for Andrew Cuomo, Governor Mario Cuomo's son, at Housing Enterprise for the Less Privileged. Cuomo had started the organization in 1986 to build and operate low-income housing for the homeless, with an abundance of social services, from job training to drug counseling. The two men developed a continuing friendship.

"I was a lost soul," Speyer said. "I asked Andrew if I could open his mail. He took me in at a tough point in my life. He was there for me, an important older brother figure at a critical moment."

After a year away from school, Rob transferred to Columbia University, where his father had been chairman of the board of trustees. He was set on becoming a political science professor and planned on going to England after graduation on a prestigious Marshall scholarship to study at Oxford University. But one day that spring he ran into a tumultuous demonstration at Columbia in support of striking campus workers. On a whim, he telephoned the *New York Observer*, a feisty weekly known for its irreverent coverage of the rich and powerful. He provided a breathless account of the demonstration and an interview with a provost whose office had been overrun by demonstrators. As Rob recounted the action, reporter Terry Golway took it down. A day later it was on the newsstands. Suddenly, Rob was hooked on journalism. He graduated but turned down the Marshall scholarship and joined the staff of the *Observer*.

"It was the most exciting experience of my life," he told me. "In that moment, I decided there was no way I was staying in school. I never considered going into the family business."[10]

Speyer spent a year at the *Observer* before moving to one of the city's tabloids, the *Daily News*. He wrote about everything from boxer Mike Tyson's love child to a riot at a New Jersey immigration center and the U.S. invasion of Haiti. During a fire drill at the offices of the *Daily News* in 1995, he was caught unawares when a colleague asked him about his father's pending purchase of Rockefeller Center in partnership with the Rockefeller family and Goldman Sachs. His love affair with journalism was about to end.

"We didn't talk much about real estate," Rob said of his father.

"I asked my father, 'What's going on?'" Rob was captivated by his father's two-year quest to buy the complex and his vision for Rockefeller Center, which treated the iconic complex as a living organism. His father wanted to buff the landmark towers while enlivening the shop fronts and plazas. "My first lesson was my father's intense focus on the deal, day and night, for a year," Rob told me. "Nothing was going to stop Jerry from getting the deal done."[11]

Rob joined his father almost immediately after they bought Rockefeller Center, starting in the management and leasing department. Even his sister Valerie, an executive at Tishman Speyer, was surprised by the move and doubted whether he would stick it out. Jerry Speyer tapped Geoffrey P. Wharton, the senior partner in charge of Rockefeller Center, to oversee Rob's apprenticeship. Early on, Rob was an eager student and a quick learner, those who know him say, but he had a tendency to be bullheaded. He had a reputation inside the company for anger-management problems and rotated through a succession of secretaries, unlike his father, whose assistant has worked for him for decades. Over time, people who know him say that he settled down.

"Jerry made it clear to me that one of my responsibilities as a partner and a friend was to make sure that Rob was ready to take over the company at the right time," recalled Wharton, who left Tishman Speyer in 2001 to run the World Trade Center.[12] Wharton narrowly escaped death on September 11, 2001, when he left a breakfast meeting on the 106th floor of the North Tower moments before terrorists flew a passenger jet into the side of the building.

Rob's first deal brought the upscale Reebok Sports Club to

the complex, replacing the U.S. passport office, whose long lines contributed to the bland, service-oriented ambiance of Rockefeller Center. Years later, he headed a team that figured out how to reopen to the public the observatory at the seventieth floor of 30 Rockefeller Plaza, the 2.9-million-square-foot centerpiece of the complex. The key was reengineering the elevators to carry visitors swiftly to the "Top of the Rock" observation deck without interfering with their demanding office tenants, such as Lazard, the 150-year-old investment bank. It turned into a gold mine, attracting two million visitors a year and throwing off $25 million in annual profits.

But even before he had chalked up his own victories, Rob was accorded respect from the real estate fraternity, which recognized that he was the heir apparent to one of New York's most powerful and politically connected families. At a late-1990s real estate party that drew over a thousand top brokers, lawyers, bankers and developers, one executive after another, many of them older and more experienced, approached Rob with deference, as if they wanted to kiss his ring. A gregarious man with a slim figure who always looked good in a suit, Rob seemed largely oblivious to their fawning.

In 1998, Rob joined the company's acquisitions and development department, where he helped modernize the headquarters of the Colgate-Palmolive Company at 300 Park Avenue, which was considered one of the ugliest buildings in midtown. Sandy Lindenbaum, one of the best lawyers at navigating New York City's arcane zoning regulations, worked with Rob on that project. Normally, Lindenbaum, who was friendly with Rob's grandfather Robert Tishman, did not bring his clients to the often-tedious meetings with zoning and landmark officials. Rob had other ideas. "I really want to learn the business," he told Lin-denbaum. "Even if you don't need me, I want to go with you."[13]

Rob's team at Tishman Speyer, which bought the twenty-five-story building for $180 million in partnership with Travelers, transformed the dowdy structure, installing a new $12 million facade of aluminum spandrels and transparent green glass. The property is fully leased and now worth an estimated $1 billion.

Rob was also instrumental in developing an office building on a rare midtown parking lot, where his partner, Travelers, owned the development rights. But the land itself was owned by a cantankerous real estate developer named Stanley Stahl, whom Rob had met as a boy. He worked out a lease for the land shortly before Stahl died and began erecting an office tower, without having a single tenant. Speculative office buildings are a rarity in Manhattan because of the extraordinary cost of land and construction and the difficulty in getting financing without a blue-chip tenant. But Speyer caught the market on an upswing and landed a prominent law firm and technology firm. He sold the building for $76 million shortly before it was completed, netting a hefty profit on a $6 million equity investment.

"It was made clear to me by my father when I was a kid that there were two kinds of people who were born to privilege," Rob said. "One kind lived off the fat of the land. My father called them consumers. The other kind is more motivated to succeed. I fell into the latter category. I always wanted to be successful."

By 2006, Rob was a senior managing director of Tishman Speyer and chairman of the management committee. He threw himself into the Stuyvesant Town deal with the same fervor with which his father had chased Rockefeller Center. That fall he visited the complexes a dozen times, he said, sometimes on a Saturday, dressed in shorts and a T-shirt, just to get a feel for the place. "It's the only place in Manhattan with a neighborhood feel," he told me in 2006. "I grew up on the Upper East Side and didn't even know my next-door neighbor."

He had a team of twenty executives at Tishman Speyer working on the deal in their own "war room," much like every other bidder, including the tenants. He worked with an equal number of executives at BlackRock, refining projections, looking for new ways to make money at the complexes with better retailers and health clubs and calculating exactly how much higher they could go, or needed to go, with their bid. About 71 percent of the apartments were rent regulated, with residents paying an average of $1,338 a month, while market-rate rents averaged three times that number, or more than $4,000 a month. They estimated that they could push the proportion of market-rate units to 63 percent over the next seven years and boost net operating income to $397 million from $105.6 million.

Rob Verrone, the thirty-eight-year-old Wachovia banker who was nicknamed "Large Loan Verrone" for his prodigious ability to make huge interest-only commercial loans to developers who put little money down, had been keen from the beginning to do a deal with Tishman Speyer and BlackRock, particularly if it meant beating out Lehman Brothers.

But before he made a commitment, Verrone had also talked with Jeff Barclay of ING Clarion on behalf of his bidding group, as well as several other rivals. Jeffrey Scott, a senior Wachovia banker based in Washington who specialized in raising equity investors for real estate deals, championed the Clarion folks, because he knew them well. Although many of the banks talked to multiple bidders, it was a tricky business.

Whichever group Wachovia ultimately selected, there were sure to be hard feelings among the losers, who would suspect that the bank was then using inside information against them in the bidding. Verrone ultimately won the battle inside Wachovia to go with Tishman Speyer and BlackRock. As predicted, the executives at ING Clarion and Apollo were not happy.

Rob Speyer and Verrone were both relatively young, almost exactly the same age and cocky. They had done several deals together in Los Angeles. Verrone expected Tishman Speyer to come out on top at Stuyvesant Town; it was a bonus that he had nabbed a traditional Lehman customer.

Verrone promised them not only a $3 billion mortgage and $1.4 billion in mezzanine, or secondary, loans but also what was known in the business as "bridge equity." This was critical to the bid because MetLife wanted to pick a winner in October and close the deal thirty days later. That did not leave enough time to prepare an offer, conduct the due diligence on the property and gather almost $2 billion from equity investors so they could write a check in November. Hence, they needed bridge equity.

It was a lucrative line of business at Lehman Brothers, but one fraught with risk. Verrone was eager to expand into bridge equity. He had been losing financing deals to Lehman Brothers in part, he figured, because they were offering bridge equity. Before Stuyvesant Town, Verrone had only included bridge equity in two far smaller deals. In essence, the bank was buying a piece of the asset, say for $2 billion, until the bank and the buyers could resell it to new investors at a 4 percent markup. But if the market turned sharply downward and the buyers were unable to complete the deal, the bank would be left holding a $2 billion bag, which was suddenly declining in value. It was a danger that ultimately contributed to the collapse of Lehman Brothers.

Rob Speyer and the top executives at BlackRock confidently predicted they would have little trouble signing up equity investors. Verrone agreed, although he split the financing and the risk with Merrill Lynch. Wachovia would provide two-thirds of the senior mortgage, the mezzanine loans and the bridge equity; Merrill would cover the rest.

The partners also brought in Jonathan Mechanic, who ran the real estate department at the Fried Frank law firm and worked on many Tishman Speyer deals, to examine the proposed purchase and sale contract distributed to the finalists by MetLife and recommend any changes, knowing that MetLife frowned on revisions. Not long after submitting the initial offer, Rob Speyer and his colleagues from BlackRock arrived at the number that they thought would win the deal. On October 16, they began printing a half dozen copies of their bid package. "About a weekend beforehand," Rob Speyer said. "We decided to put our best foot forward in the second round, hopefully grabbing the deal and short-circuiting other rounds. We took a chance."[14]

Similar meetings and calculations took place all over Manhattan, with the Related Companies, Simon Glick and others. Glick's plan was not that different from the other bidders' in seeking to convert regulated apartments to market rents. But the pricing was not about some multiple of cash flow, the way buyers traditionally derived the worth of a property. That kind of thinking was passé. Wall Street lenders were willing to lend 70, 80, even 90 percent of the property's value, making a bet that the real estate boom would continue. The change in approach on underwriting fueled a surge in prices. Why not? The mortgages quickly dropped off their balance sheets, after being combined with other loans into a security and sold to other investors. On the first day a new landlord took over Stuyvesant Town–Peter Cooper Village, the rental income wouldn't even cover the debt service. But buyers, lenders and investors imagined that revenues would increase quickly in an ever-rising market.

"The price was dictated by the amount of debt you could put on the property," Glick said. "The assets were worth as much as the banks were willing to lend."[15]

Five blocks to the south, a dozen senior members of the Apollo group sat around a long table in a conference room at ING Clarion's office in the landmark Beaux Arts–style tower at 230 Park Avenue at East Forty-Sixth Street. Richard Mack and Andrew MacArthur had spent weeks visiting with state pension fund executives in an attempt to raise almost $3 billion in equity capital, so they could limit the amount they would have to borrow. They knew they were locked into battle with Tishman Speyer, but they also worried that they were getting "brokered up," meaning the broker was urging them to raise their offer higher than necessary to win. The debate over whether to increase their bid incrementally or go for a knockout punch dragged on for hours. Before lining up with Tishman Speyer, Verrone, the banker from Wachovia, had asked them, "Why are you bidding so low?" But Stephen J. Furnary, the chairman of ING Clarion, wondered whether it was possible to make money on a $5 billion deal. To resolve the dispute, they each agreed to write down the number they thought it would take to win the deal and drop it into a hat. Their scribbling sounded loud in the suddenly hushed room.

Furnary unfolded the slips and read out the numbers. The

spread was $5.2 billion to $5.45 billion. Furnary and Neibart, the voices of "moderation," were on the low end. Andrew Mac-Arthur of Dermot, and Richard Mack and James Simmons of Apollo, were in between. Dickey, chairman of Dermot, wanted to go all in. Most of the people in the room were surprised when Barden Gale, usually a conservative investor, agreed with Dickey, arguing that once you got above $5 billion, it hardly made a difference whether they offered $5.3 billion or $5.5 billion. Gale was chief investment officer for APG Investments, a subsidiary of the largest pension fund administrator in the Netherlands, and a financial partner in the deal.[16]

Still, it took several more hours to come to an agreement. The next morning, October 17, the Apollo group was printing six copies of the bid documents and the purchase and sale agreement when the machine suddenly jammed. Jeff Barclay of ING Clarion called Stacom in a panic, saying he'd had a technology breakdown and would not be able to meet the noon deadline. Stacom urged him to get it to her as soon as possible. "I personally walked it across Forty-Fifth Street myself, took it up to her office and handed it to the receptionist," Barclay said. "It was a surreal moment. I don't think I'd ever handed over a bid package with a $5.33 billion offer. I didn't trust anyone else to do it."[17]

Meanwhile, Grunstein and Gallagher were scrambling to keep the tenant bid from unraveling. Their offer was different from the others in that Garodnick and Doyle were committed to retaining what they viewed as the ideals of Stuyvesant Town by converting the rental property to a cooperative. Although they were lining up the same kind of jumbo loans as the conventional bidders, the tenant plan envisioned paying off a chunk of the debt quickly through the sale of apartments to existing tenants at a discount and to outsiders for full price. Rent-stabilized tenants who did not want to buy could remain in place. The AFL-CIO pension funds were lined up for about $250 million to $300 million in equity.

Maura Keaney, deputy chief of staff for council speaker Quinn, worked with Garodnick, helping to set up meetings and assess the political landscape. But as Grunstein rejiggered the bid again and again in an effort to compete with the other bidders, Keaney got nervous. It was a case of diminishing returns, she thought, if your goal was affordable housing for teachers, construction workers and firefighters. "Every time you added a zero," Keaney said, "you lost something that was the whole reason for doing this."[18]

All the bidders, with the sole exception of Tishman Speyer, had met with Garodnick or Grunstein or both. They wanted to establish a friendly relationship with the tenants association, if not a partnership. If they won, they also wanted to avoid a potential lawsuit. Both Related and the Apollo group had talked to them about preserving a block of rent-stabilized apartments. "It was agreed that, if we won, the tenants would have a voice," Simmons said vaguely.[19]

"We met with all of them but Tishman Speyer," Garodnick said. "Everybody wanted to partner with the tenants if they could. But Tishman Speyer did not."[20]

But the enthusiasm of the tenants' partners in the bidding, the billionaire Ruby Schron and Colony Capital, waned after Mayor Bloomberg made it clear that the city would not intervene on behalf of the tenants. JPMorgan Chase had provided a $4 billion financial proposal, but it was marked "preliminary," not the rock-solid commitment that MetLife wanted. At the last minute, another participant in the deal, SL Green, pulled out. In a flurry of last-minute phone calls, Gallagher plugged that hole with help from a Deutsche Bank real estate fund.

"I hope the tenants are able to swing this," said Soni Fink, a resident of Peter Cooper and a tenant activist. "We want to buy this thing. It looks very good if they give us any kind of break at all."[21]

CHAPTER EIGHT

What $5.4 Billion Gets You

On October 17, 2006, messengers dropped off six thick bid packages for Stuyvesant Town-Peter Cooper Village on the fifteenth floor of the fifty-nine-story MetLife Building. Darcy Stacom collected the documents for the biggest sale of her or any other broker's life and took the elevator up to the MetLife offices, where Robert R. Merck, David V. Politano and Kevin Wenzel sat waiting. With some trepidation, she slit open the first package, from Related and Lehman Brothers. A sharp intake of breath greeted the $4.7 billion offer that sat on the page like a rotten egg, spoiled and sulfurous. It was well south of what they expected. Could it be a harbinger of what was to come?

"The first one was really low, $4.7 billion, from someone I expected to be really high," Stacom confided to a friend. "I had a heart attack. My career flashed in front of my eyes."

Stacom passed it around as she reached for the next thick manila envelope, and the next, as the afternoon wore on. There was a $5.1 billion bid from the billionaire Simon Glick and the Morgan Stanley Real Estate Fund. Steven Roth of Vornado

Realty Trust, with backing from the Emir of Qatar, came in at
$4.5 billion. The tenant bid remained at $4.5 billion, with a
slight twist, in which Grunstein offered what he described as a
significant tax savings for MetLife by leasing the property for
ninety-nine years, instead of buying it. But without hard commitments from its partners, the tenants' offer appeared to
MetLife to be held together with Scotch tape and chewing gum.

The offer from the Apollo–ING Clarion–Dermot group was
$5.33 billion. That was more like it. But Tishman Speyer edged
them with a bid of $5.4 billion. Theoretically at least, there was
an extraordinary amount of capital on the table from the nine
bidders and only a $70 million gap between the front-runners,
just over 1 percent. But price was not the only issue that concerned MetLife. How solid was the financing? Could they close
within a month? How big was the down payment? How much
did the bidder alter, or "mark up," the sales contract proposed
by MetLife? Equally important, did they provide the indemnification that the company wanted?

Stacom, Merck and Politano then took the two highest offers
back down to the fifteenth floor and MetLife's lawyer Robert J.
Ivanhoe, chairman of the two-hundred-member global real estate practice at Greenberg Traurig. They asked Ivanhoe to sift
the offers for distinguishing features or potential problems in
any contract changes requested by either bidder. They waited
while the lawyer pored over the documents.

"We had a provision where the buyer wasn't just releasing
MetLife from environmental liabilities, meaning the buyer
couldn't sue MetLife. That's not unusual," Ivanhoe said. "We
also had the buyer assuming all the obligations and indemnify-
ing the seller from environmental liabilities. The Apollo bid
crossed that out and Tishman Speyer did not."[1]

MetLife very much did not want anything from Stuyvesant Town-Peter Cooper Village coming back to haunt them. Consolidated Edison Company had already entered into a voluntary cleanup agreement with the state Department of Environmental Conservation concerning coal tar pollution from a manufactured gas plant and related storage facilities that were knocked down to make way for Peter Cooper Village and Stuyvesant Town. A by-product of gas production was a toxic oily liquid called coal tar that had seeped into the ground long ago. A Con Ed report, approved by the state, found that there was no risk to tenants from the historic groundwater and subsurface soil contamination. But any company in the chain of ownership of the properties was potentially liable if more serious problems were uncovered in the future.

Both the Related Companies and the Apollo–ING Clarion–Dermot group had balked on the indemnification. Bruce Beal, a partner at Related, said the company had spent $500,000 on its own environmental study and did not want to "read about 'Toxic Town' on the front page of the *New York Post*" at some point in the future. The Apollo group had also commissioned its own environmental study and talked to state officials. They concluded that the problem was "manageable" but they were worried investors might panic so they refused to provide indemnification. But if the environmental issue was not enough of a hurdle, MetLife also wanted indemnification against any legal claims brought by tenants for past actions by the owner over rents. Like Glick and Morgan Stanley, Related and Lehman Brothers, the Apollo group had made extensive revisions to MetLife's proposed contract, effectively cutting the value of their offer.

Tishman Speyer and BlackRock, which subsequently bought

a ten-year pollution insurance policy for $8 million, were unde-terred by either risky issue and changed relatively little of the language in the purchase and sale agreement.[2] They figured that Con Edison had already agreed to cover the cost of any neces-sary decontamination effort and they were not planning to start digging deep holes that might disturb the coal tar.

For MetLife, Tishman Speyer had not only the highest bid but also one that complied with all its demands. So when Ivan-hoe wrapped up his review, Kandarian and Merck took the el-evator to the fifty-seventh floor, where MetLife's fourteen directors were holding a special session in the company's his-toric boardroom. Several directors participated via telephone.

Harry P. Kamen, a former MetLife chairman and a MetLife employee for thirty-nine years, felt compelled to disclose that he had received a telephone call the night before from Jerry I. Speyer, Rob's father. Although Jerry did not participate in any of the negotiations and deal making, he wanted to make last-minute contact with an old friend, just in case. The two men had met when Speyer served as chairman of the Partnership for New York City and Kamen was treasurer. Turning to the cur-rent chairman, C. Robert Henrikson, Kamen said, "Bob, Jerry called me last night to say that he was bidding. If there is a ques-tion about his integrity, he was hoping I could speak to it."[3]

Henrikson responded, "Don't worry about it. He's the high bidder anyway."

Kandarian and Merck recommended that the board accept the $5.4 billion offer from Tishman Speyer–BlackRock pending final negotiations on the contract. They did, and at about 5:00 P.M., Stacom called Rob Speyer at Rockefeller Center and asked him to discreetly bring his team to Greenberg Traurig's fifteenth-floor offices at 200 Park Avenue, the MetLife Build-

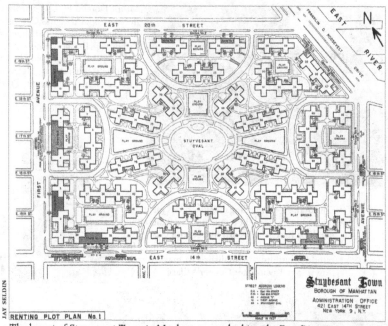

The layout of Stuyvesant Town in Manhattan, overlooking the East River.

A cartoon from a MetLife magazine illustrating Frederick H. Ecker's career at Metropolitan Life Insurance, starting at sixteen in the mailroom and rising to become the company's longest-serving chairman.

Frederick H. Ecker, chairman of Metropolitan Life Insurance, conceived of Stuyvesant Town-Peter Cooper Village as a home for returning veterans of World War II. All told, he built more than thirty thousand apartments for the middle class in the 1940s in New York, Virginia, and California. He said, "Negroes and whites don't mix," when he imposed a strict policy barring black and Hispanic families from renting in the complexes.

Mayor Fiorello H. La Guardia swears in New York City Parks Commissioner Robert Moses as chairman of the Triborough Bridge Authority, November 14, 1936. Moses would become La Guardia's emissary to Metropolitan Life Insurance chairman Frederick Ecker for the Stuyvesant Town-Peter Cooper Village project.

One of the foul-smelling manufactured gas storage tanks that inspired the name for the neighborhood north of East Fourteenth Street, the Gas House District. The tanks and gas plants were among five hundred buildings demolished to make way for Stuyvesant Town-Peter Cooper Village.

The lunar landscape that remained in 1946 after the demolition of the Gas House District between Fourteenth and Twenty-Third Streets, east of First Avenue. The Empire State Building is in the background in the center, and the Chrysler Building is to the right.

The razing of five hundred tenements, churches, factories, and warehouses in the Gas House District started in 1945. The first buildings opened in 1947.

Stuyvesant Town's thirty-five cross-shaped buildings take shape, 1947.

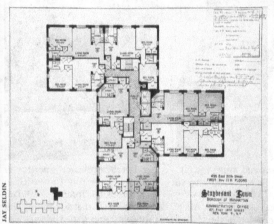

For decades, MetLife provided prospective Stuyvesant Town tenants with a floor plan of a vacant apartment but not a tour of the unit.

The apartment houses at Stuyvesant Town radiate out from Stuyvesant Circle at the center of the complex.

Stuyvesant Town-Peter Cooper Village covers a wide swath of Manhattan, between Fourteenth and Twenty-Third Streets, east of First Avenue, 1950s.

Lee Lorch, a mathematics professor and army veteran, helped to form the Town and Village Tenants Committee to End Discrimination in Stuyvesant Town, with his wife, Grace, who died in 1974, and five-year-old daughter, Alice, in 1949. Unable to get a teaching position in the United States because of his civil rights activism and left-wing views, Lorch and his family eventually immigrated to Canada.

Lee Lorch, professor emeritus of mathematics at York University, in his apartment in Toronto, 2010. Two of the schools that fired him, Fisk University and City University of New York, later awarded Lorch with honorary degrees.

A three-year-long battle with MetLife began in August 1949 when Jesse Kessler of the Town and Village Tenants Committee to End Discrimination in Stuyvesant Town invited a fellow union member, Hardine Hendrix; his wife, Raphael; and their six-year-old son, Hardine Jr. to stay in his apartment at Stuyvesant Town.

Robert R. Merck, MetLife's senior managing director in charge of real estate investments, ran the sale of the company's biggest asset: Stuyvesant Town-Peter Cooper Village.

Steven A. Kandarian, who joined MetLife in 2005 as chief investment officer, ordered the sale of Stuyvesant Town-Peter Cooper Village, which netted the company a $3 billion profit. Kandarian was subsequently promoted to chairman, president, and chief executive of MetLife.

William M. Shanahan and his partner, Darcy A. Stacom, the top sales brokers at CB Richard Ellis, sold $9.4 billion worth of real estate in 2006, including Stuyvesant Town-Peter Cooper Village, the biggest deal of their lives.

Robert J. Ivanhoe, MetLife's lawyer and the chairman of the global real estate practice at Greenberg Traurig, approved the $5.4 billion contract for sale to Tishman Speyer and BlackRock.

Richard S. LeFrak, a billionaire real estate tycoon, raised his bid for Stuyvesant Town-Peter Cooper Village to $4.5 billion in 2006 after bankers told him, "The more you spend, the more we can lend against it." He ultimately pulled out of the auction rather than raise a bid that he already thought was outlandish.

Rob Speyer spent $21.8 million on landscaping, signage, and new storefronts to create a lush environment at Stuyvesant Town-Peter Cooper Village. The new shrubs and trees blocked the views of some security cameras, angering tenants, who dubbed the thickened landscaping Rape Forests.

Rob Speyer and his father, Jerry I. Speyer, on a rooftop at Stuyvesant Town not long after buying the property for $5.4 billion, a record-setting price for a single real estate asset. The Speyers invested $112.5 million, or 2 percent of the purchase price.

The pension funds that were invested in the Stuyvesant Town deal lost more than $3 billion, but the subsequent financial debacle barely dented the reputation of Laurence D. Fink, chairman and chief executive officer of BlackRock, or his partners, the Speyers.

Robert "Big Loan" Verrone, the Wachovia banker, erected the financial architecture for a deal that many analysts said was doomed from the start.

The ten-pound crystal trophy that was given out at the closing dinner at Top of the Rock to top MetLife executives, brokers, lawyers, and buyers responsible for the record-setting $5.4 billion Stuyvesant Town sale.

Officials back a tenant-led bid to buy Stuyvesant Town–Peter Cooper Village at a rally in Stuyvesant Town on September 5, 2006, just as MetLife put the complexes on the auction block. (Left to right: Senator Charles E. Schumer, Assemblyman Jonathan Bing, resident Granville Leo Stevens, City Councilman Dan Garodnick, Manhattan Borough President Scott Stringer, State Senator Tom Duane, State Senator Liz Krueger, Assemblywoman Sylvia Friedman, Congresswoman Carolyn Maloney, and Central Labor Council President Edward Ott.)

Al Doyle, president of the tenant association and a second-generation resident, and Dan Garodnick, a newly elected councilman and second-generation resident, were the Mutt and Jeff team that led the fight to preserve Stuyvesant Town–Peter Cooper Village as a rare haven for the middle class in high-priced Manhattan.

ing. Speyer's lawyer Jonathan Mechanic and several associates walked over from the nearby Seagram Building on Park Avenue. The lawyers shuttled between the Tishman Speyer conference room and the MetLife room as negotiations dragged on until early the next morning. Speyer and Merck, whose soft-spoken Southern accent contrasted with his counterpart's seventy-miles-per-hour New Yawkese, were only in the same conference room twice over a fifteen-hour span. After the lawyers on both sides had stopped haggling early the next morning, Stacom went out to Forty-Second Street for doughnuts and a jug of coffee from Dunkin' Donuts to revive the weary participants. Rob Speyer, then thirty-seven, signed the $5.4 billion contract, had a $400 million nonrefundable deposit wired to MetLife and shook hands with everyone in the room.

MetLife and Tishman Speyer each issued a press release announcing the sale and within an hour, media websites around the world were rumbling with headline news of the $5.4 billion deal, the most money ever paid for a single asset in the United States. The comic Bill Maher joked during an episode of HBO's *Real Time*, about the stunning price tag for the complex in which he was conceived, while Robert Siegel on National Public Radio's *All Things Considered* provided a sentimental look back at his "childhood home."

"It was an inner-city oasis with no rich people and no poor people," Siegel concluded. "It has been sold in an age that celebrates the virtues of markets. It was built in a simpler time, when the glaring failures of the market, like no affordable housing, were considered targets for public action."[4]

After donning a fresh shirt and holding a hoarse conversation with his father, who offered an affectionate congratulations, Speyer got back to business. He knew he had to deal with the tenants. He sent out a brief letter to the residents of Stuyvesant Town-Peter Cooper Village with what he hoped would be a comforting message: "We are committed to maintaining the unique character and environment that have made Peter Cooper Village and Stuyvesant Town such a wonderful place to live for so long."

He also called Garodnick, whom he did not know, saying he looked forward to sitting down with him now that he had signed the purchase contract. He assured the councilman that they did not intend any major changes; they wanted to be good stewards of the property. "We love Stuyvesant Town and we're very excited," Speyer told him. "We want to work with you."[5]

"I told him I appreciated the call," Garodnick said, "but I asked him his plans for preserving the long-term affordability of the place. He avoided the question. I thought, 'This is going to be a problem.'"[6]

A few days later, Speyer invited the tenant leaders to his office at Rockefeller Center for a get-acquainted meeting. Doyle brought along Susan Steinberg, the association's executive vice president, and Jim Roth, a retired FBI agent and staunch tenant advocate. They were impressed by the colorful, oversize pieces of contemporary art that seemed to leap from the stark white walls of Tishman Speyer as they trooped into a small conference room. There were more white walls and white marble in the conference room, where Rob Speyer sat with David Dishy, a residential real estate executive whom Speyer had hired away from a rival developer to head the company's housing division. "In another year," Rob told the tenant leaders as a smile spread across his face, "you guys will be happy how we turned things around. We pride ourselves on service."[7]

But Doyle wanted to know what Tishman Speyer was going

to do about preserving the complexes as an affordable oasis for the middle class. "Other than saying he would turn the place around, he did not make any comments about searching for ways to keep the place affordable," Doyle recalled. "He couldn't do that because he had to make his mortgage payments. We were cognizant of that fact."

But if Doyle was still willing to give Speyer a chance, Roth was not. "When Al Doyle asked what they were going to do for affordable housing, the temperature went down about forty degrees," Roth recalled. "Shortly afterward, we were invited to the Christmas tree-lighting ceremony at Rockefeller Center. I said to the others, 'If you go, I'm going to rat you out to the neighborhood and *Town & Village*. They're trying to buy you off.'"[8]

None of the tenant leaders attended the glittering tree-lighting that is viewed by millions of people every year.

For MetLife, the results of the Stuyvesant Town-Peter Cooper Village transaction could not have been better. The sale sent the company's share price to a fifty-two-week high of $58.60 and MetLife's end-of-the-year accounting revealed that it had reaped an incredible $3 billion gain, net of income tax, on the deal, or half the $6.16 billion in net income, or profit, for all of 2006. MetLife also reported that its net investment income from the two complexes was $73 million in 2006, up from $70 million in 2004.[9] So it had not been losing money on the property. But the gains from the sale were nothing short of spectacular.

Over the prior four years, MetLife had sold twenty properties for more than $10.5 billion. It only made $85 million on the $835 million sale of the Sears Tower, where it had foreclosed on a loan. But the other buildings had been built or purchased by the insurer decades ago, so most of the purchase price was profit. MetLife's former headquarters building at 1 Madison Avenue brought in $918 million. After buying the MetLife Building in Manhattan for $400 million in 1980, the company sold it twenty-five years later for $1.72 billion. The $3 billion gain on Stuyvesant Town-Peter Cooper Village was unparalleled.

No wonder MetLife, in preparing for the traditional "closing dinner" for the brokers, lawyers and company executives who worked on the deal, wanted something more substantial than the traditional Lucite block, known as a "tombstone," emblazoned with the names of buyer, seller and broker.

The insurer commissioned a crystal wedge that stood eight and a half inches high and weighed a full ten pounds. It was nestled in a velvet-lined black box. The company logos were affixed in their respective colors: blue for MetLife, green for CB Richard Ellis, silver for Tishman Speyer and black for Black-Rock. Hovering inside the glass was a laser-etched schematic of the layout of the buildings at Stuyvesant Town-Peter Cooper Village. The inscription read: "Peter Cooper Village; Stuyvesant Town; Largest Real Estate Transaction in World History."

The tombstone was distributed to about 30 people at the closing party at Top of the Rock, the observatory atop 30 Rockefeller Plaza in midtown. From that perch 850 feet above the street, Rob Speyer and Steven A. Kandarian, MetLife's chief investment officer and soon-to-be chief executive officer, had unobstructed views of Stuyvesant Town-Peter Cooper Village, 1.5 miles to the south. Feeling expansive, Kandarian wished Speyer well, although he did not want to see him turn around and sell it for an even higher price tomorrow, a crazy possibility in the rollicking market. There was not a whisper of doubt among this gathering of some of the country's shrewdest real estate investors that the market would continue its upward march. "I sincerely hope you do well with this transaction," Kandarian said to Speyer, "just not too soon."[10]

Kandarian need not have worried that he had undersold Stuyvesant Town-Peter Cooper Village. Four years later, he looked uncannily prescient in selling the property at the peak of the market, before the boom collapsed in a devastating recession. The Stuyvesant Town deal, along with his decision to steer the company away from investments in automakers and subprime mortgages before the crisis, contributed to his being named in 2011 president and chief executive officer of MetLife.

Jerry I. Speyer was the doting father after his son won. Tishman Speyer was a family business even before Rob joined the company. Rob's sister, Valerie Peltier, was a managing director and his stepmother, Katherine G. Farley, was a senior managing director. In recent years, Rob had taken on increasing responsibility at the firm. But the $5.4 billion Stuyvesant Town deal marked his ascension to his father's side in a very public way.

"Obviously, Rob is on the deal side and has taken a leading role in the company as the heir apparent," Jerry told me shortly after they won the auction. "I expect he'll be far more successful than I was. He has great vision, wonderful people skills, and above all, he loves what he does."

The elder Speyer confided that he had received a "lovely note" from a fellow real estate magnate, Mortimer Zuckerman, the chairman of Boston Properties and the owner of the New York *Daily News* and editor in chief of *U.S. News and World Report*. Zuckerman, who had once hired Rob to work as a reporter at the *Daily News*, described him in glowing terms. Now Jerry and Rob were working in tandem, the hope of perhaps every father and son. "He said, 'You're a very lucky guy,'" Speyer said. "I was thrilled."

The deal not only confirmed Rob Speyer's ascension to the top ranks of real estate and goosed MetLife's earnings, but it also burnished the reputations of Verrone, Wachovia's big-deal banker, and Tishman Speyer's lawyer Jonathan L. Mechanic, who was named the Dealmaker of the Year by *The American Lawyer* for his role in the $5.4 billion sale. Darcy Stacom chalked up a personal best in 2006, selling $9.4 billion worth of commercial property. City and state government also scored, hauling in $262 million from the transaction: $162 million from MetLife in transfer taxes and $100 million from the buyer in mortgage recording taxes.

Richard and Bill Mack, William Dickey and Jeff Barclay from the Apollo–ING Clarion–Dermot Group were stunned by the news that Tishman Speyer and BlackRock had won. With information gleaned from the gossip-ridden real estate and banking industries, they figured their $5.33 billion offer had put them ahead of all rivals. Members of the group wondered aloud whether MetLife had given Tishman Speyer a "last look" and the opportunity to top the Apollo group's offer because of Jerry Speyer's ties to executives at MetLife. William P. Dickey, the founder of Dermot, called the real estate brokers, Darcy Stacom and her partner William Shanahan.

"I was concerned that Tishman Speyer and BlackRock had gotten a last look. Bill and Darcy told me point-blank that that was not the case," said Dickey. He paused and laughed before continuing. "But I also know that Tishman Speyer and Black-Rock had better relationships with MetLife than we did."[11]

For many in the real estate industry, it seemed like déjà vu all over again. After MetLife's $1.72 billion sale of the MetLife Building at 200 Park Avenue to Tishman Speyer in 2005, a similar controversy arose. A rival bidder, Scott Rechler, then chairman of Reckson Associates Realty, had complained to many of his real estate brethren that he had actually won the auction, not Tishman Speyer.

Although MetLife executives attribute the story to "sour grapes," Rechler insisted that MetLife or their brokers initially called him to say that he was the high bidder and the winner, pending negotiations over a lease with the insurance company for the penthouse space at the top of the tower. He said his company had completed the due diligence, marked up the proposed contract and demonstrated an ability to finance the deal. The deal played out while Rechler was in Orlando, where he spent most of his time trailing ten steps behind his children at Disney World while tracking the progress of the deal on his cell phone.

At the last minute, Rechler said, he got a second call, from MetLife's broker, saying there had been a change in plans. Rechler said he was told that the chairman of MetLife had decided to sell the building to Tishman Speyer, which had offered $10 million less than Rechler. Top bankers at Lehman Brothers, which was working with Tishman Speyer, had called MetLife on behalf of their client. (In this internecine world, Fuld, Lehman's chairman, and Jerry Speyer were close friends, and both men served on the board of the Federal Reserve Bank of

New York.) MetLife, in turn, decided that the $10 million dif-
ferential was less important than its relationship with Lehman
Brothers.

"We thought we had jumped ahead of the pack with our final bid," Rechler said. "We got a call from MetLife saying, if we
can resolve the lease terms, we're ready to go forward. Then
they told us it was a Lehman play. I couldn't even look at the
MetLife Building for a year."[12]

But MetLife executives and Stacom insist that the sale of
Stuyvesant Town-Peter Cooper Village was a proper auction
without any hint of favoritism. Merck told me afterward that
the company was "not happy" about the rumors. "This was a
very clean and detailed sales process and everyone was treated
fairly," Merck said in 2006. "Any rumors to the contrary are
totally false."[13]

A private owner can sell property to anyone at any price.
The presumption is that it will go to the highest legitimate offer. Like most bidders, the Apollo group, which spent more
than a million dollars preparing their offer, did not like being
used as a stalking horse for a preordained winner. Still, in trying
to sort out the claims and denials, it is also clear that the Apollo
group was unwilling to comply with some of MetLife's contract
stipulations concerning environmental indemnity, which would
have reduced the value of their offer in MetLife's eyes.

In any event, the Apollo group was so incensed about the
outcome that they took the highly unusual step of holding a
"closing dinner" for thirty people at Café Gray, an upscale restaurant in the Time Warner Center. Traditionally, the winner
of a real estate auction holds a "closing dinner," never the
second-place finisher. Nevertheless, Richard and William Mack,
Jim Simmons and Lee Neibart of Apollo; Bill Dickey and

Andrew MacArthur of Dermot; and Barclay from Clarion marked the occasion on October 30 with their bankers at Morgan Stanley, who distributed blank Lucite tombstones commemorating the occasion. "We felt we deserved a closing party," Richard Mack said in 2006. "We all worked hard."

Afterward Barclay of ING Clarion was more forgiving. "It's a great investment these guys have made," he told me in 2006. "We'll look back on this in ten or fifteen years as the one that got away."

Several years later, Barclay would point to the blank Lucite sitting on his desk and say to friends, "That was what was between my ears when we submitted our bid."

The political issues, however, did not subside. Michael McKee, treasurer of the Tenants Political Action Committee and a veteran of New York's tenant-landlord wars, called the Stuyvesant Town sale a "dark day for affordable housing." "I think it's deplorable that the mayor did not step up to the plate," McKee said at the time. "If he had, this might've turned out differently. Our rent-regulated housing is disappearing. It's not slow. In the last ten years, we've lost close to 300,000 units."[14]

Three days after the sale of Stuyvesant Town-Peter Cooper Village to Tishman Speyer and BlackRock, Mayor Bloomberg hurriedly announced his own plan for addressing the housing crisis for New York's middle class. He proposed building the largest middle-income housing complex in New York in more than thirty years on a twenty-four-acre parcel of crumbling industrial land on the waterfront in Queens, across the East River from midtown Manhattan. Under the proposal, the city would create a tree-shaded community with restaurants, shops and a mix of five thousand rent-regulated and market-rate apartments. He said the apartments would be for families of four earning between $60,000 and $145,000 a year. Residents would pay $1,200 to $2,500 in rent. "Not only will it give birth to a new community that's going to complement our efforts to revive the city's waterfront," the mayor said, "it will also provide much needed housing for the real backbone of our city, our teachers, nurses, police officers."[15]

It was a bold move cooked up by Deputy Mayor Doctoroff after he decided against intervening on behalf of the tenants at Stuyvesant Town. Doctoroff had planned to build an Olympic Village for athletes on the Queens site as part of the city's ill-fated bid for the 2012 Olympic Games. Doctoroff dusted off his Olympic Village proposal and put the administration's new venture in the context of affordable housing, more specifically workforce housing, for the middle class. He told reporters that the Queens project was a more efficient use of public subsidies: It would have cost the city about $107,000 per apartment to preserve Stuyvesant Town and Peter Cooper as an affordable complex, while the units in Queens would cost about $54,000 each to build. "So we can get two units here for every one there," Doctoroff told reporters at a press conference in Queens, "plus we get a major increase in the housing stock."

Tom Waters, a housing analyst with the Community Service Society, a nonprofit planning agency, did not buy it. He said that the construction of new housing would never keep pace with the loss of rental units rapidly moving from regulated to market-rate rents.[16] A 2006 study by the Community Service Society found that between 1990 and 2005, nearly a quarter of the roughly 121,000 apartments built under federal and state subsidy programs, dating from the 1960s and '70s, left those programs. In return for government aid, building owners were required to keep rents affordable to low- and moderate-income people for, usually, twenty years, before they could withdraw from the programs. A separate study by the city comptroller's office found that 25,000 units had been withdrawn from the state's Mitchell-Lama moderate-and-middle-income program since 2004 or had begun the process. That number was greater than the 24,000 units that left the program prior to 2004.

In 2006 alone, the CSS study said, New York City would lose more than 5,000 apartments for low- and moderate-income families. A third study, by the Brookings Institution, noted the sharp decline in middle-income neighborhoods since 1970 in cities from Baltimore and Philadelphia to Los Angeles–Long Beach.

Bloomberg's $7.5 billion housing program was far more ambitious than that of any other big-city mayor. But many analysts disputed Doctoroff's math when it came to Stuyvesant Town. It almost always costs more to build new apartments than it does to rehabilitate existing buildings, they said, even if the price for Stuyvesant Town-Peter Cooper Village was a record-setting number. Indeed, it subsequently cost the city $275 million just to buy the property in Queens, cleanse the land of toxic waste, create a ten-acre park and build roads and water and sewer lines. The project would need tens of millions more in subsidies and tax breaks. Although the city selected a developer for the first one thousand apartments, construction of the first building was not scheduled to start until December 2012.

Emily Youssouf, the former president of the city's Housing Development Corporation who had disagreed with the administration's position, said the implicit message was that the middle class should live in Queens; much like manufacturing, they don't belong in Manhattan anymore. "I was outraged," she said during an interview in 2011. "It was so elitist. I always thought that economically integrated buildings were the best way to go. Even if it had become a prime neighborhood, why can't middle-income people continue to live in housing built to be affordable to them twenty, forty, or even sixty years ago?"

Still, there was no disputing that Mayor Bloomberg's project in Queens would be the largest middle-class development built in New York since 1974 and the opening of Starrett City, a 140-acre complex of 46 high-rise towers on Jamaica Bay, at the far eastern end of Brooklyn, 12 miles from Manhattan. But subsequent events highlighted the city's rapidly dwindling supply of affordable housing, not Mayor Bloomberg's initiative in Queens. In December 2006, Starrett City went on the auction block in what promised to be another blockbuster sale that would reunite Stacom and Grunstein, the lawyer who had represented the tenants at Stuyvesant Town. The immediate and widespread opposition to the sale, however, signaled that the very public Stuyvesant Town-Peter Cooper Village battle had fed a backlash to the unbridled speculation over what many regarded as one of the city's most precious resources: its supply of affordable housing for impoverished New Yorkers as well as nurses, construction workers, firefighters, teachers and municipal clerks.

Starrett City, which had its own schools, churches, synagogues, shopping center, post office and power plant scattered among 5,881 apartments, had been a safe haven for poor and working-class New Yorkers for thirty years. Unlike the red brick buildings at Stuyvesant Town-Peter Cooper Village, Starrett City's eleven- and twenty-story towers have a modern appearance with light-colored brick, exterior balconies and neatly manicured lawns. "It has a blend of all kinds of races and religions, and maintenance is really good and security is really good," said Pasquale Santaniello, a retired carpet installer. "It's one of the safest neighborhoods in America."[17]

But the fifteen thousand residents of Starrett City, the nation's largest federally subsidized housing development, were less prosperous than those of Stuyvesant Town and Peter Cooper Village. Starrett City's longtime owners, seeking to take advantage of a red-hot real estate market, hired Darcy Stacom to market the property. She and the owner set the target price at more than $1 billion.

The original partnership group led by Disque D. Deane tried to mollify tenant fears by saying, "This is a sale of a nearly totally subsidized development where the tenants will continue to be subsidized, no matter who eventually buys it." But the Starrett City tenants association, low-income housing advocates, elected officials and even the Bloomberg administration expressed concern that anyone paying such an exorbitant price would be forced to cut services and raise rents substantially in order to meet the mortgage payments. "The big complexes are falling like dominoes," said Michael McKee, treasurer of the Tenants Political Action Committee. "Affordable housing is simply disappearing."[18]

Starrett City received nearly every available federal, state and city housing incentive, an estimated $75 million annually in rent subsidies and tax breaks. About 90 percent of the tenants received some type of government assistance for shelter. But even in far-off Brooklyn, the demand for housing continued to push rents higher. After David Bistricer emerged as the winning bidder with an offer of $1.3 billion in February 2007, he was nearly buried under an avalanche of criticism and scandal. Bistricer was represented by Leonard Grunstein, who desperately tried to curry favor with labor leaders and prominent African-American ministers. But Attorney General Andrew M. Cuomo, who had been silent during the sale of Stuyvesant Town-Peter Cooper Village, blasted Bistricer's "long and troubled history of tenant abuse" in New York City. He was referring to a court order forcing Bistricer to make $450,000 in restitution to tenants in two Brooklyn buildings and a 1998 court order obtained by the attorney general's office barring Bistricer for life from converting rental buildings in New York to condominiums.[19]

Mayor Bloomberg, who had taken a political hit over his decision to sit out the Stuyvesant Town-Peter Cooper Village fight, complained of Bistricer's "worrisome" history of building violations at Flatbush Gardens, a troubled housing project in Brooklyn where the entertainer Barbra Streisand had grown up.[20] He painted Bistricer as a bad landlord, in contrast with the Speyers. But unlike Stuyvesant Town-Peter Cooper Village, Starrett City offered a clear regulatory hook for public officials to derail the sale. Because of the extraordinary level of subsidies at Starrett City, state and federal officials had to approve the sale. The Bloomberg administration joined Senator Charles E. Schumer, community activists from the Association of Community Organizations for Reform Now (ACORN) and Cuomo, who would become New York's governor in 2009, in calling on U.S. secretary of housing and urban development Alphonso R. Jackson to reject Bistricer's application to buy Starrett City.

Aside from his checkered legal history, Bistricer, who lives in Brooklyn and is not a member of either the Real Estate Board of New York or the Partnership for New York City, did not have the social and political connections enjoyed by the Speyers. Federal officials scuttled Bistricer's attempt to buy the property on two separate occasions before he finally acknowledged defeat. But Bistricer's loss was rooted in the battle at Stuyvesant Town-Peter Cooper Village, which gave voice to average New Yorkers dismayed by the escalating cost of housing.

"I believe that the Stuyvesant Town battle in 2006 gave birth to the city's opposition to the sale of Starrett City," Garodnick said. "It's not a totally fair comparison because they had a much bigger hook. But people realized the failure at Stuyvesant Town and wanted to correct it at Starrett City."[21]

The month after the sale was a mad scramble for Tishman Speyer and BlackRock to finalize the financing for the deal with Wachovia and Merrill Lynch in order to close by November 17, MetLife's deadline. The Tishman Speyer–BlackRock joint venture had signed a contract to pay $5.4 billion for the property, but the total bill for the transaction came to an even more eye-popping number: $6.3 billion. Aside from the purchase price, there were $240 million in acquisition costs and $650 million in reserve funds required by the lenders.[22]

The whole deal was about OPM, other people's money. Robert Verrone, the banker who was instrumental in making Wachovia the number one underwriter of securitized commercial debt during the boom, orchestrated the financing. The superlatives surrounding the deal did not stop with the sale price. The $3 billion, ten-year, interest-only mortgage, which Wachovia and Merrill Lynch planned to combine with other loans into a commercial mortgage-backed security and sell to investors, was the largest ever for a single property. The second item in the debt stack was $1.4 billion in secondary loans, which were ultimately obtained from eleven different parties.

But in addition to borrowing $4.4 billion, the partners needed to raise another $1.89 billion from equity investors to cover the total cost. Tishman Speyer and BlackRock Realty kicked in a combined $225 million, or a mere 3.6 percent of the total capitalization. The buyers were able to pull off a record-breaking deal by putting only a relatively small amount of their own money at risk. And the interest-only mortgage itself was nonrecourse. If there was a default, the lenders could only come after the property, not either company's other assets. It's all part of what made this and other deals so enticing. Half of Tishman Speyer's $112.5 million share came from their most consistent partner and investor, the billionaire Lester Crown of Chicago. This was big-time deal making that the average home buyer could only imagine.

Few of the bankers involved in the deal actually understood the mechanics or the intricacies of the unique system of rent regulation in New York. The main question in their minds was: Can we sell the debt and equity so it's not on our books? "Outside of the real estate area, nobody really understood it," one banker confided. "It was all about, can we move the risk? That was the sole and only criteria. I think we all talked ourselves into believing the deal was going to work financially. We drank the Kool-Aid."

Larry Fink, Dale Gruen, Fred Lieblich and Rob Friedberg of BlackRock had expected to enlist $500 million each from the California Public Employees' Retirement System, or CalPERS, and the California State Teachers' Retirement System, or CalSTRS, by the date of the closing in November. Afterward, BlackRock, Tishman Speyer and the bankers would only need another $600 million or so to hit their goal of $1.89 billion of equity. But not everything went according to plan.

By the time the contract closed in November, CalPERS, the country's largest pension fund, was on the phone with

$500 million. It took a 26.5 percent stake in the property. The partners promised a 13.5 percent internal rate of return.[23] CalPERS itself had turned to higher-risk real estate investments for just those kinds of returns to fill their coffers and meet their obligations to pensioners. Any shortfalls could force communities to raise taxes to cover the gap—political anathema.

The closing itself—done in a conference room in the Seagram Building, at 345 Park Avenue, where Tishman Speyer's lawyer Jonathan Mechanic had his offices—was something of a nonevent, without any of the drama or headlines created by the auction. "We had the ability to write all the debt and provide bridge equity," said Verrone, who even four years after the event could not help bragging about the deal. "Ultimately, we brought in Merrill for 35 percent. We ran the deal. It was an aggressive underwriting, but it didn't feel outlandish. There were a lot of deals afterward that were considerably more outlandish."

CalSTRS, however, was not on board. The pension fund had been very receptive to BlackRock's offer. But a key adviser to CalSTRS, Nori Gerardo Lietz, was vehemently opposed. Lietz, a founder of the Pension Consulting Alliance, was a rigorous, blunt analyst who was ranked among the "30 most influential people in private equity real estate" by a business magazine in 2006.

Lietz advised not only CalSTRS, but also CalPERS and the Oregon Public Employees Retirement System. A positive recommendation from her could release a gush of investment dollars from the country's largest pension funds. A negative declaration could leave fund-raisers parched.

"It was a bad deal," Lietz said. "I advised CalPERS and CalSTRS against it. It was abundantly clear to anyone who looked at it that it would not work. It was overfinanced and based on aggressive assumptions. They grossly underestimated how difficult it would be to do the conversion."[24]

What did she see that the biggest names in real estate did not? "It had [a $400 million] interest reserve," she said. "That was a huge red flag. It was not cash-flowing on day one."

At the time, she said, she spoke to Ralph L. Schlosstein, the cofounder of BlackRock, who assured her that it was a great opportunity with a lot of upside potential as previously regulated apartments moved to market rents.

"He said, 'I'd put my mother's money in it,'" Lietz recalled.

"I said, 'You are putting my mother's money into it; she's a beneficiary of CalPERS.'"

"He said, 'You can take it to the bank.'"

"I hope so," Lietz responded, "but I don't believe so."

But Al Fernandez, the senior portfolio manager at CalPERS, liked the deal and had the authority to make the investment without her consent. The teachers' retirement fund was another matter. CalSTRS asked her what it should do. Once more, Lietz counseled against the investment. But, the CalSTRS executives said, they had already promised to put up $500 million. It would undermine their credibility if they went back on their word. Lietz suggested that they reduce their commitment to a minimum. So CalSTRS reconsidered and missed the closing.

"I remember getting a call from BlackRock saying CalSTRS was out," said one banker who worked on the deal. "That sent shivers down our spine. We now had a billion dollars in bridge equity to sell."

Like several people involved in the Stuyvesant Town purchase, the banker did not want to be identified by name because so many people had lost so much money on the deal. But most executives at BlackRock, Tishman Speyer, Wachovia and Merrill Lynch considered the AWOL CalSTRS to be a mere bump in the road.

The banks underwrote the property on the assumption that the two complexes would be worth an appraised value of $6.9 billion by 2011. Speyer and Lieblich from BlackRock told bankers, lenders, and later, bond-rating agencies that net income from the property would triple to $336.2 million in five years. Verrone and the partners described the property as the "Rockefeller Center of Manhattan residential real estate," as part of a forty-seven-page presentation to bond-rating agencies in December by Wachovia and Merrill Lynch, who paid the rating agencies to evaluate the creditworthiness of the loans and the level of risk to investors. The partners and the bankers wanted an investment-grade rating for the $3 billion mortgage so they could more easily sell it to investors without having to offer higher interest rates.

The presentation outlined many opportunities for boosting the net income, ranging from the parking garages, where rates were said to be 70 percent below market, to the retail spaces, where rents were roughly half the market rate. There was enough underdeveloped land, it said, that the new owners could also build seven hundred thousand square feet of valuable residential and retail space. But the big upside would come with the conversion of regulated apartments to market rates. New York had some of the highest rents in the country and the lowest vacancy rate. Demand was strong.

The new owners portrayed MetLife as a lumbering landlord that had failed to capitalize on its asset. Although the insurance company had deregulated more than three thousand apartments, the new owners could easily double MetLife's pace because the "previous owner did not aggressively pursue illegal sublets or tenants that did not meet rent regulation guidelines. The new owners anticipate that the percentage conversion to market will increase significantly as the sponsorship actively enforces subletting laws and market deregulation."[25] Tishman Speyer and BlackRock were eyeing as many as 1,600 apartments that were illegally sublet, or leased to tenants who did not qualify for rent regulation, and could easily be converted.[26]

Despite the fact that on day one income from the property covered only 40 percent of the debt service, Fitch Ratings, Standard & Poor's and Moody's Investors Service all believed that the shortfall would diminish over time as the new owners converted regulated apartments to market rates at a faster pace than either MetLife or most other landlords in New York had ever achieved. No small item, the gap between income and debt obligations was $172 million, based on 2006 financial results. So the loans did not get the highest, AAA rating, but they did manage a passing grade, one notch above a speculative or junk bond rating. The rating meant that there was a low to moderate risk of default, although market conditions could adversely affect the borrower's ability to make the mortgage payments.

The reports did not outline what might happen if any one of their assumptions about the strength of the rental market, the desirability of Stuyvesant Town apartments, the turnover rate and rent hikes did not pan out, let alone all of them.

"We convinced the rating agencies that a $3 billion mortgage was investment grade," Verrone said. "From a financing standpoint, everything went right for Wachovia and Merrill."

It sure did. By the time the deal closed six months later, after the $3 billion senior mortgage was sold to investors, after

$1.89 billion in bridge equity was sold to pension funds and others, and after $1.4 billion in junior loans were secured, one Wachovia banker who worked on the deal estimated that the bank had made $140 million. Merrill Lynch, in turn, pulled in about $70 million.

Rob Speyer finished 2006 by selling the skyscraper his grandfather built at 666 Fifth Avenue for a record $1.8 billion to another young scion, Jared Kushner. The Kushner family was selling its residential holdings in New Jersey and Pennsylvania and was willing to pay up for Manhattan real estate to make a splash. The price broke a record set by Speyer himself when he bought the MetLife Building at 200 Park Avenue for $1.72 billion. The market was still booming not only in New York but also nationally. There were twenty-two transactions for real estate investment trusts over the course of 2006 with a total value of $102.8 billion, including debt.

Early in January 2007, Verrone called Rob Speyer saying that senior executives at Wachovia's headquarters in Charlotte, North Carolina, wanted to meet him and talk to them about their progress in raising $1.165 billion in equity; Wachovia wanted the bridge equity off their books. Speyer, Galiano and Verrone boarded Wachovia's brand-new Challenger jet for a quick flight to Charlotte. The meeting went relatively smoothly as Rob spent the afternoon assuring a half dozen bankers from the commercial real estate group that his organization and BlackRock were already tapping into their network of institutional investors and sovereign funds.

The jolt came on the return flight. As the jet went into a landing pattern on the approach to Teterboro Airport, directly east of Manhattan in New Jersey, the pilot suddenly pushed the jet into a steep ascent, back into the sky, nearly taking out a passing helicopter. Apparently the landing gear had failed to release. The jet veered south and made a successful emergency landing at Newark Liberty International Airport, where emergency vehicles with whirling lights lined the runway.

It did take about six months for Tishman Speyer, BlackRock, Wachovia and Merrill Lynch to line up equity partners who shared their optimism. That was a little longer than they originally anticipated, because the headlines about tenant unrest and a lawsuit brought by current and former residents in January had unsettled some potential American investors. It was more evident than ever to the bankers and partners that they would need to go overseas as well to fill out the equity roster.

The much-admired CalPERS served as the flypaper for attracting the remaining $1.165 billion in equity because its successful investment strategies were scrutinized, admired and copied by pension funds from the United States to Europe and Asia. "CalPERS has the reputation of being the gold standard of pension investing, largely by virtue of its size," Edward Siedle of Benchmark Financial Services told HedgeWorld, a news service for the hedge fund industry.

The pitch from BlackRock, Tishman Speyer and the bankers was that even at $5.4 billion Stuyvesant Town-Peter Cooper Village was a bargain. It cost $498 a square foot, or an average of $480,810 per unit, less than half what it cost to buy the average condominium in that neighborhood. With rents at "leading rental properties in Manhattan" 15 to 30 percent higher than market-rent apartments in Stuyvesant Town-Peter Cooper Village, there was a lot of room for revenue enhancement. Their confidential investment memorandum cited a new rental building across First Avenue from Peter Cooper Village that commanded rents of $68 per square foot, the equivalent of $6,930 a month for a two-bedroom unit at Peter Cooper. But a newly built condominium tower with a doorman and various amenities was not a proper match-up for plain brick buildings without doormen, with sixty-year-old plumbing and with only one bathroom in the two- and three-bedroom apartments. Stuyvesant Town apartments were always going to rent at a discount to newly built residential towers.

Still, CalPERS, which had a 250-member investment staff, embraced the deal and others like it. The managers sought high-return real estate investments in order to meet their swelling obligations to retirees. As the real estate market surged in the early 2000s, the fund increasingly ceded decision making over property deals to outside advisers and moved from a focus on "core investments" that provided steady if unremarkable returns to riskier, highly leveraged joint-venture projects that theoretically offered better returns, like the 13.5 percent return projected in the Stuyvesant Town-Peter Cooper Village deal. In 2005, CalPERS and its real estate partner Rockpoint Group invested in the acquisition of another project built by MetLife, Riverton in Harlem.

After the closing Jerry Speyer set up a secret meeting with John E. Sexton, the president of New York University, whose seemingly insatiable appetite for dormitory space was creating tensions with residents of Greenwich Village. NYU had leased dozens of apartments at Stuyvesant Town in the past. But Speyer, who had served with Sexton as a director of the Federal Reserve Bank of New York, had something bigger in mind, an investment. Jerry Speyer's initiative illuminated the way in which father and son interacted. Rob was the heir apparent and a key decision maker, but it was still Jerry who had the relationships and set the table for the deals.

Of course, Larry Fink had his own connection to Sexton and NYU; he was a university trustee. Jerry Speyer attended the meeting at NYU, but Rob ran it, proposing that NYU become a partner in the Stuyvesant Town-Peter Cooper Village deal, investing more than $200 million and leasing a block of apartments for faculty housing. Rob Speyer suggested that over time the new owners would be able to assemble a contiguous block of apartments for NYU faculty for an academic community within a community. While that sounded intriguing, Sexton, according to two people who attended the meeting, was concerned whether NYU's investment would ignite a political firestorm. NYU never did put money into the project, but the university did lease about eighty apartments for use by undergraduates and another twenty-five for graduate students and faculty, according to Tishman Speyer.

BlackRock Realty continued to press the California teachers' pension fund to invest in the deal. BlackRock was already advising CalSTRS on multifamily housing projects. Christopher Ailman, CalSTRS's chief investment officer, and Michael DiRe, the real estate director, flew to New York to tour Stuyvesant Town-Peter Cooper Village and talk to tenants. The fund mulled over the investment for several months before finally giving it a green light in May, but for $100 million, not $500 million. CalSTRS's real estate portfolio was oriented toward "core" investments, properties that produced a positive cash flow from the first day. They determined that the Stuyvesant Town deal fell into a different category. "Staff concluded it should be classified as a tactical investment, with higher risk and potentially a higher return," said Ricardo Duran, a spokes-man, "and lowered the allocation to $100 million."

At the same time, BlackRock contacted Florida's State Board of Administration, another pension fund that it advised, about a partnership stake in the deal. The board invested more than $100 million on behalf of one million current and future retir-ees. Early in January 2007, five BlackRock executives flew to Tallahassee to present the deal to Steve Spook, a senior acquisi-tions manager in the real estate unit; Doug Bennett, the senior investment officer; and Kevin SigRist, the board's deputy ex-ecutive director. In March, Bennett and Spook recommended approval of a $250 million investment in the partnership. Spook's seventeen-page confidential analysis is remarkable for how closely it mirrors the investment memorandum, including notes on rent projections and apartment turnover, as well as the environmental and market risks associated with the deal and the unusually high cost of bridge financing. "Unless net operat-ing income from the Property increases materially, the Partner-ship will not be able to meet its interest payment obligations, in which event it would default on the Ten-Year Debt," Spook's March 12, 2007, memo states.

But Bennett, like Spook and SigRist, enthusiastically endorsed the partners' strategy of replacing rent-regulated residents—who were very much like the pensioners represented by the fund—with tenants paying higher, market rents. They figured it was a potentially lucrative investment that over seven years would "add to [their] high return bucket." Curiously, Spook also said that "both venture partners have extensive experience in managing rent-regulated apartments," a claim that is not made in the Tish-man Speyer–BlackRock investment memorandum.

Asked why Tishman Speyer, which was known for its portfolio of commercial buildings, was suddenly plunging into the
multifamily residential market, Jerry Speyer told me the day
that his son signed the contract that Tishman Speyer was not a
newcomer to the housing field. He said he had built a five-
hundred-unit residential tower in Manhattan in 2000, although
the company sold it two years later for $209 million. "We were,
at one point, one of the largest developers of residential properties in France. We've done residential in Germany. We have a
significant residential business in Brazil and we're planning a
large undertaking in India."

But while Tishman Speyer developed residential projects, it
did not manage the properties and none of the buildings were
rent-regulated housing. Indeed, the investment memorandum
states that Tishman Speyer "has limited experience in managing multifamily rental properties." The memorandum did say
that a BlackRock subsidiary managed apartment properties for
the company's clients, but there was no mention of the very
peculiar residential subset of rent-regulated units.

Nevertheless, investors from around the world found the arguments made by Tishman Speyer and BlackRock compelling. They
also liked the idea of owning a piece of Manhattan. The projected
internal rate of return, 13 percent, was a good deal better than
many of their other investments. Tishman Speyer brought in the
Church of England, which invested $75.7 million. The Wellcome
Trust, a British trust for health-related research, took a $177.2
million limited partnership interest. KB Financial Group of Korea
invested $155 million, after a meeting in a New York boardroom
with twenty Korean investors and an equal complement of trans-
lators. The Ontario Municipal Employees Retirement System put

in $75.7 million, as did PKA, a Danish pension fund. BlackRock was already a PKA adviser. "We thought it was a great opportunity to get into a core investment with a lot of potential," Nikolaj Stampe of PKA told one real estate magazine. "We didn't necessarily decide that we wanted to be in the US, but when the opportunity came along, it sounded interesting."[27]

Wachovia and Tishman Speyer, which is an active developer in India and China, landed the Government of Singapore Investment Corporation (GIC).

EQUITY INVESTORS[28]
Stuyvesant Town-Peter Cooper Village

CalPERS	$500 million
Florida State Board of Administration	$250 million
Government of Singapore Investment Corporation	$189.4 million
Wellcome Trust, England	$177.2 million
KB Financial Group, Korea	$155 million
Tishman Speyer Properties	$112.5 million
BlackRock	$112.5 million
CalSTRS	$94 million
Church of England	$75.7 million
Ontario Municipal Employees Retirement System, Canada	$75.7 million
PKA, Denmark	$75.7 million
Norinchukin Bank, Japan	$25 million
Credit Suisse First Boston	$15 million
Tishman family and friends	$12.9 million
Daiwa, Japan	$9.7 million
Gen Re	$9.3 million

THE DEBT STACK
Stuyvesant Town-Peter Cooper Village

Class	Class Size	Participants
Mortgage	$3 billion	Securitized Debt: WBCMT 2007-C30; WBMCT 2007-C31; Cobalt CMBS 2007-C2; MLCFC 2007-5; MLCFC 2007-6
Mezzanine 1–3	$300 million	Hartford Financial $100 million Deutsche Genossenschafts-Hypothekenbank AG $100 million Allied Irish Banks $50 million Winthrop Realty Trust $25 million Wachovia $25 million
Mezzanine 4–9	$600 million	GIC $575 million Brookfield Asset Mgmt. $25 million
Mezzanine 10	$300 million	CWCapital $90 million Fortress $50 million NY Credit $25 million JER $60 million Bracebridge Capital $75 million
Mezzanine 11	$200 million	SL Green $200 million

GIC was initially only interested in providing a $575 million secondary loan. But the partners convinced GIC that it should also buy a $100 million stake in the partnership. Rob Speyer was instrumental in 2004 in forming a strategic alliance with GIC, which managed a multibillion-dollar portfolio of direct and indirect property investments around the world. That year the two companies jointly purchased a dozen major office buildings in eight U.S. cities, including the Colgate-Palmolive Building on Park Avenue in Manhattan. Tishman Speyer handled management and leasing at the properties.[29]

One pension fund that did not heed the siren call from Tishman Speyer or BlackRock was the Washington State Investment

Board, which manages about $52 billion in state retirement and public trust funds. Joseph A. Dear, then the executive director of the Washington investment board, recalled getting a call from a senior executive at BlackRock asking whether he was interested in a limited-partnership stake in Stuyvesant Town–Peter Cooper Village. When BlackRock called, you listened. Dear, who grew up in MetLife's Parkfairfax complex outside Washington, DC, quickly sent off a note with BlackRock's investment memorandum to Gary Bruebaker, his chief investment officer in Olympia, Washington. He suggested to Bruebaker that it might be time to develop a closer relationship with BlackRock. But by the end of the day, Dear got his response and it was an emphatic no thanks.

"The price looked a little high," Bruebaker recalled. "The terms were not anything we would ever accept. The fees were kind of rich for the manager. But the biggest thing—the structure didn't work for us."[30]

The Washington investment board preferred to invest in real estate operating companies, where they were the principal owner and had a great deal of control, instead of making do with an impotent seat on an advisory committee for a limited partnership. Whatever the outcome of the investment, the Stuyvesant Town partnership structure entailed several ongoing revenue streams flowing to the operating partner. There was a 1.5 percent property-management fee based on gross residential revenues, which would amount to an estimated $3.2 million in 2007, plus reimbursable expenses and leasing commissions. That was typical in Manhattan. But then there was the 3.5 percent "supervisory fee" for a planned $100 million in future capital projects, total: $3.5 million. The asset management fee amounted to $10 million a year for a limited partner with a

$500 million investment and $2.5 million from a $100 million investor. The general partners received a 20 percent "promote," or percentage of profits, after the limited partners got a preferred 9 percent return on their investment.

The Washington analysts were concerned that the Stuyvesant Town-Peter Cooper Village acquisition was highly speculative, one in which the new owners did not take into account the fluctuating demand for market-rate apartments or the ebbs and flows of the real estate markets and the economy. "The plan was for perfection," Bruebaker said. "They never put together a contingency plan. That coupled with the controversy over affordable housing on day one was not a good combination."

CHAPTER NINE

"What Do They Have Against Trees?"

Tishman Speyer Properties, the large, well-regarded organization credited with rejuvenating signature commercial properties like Rockefeller Center, the Chrysler Building and the MetLife Building, turned its attention to the sprawling Stuyvesant Town-Peter Cooper Village complexes on the East Side of Manhattan. Although Tishman Speyer had never owned or operated a housing complex as large as the eighty-acre development, Rob Speyer and his company had big plans for transforming the sixty-year-old housing development into "an exciting, vibrant, desirable residential community."

The two complexes, their business plan said, suffered from a rather "modest" image in the Manhattan marketplace and a distinct lack of the amenities that would allow them to reposition Peter Cooper Village in particular as a "luxury product." They planned to spend $160 million to build an upscale health club, roof decks, children's playrooms and a concierge center, as well as remodel apartments with stone counters and high-end appliances, improve the outdoor lighting, refurbish the lobbies and establish a shuttle to transport residents to and from subway and bus stops.[1] Rob Speyer took a particular interest in turning the landscaped grounds into the kind of lush flower show you'd find at a botanic garden.

The new owners were going after a whole new demographic. The teachers, government workers and firefighters of yesteryear were out of fashion in Manhattan. If Stuyvesant Town-Peter Cooper Village had been created on the ruins of a demolished working-class neighborhood, Tishman Speyer now wanted to push the complexes farther up the economic ladder by appealing to younger, more well-heeled, upwardly mobile New Yorkers working in finance, advertising and communications. "When we first looked at the property, we thought there were quality of life issues that made it less desirable than other Manhattan properties," Rob Speyer told *New York* magazine. "Access to public transportation was a challenge, so we introduced a trolley. There were few entertainment options, so we created an event series. We tried to improve a stark living environment, so we planted trees and we invested in a health club."[2]

The first order of business, however, was to increase revenues by dislodging tenants who did not qualify for rent-regulated apartments and shifting previously rent-regulated units to market rents. The recovery of rent-regulated units was a preoccupation of the weekly staff meetings. Their obsession with the turnover rate was understandable given that the annual debt service on $4.4 billion in loans was $284.4 million, while annual net income in 2006 was just over $100 million. They had a $400 million reserve fund to make up the difference in the early years, but it would not last forever, unless they boosted rental income. But it soon became clear that Tishman Speyer had something to learn about managing rent-stabilized housing in New York, where every tenant complaint, no matter how specious, and every corporate misstep would find its way into the tabloids, the real estate trade papers and the often eviscerating blogs that sprang up to chronicle Rob's misadventures. It was unfamiliar terrain for a buttoned-down company that preferred to do business outside the public spotlight.

Early on, Adam Rose, the co-president of Rose Associates, who was managing the property at the time, caused a ruckus at one staff meeting in a boardroom at Rockefeller Center when he told the Tishman Speyer executives that they were unrealistic in assuming a double-digit recovery of rent-stabilized apartments in the first year. Their presentation to the bond-rating agencies in December estimated the conversion rate at "15 percent for the first year and 12 percent in the second year."[3]

"We've been screening the rent-stabilized tenants for years," Rose recalled telling them. "You'll get a four to five percent turnover. They said, 'Oh no. Our pro forma shows more than 10 percent.'"[4]

The exchange grew heated as a disembodied voice, presumably an investment partner from California who dialed into the meeting via telephone, demanded, "Where did those numbers come from?" And one young executive from Tishman Speyer became, in Rose's words, "apoplectic." Rose, scion of another prominent New York real estate family whose company managed thirty thousand apartments in New York, was steadfast. "This is my experience," he said. "This is what I believe."

Within two months, Rose was gone. Rose felt double-crossed. He said Rob Speyer had assured him that Rose Associates would continue to manage Stuyvesant Town-Peter Cooper Village. The complexes accounted for one-third of the thirty thousand apartments his company managed. He had gone to Yale University, working during the summers as an auxiliary policeman in

Provincetown, Massachusetts, before going into the family business. Usually a genial, talkative executive, he became a bitter critic of Speyer's tenure at the complexes. And years later he would get his revenge when he was brought back in to manage the complexes after Tishman Speyer left.

Tishman Speyer, which took over day-to-day management, had repeatedly told investors, lenders and the rating agencies that it would take a more aggressive approach to turnover than the "passive," or lackadaisical, strategy employed by MetLife. But after the dispute with Rose over the projected turnover rate, Tishman Speyer did adjust their numbers, somewhat. The investment memorandum that went out to pension funds in January and February 2007 indicated that the anticipated conversion rate was 7.5 percent in 2007 and 11 percent in both 2008 and 2009, on a declining number of rent-regulated apartments. By that time, net operating income was to have more than doubled to $253.2 million.

Tishman Speyer hired not one but three law firms to pursue cases against what it described as "illegal" tenants, mainly those residents who wrongfully sublet apartments without approval by the landlord, or tenants who did not qualify for a rent-stabilized apartment because their primary residence was outside Stuyvesant Town or Peter Cooper. Fred Knapp, a private detective once described by the *New York Times* as the "scourge of illegal tenants," was brought in to dig into the background of tenants whose leases were up for renewal. Knapp made a good living hunting through property records and other public documents for New York City tenants who had a home or employment elsewhere.

The first wave of lease-renewal notices from the new landlord sent a shock wave through Stuyvesant Town and Peter Cooper Village, as tenants saw their rents jump by anywhere from 15 to 33 percent. There was a great deal of hand-wringing during the sale over the fate of the elderly, rent-stabilized residents. The truth was that those tenants were locked in, protected by state law from eviction and hefty rent hikes. It was the market-rate tenants who were taking a beating. Dara Kane had grown quite fond of her spacious two-bedroom apartment in Peter Cooper Village, her friendly neighbors and the parklike setting of the complex where her seven-year-old played. Her renewal notice stated that the rent was going up $700 a month to $4,450 beginning February 28. MetLife was no piker when it came to rent hikes; her rent had gone up $500 a month a year earlier. But the jump to $4,450 was more than Kane and her family could afford.

"It's a really special place," said the departing Kane. "But they are not interested in retaining any stable tenancy. When people like us leave, you have to wonder. How are the public schools going to survive? How will the 14th Street Y sustain itself? All those things are going to suffer."[5]

Every weekend seemed to bring another convoy of moving trucks that deployed around Stuyvesant Oval, a rare sight in the past when tenants lucky enough to get an apartment would stay for years, even decades. Evan Horisk, a television producer for PR Newswire who had lived at Stuyvesant Town for four years, was forced to give up his newly renovated two-bedroom apartment in Stuyvesant Town when the rent jumped 26 percent to $3,350, from $2,660 a month. "It flipped my life upside down," Horisk said two weeks after he moved to a smaller apartment blocks away. "Living there was great. The renovations were superb. The maintenance was top-notch." But he continued, "I didn't get a big raise this year that can compensate for that kind of increase."[6]

The rent history for Horisk's apartment provides a glimpse of how the system worked. Prior to 2002, the rent for the two-bedroom unit had been a rent-regulated $888.87. But once it became vacant, MetLife and Rose Associates spent $42,204 renovating the apartment. To offset that expense, state housing laws allowed the landlord to bump the rent by $1,055.11 per month. The owner was also permitted "vacancy increases" of $309.33. So the total monthly rent for Horisk and his room-mates came to $2,253.31 in January 2003, and since that was above the $2,000 threshold, the apartment was also deregu-lated. The rent rose to $2,495 in 2004, $2,550 in 2005 and $2,660 in 2006, before leaping to $3,350 in January 2007.[7]

Rob Speyer was unimpressed by the complaints from tenants like Horisk. After all, 80 percent of the tenants were renewing their leases, despite the increases. He figured he was only rais-ing rents to market levels, a process begun by MetLife in 2001 when for the first time it hired an outside manager for the com-plexes and began deregulating apartments in earnest. The new owner pushed the rents hard. By Tishman Speyer's calculations, rents for deregulated apartments at Stuyvesant Town and Peter Cooper Village were running at least 12 percent below what was being charged at comparable buildings nearby, while rents for rent-stabilized apartments were 30 to 40 percent below market. "We're generating significant demand from existing residents as well as from the outside," Speyer countered. "Our rents are well within the market, and our renewal rates demon-strate that."[8]

The rumblings over the subprime mortgage crisis started to get louder by the spring of 2007. But whatever the problems with home mortgages, few developers, bankers or analysts expected the crisis to radically affect the booming commercial credit market for hotels, shopping centers, multifamily housing or office buildings. No one anticipated defaults on those loans.

Both trends emerged in an era of lax lending standards, high-risk mortgage products and heavy betting that property values would continue to rise.

Banks make high-interest subprime loans to buyers who lack the income or the strong credit history needed to qualify for traditional mortgages. Most banks in the past refused to grant mortgages in black, Latino and poor communities.

Under the Community Reinvestment Act the federal government encouraged institutions receiving Federal Deposit Insurance Corporation insurance to end discriminatory lending practices in low-income neighborhoods. Federal banking agencies assess a bank's performance in meeting credit needs in communities in which they operate before approving applications for new branches or for mergers and acquisitions.

Historically, subprime lending only accounted for a sliver of all home mortgages. But starting in the late 1990s subprime lending became big business.

Independent mortgage banks like Countrywide, Ameriquest and New Century, which operated outside of federal regulation, including the Community Reinvestment Act, began aggressively marketing subprime loans as their higher interest rates made them more profitable. The banks also tapped into the global capital markets, gaining access to seemingly unlimited amounts of capital. Ultimately, the default rate on the loans originated by this fast-growing industry, unshackled by regulation, would reach epidemic proportions, while FHA and other government-backed loans proved to be far more successful.

The new private lenders typically offered easy initial terms—lower interest rates, called teaser rates—to encourage homeowners and buyers to take on difficult mortgages. After an initial period of time, say one year, the teaser rate was replaced by the regular, higher interest rate.

The effect on the homeowner was crushing. The monthly payment on a $500,000 mortgage at a 4 percent interest rate was about $2,400. But the same loan with a 10 percent rate would require a $4,220-a-month payment.

As home prices continued their rise, owners were encouraged to refinance again, at more favorable terms.

In many cases, mortgage brokers received bonuses for steering borrowers into high-interest loans larded with extra fees, even if they qualified for a traditional mortgage. The whole business was based on the assumption that house prices would never falter. But the securities were often so complex that it was difficult to assess the risk.

Wells Fargo, Bank of America, HSBC and other money center banks followed the lead of the independent banks, either acquiring subprime lenders or starting up their own operations.

These banks pooled the worst of their subprime loans with regular mortgages and sold these complex securities to investors around the world.

The percentage of lower-quality, subprime mortgages soared to 20 percent by late 2006, from 8 percent in 2003. In Florida, Southern California and Arizona it was even higher. By March

2007, the value of subprime mortgages had reached an estimated $1.3 trillion, with 7.5 million first-lien subprime mortgages outstanding.[9]

But once interest rates began to fall and housing prices slipped, modestly at first, homeowners could no longer refinance. Defaults and foreclosures escalated as the initial terms expired, higher interest rates kicked in and monthly payments jumped substantially. The securities packed with subprime loans suddenly turned toxic as investors fled, shaking the foundations of the world financial system.

"This is no longer a niche market that can be dismissed," said Keith Ernst, senior housing counsel at the Center for Responsible Lending. "It's a major component of the mortgage market and the growing rates of foreclosures should be a cause for alarm."[10]

The Center for Responsible Lending, a research group based in Durham, North Carolina, warned at the end of 2006 that 1.1 million homeowners who had taken out subprime loans in the prior two years would lose their houses by 2009. The foreclosures would cost those homeowners an estimated $74.6 billion, primarily in equity.

Still, the industry downplayed the growing crisis. Douglas Duncan, chief economist for the Mortgage Bankers Association, told the *New York Times* that the center's report was too pessimistic. "Every forecast models assumptions," he said, "but it seems they picked the worst-case scenario."[11]

The continuing fall in house prices meant that by one estimate nearly a quarter of all U.S. homes were worth less than their mortgage. The repercussions were felt in Florida and Arizona, where entire subdivisions looked like ghost towns as banks foreclosed on the properties.

The crisis had a particularly devastating effect on largely

black and Latino communities, where even the middle class turned to subprime rather than traditional mortgages. In some neighborhoods in New York City, for instance, houses on block after block sat boarded up and vacant in once-thriving communities.

"This was not only a problem of regulation on the mortgage front, but also a targeted scourge on minority communities," Shaun Donovan, the secretary of housing and urban development, said in a speech at New York University. "Roughly 33 percent of the subprime mortgages given out in New York City in 2007 went to borrowers with credit scores that should have qualified them for conventional prevailing-rate loans."

Tishman Speyer had other problems to contend with. Only two months after the company took over, a group of nine current and former market-rate tenants at the complexes filed a class-action lawsuit in state supreme court on January 22, 2007, claiming that Tishman Speyer and MetLife had illegally charged market-rate rents for more than three thousand apartments after "wrongfully pocketing nearly $25 million in New York City tax benefits." The tenants said that MetLife had received $24.5 million in tax breaks since 1992 under the city's J-51 property tax program, which, they argued, prohibits a property owner from deregulating apartments. The J-51 program was designed to encourage residential property owners, particularly landlords with older buildings, to refurbish their properties and make capital improvements, be it new elevators, boilers or windows. The plaintiffs wanted the court to roll back rents at Stuyvesant and Peter Cooper Village and issue a formal declaration that all of the units at the complexes would remain rent stabilized until the J-51 tax breaks expired in 2020. The tenants also wanted hundreds of millions of dollars in rent rebates and damages.

"Even though this was the largest real estate transaction of all time, and MetLife certainly has a right to make as much profit as it could, the tenants who have rights under the law need to be protected," said Stuart M. Saft, a well-known real estate lawyer who filed what became known as the "Roberts case."[12] "Roberts" was a reference to the lead plaintiff, Amy L. Roberts, who remained in her sixth-floor apartment on Twentieth Street, on the north side of Stuyvesant Town.

The lawsuit brought a curt "No comment" from MetLife and a dismissive wave from Tishman Speyer, which declared that the lawsuit had "no merit." It had been common practice for years for landlords, primarily in Manhattan, to simultaneously take advantage of the city's J-51 program and deregulate apartments. The state housing agency sanctioned it, Speyer's lawyers said. Rents were substantially lower in the city's other four boroughs, Queens, Brooklyn, the Bronx and Staten Island, and therefore landlords were less likely to reach the $2,000-a-month threshold for deregulation. Tishman Speyer's lawyers argued that the plaintiffs had voluntarily signed leases agreeing to market-rate rents so nothing had been taken away from them. Although anything could happen in court, most real estate experts confidently predicted that the lawsuit had no chance of success, and even many tenant activists were skeptical.

The case, which began as a Hail Mary effort to stymie Tishman Speyer, had been hatched months earlier by Leonard Grunstein, the rotund, silver-tongued lawyer who represented the tenant bid for Stuyvesant Town-Peter Cooper Village.

Grunstein had actually learned about the J-51 issue during

a meeting with Michael Lappin and Kathleen Dunn of CPC Resources, an outfit with ties to ninety banks and insurance companies that finances affordable housing. Their lawyer, Stuart Saft, was also there. CPC had revived another MetLife project, the 12,271-unit Parkchester complex in the Bronx, and was considering a bid for Stuyvesant Town-Peter Cooper Village. They were discussing the history of the complex when Dunn, a former deputy housing commissioner for the city, paused. "It's clear to me that you can't deregulate while you're taking J-51 benefits," Dunn exclaimed.[13] At first Grunstein doubted her. But he subsequently had associates at his law firm dig into the history of the state housing laws.

Soni Holman Fink, the tiny, vivacious eighty-six-year-old woman who serves as the tenants association's co-director of communications, recalled the meeting when Grunstein first broached the idea of a J-51 lawsuit. As she often did, Fink played host to the association's monthly gathering at her Peter Cooper Village apartment, whose picture window offered a mesmerizing view of the East River. "I can still see the grin on his face," Fink said of Grunstein. " 'We're going to stick it to them.' "[14]

But John H. Marsh III, the treasurer, and James J. Roth, the retired FBI agent, were the only ones on the seven-member board who really wanted to pursue it. "Half the people were saying that the laws allowed for landlords to deregulate," Marsh said. "There wasn't enough legal footing. But Jim and I felt, why not? We had just been through a grueling time with the sale."[15]

Grunstein, however, had to turn the case over to Saft because Grunstein's firm, Troutman Sanders, had a conflict of interest: It did work for MetLife. Saft, in turn, went to Councilman Garodnick, who put him in touch with market-rate tenants like Roberts and Horisk who were willing to put their names on the lawsuit. "I thought all along it was promising, but never a gimme," Garodnick said. "The law was clear but with so many years of common practice it would be a tough battle."[16]

Six months later, State supreme court judge Richard B. Lowe dismissed the tenants' lawsuit, handing a victory to MetLife and Tishman Speyer, which was busily repositioning Stuyvesant Town-Peter Cooper Village. There was very little media coverage of the decision, an indication, perhaps, that it had been widely regarded as a futile fight. The tenants' appeal would not be decided for a year and a half. By then, everything would have changed in Stuyvesant Town, in New York and across the country.

Stuyvesant Town-Peter Cooper Village was not the only thing on Rob Speyer's mind in 2007. His company operated on four continents and the real estate markets were still booming, even if there were some faint rumblings about troubled subprime home mortgages that had been turned into securities and sold to banks, insurance companies and pension funds. His company bought ten office buildings in Frankfurt, Berlin, Hamburg, Dusseldorf, Munich and Stuttgart while he flew between development projects in India, China and Brazil.

In May 2007, Rob Speyer sold the former headquarters of the *New York Times* in Times Square to an Israeli billionaire for $525 million, three times the $175 million Tishman Speyer paid in November 2004. The *Times* was building a new headquarters three blocks to the south. Rents for office space were up, but not by 300 percent or even 30 percent in 31 months. Yet, buyers seemed willing to pay almost any price to get ahold of prime property. Rob Speyer had planned on turning the building into first-class office space, but the offer was too good to resist. The Israeli investor, Lev Leviev, had not even visited the fifteen-story building before signing the contract. Rob Speyer was in the airport in Dubai at midnight after meeting with an investor when he got a call from his broker, Darcy Stacom, saying she had a buyer at $525 million, "willing to go hard."

"Sign it up," Speyer replied, laughing, hardly believing the number. "What're we on the phone for?"[17]

Speyer also sold the famed Lipstick Building, an elliptical, thirty-four-story office tower on Third Avenue designed by Philip Johnson and John Burgee, for $648.5 million. It was yet another illustration of just how fast the market was moving. Speyer and his partner, the New York City Employees' Retirement System, had bought the building three years earlier for $235 million. Having sold 666 Fifth, the New York Times Building, the Lipstick Building and $2 billion worth of property in London, Tishman Speyer raked in spectacular profits for its partners and itself on $5 billion in sales.

But the Lipstick deal also emitted a warning bell. The new owner, a group led by two Israeli investors, had planned to pay $44.8 million cash and finance 90 percent of the purchase with a loan from none other than Robert Verrone at Wachovia. But with the market jittery over the gathering storm in the subprime mortgage market, Verrone suddenly demanded a higher interest rate and less leverage. The Israelis were forced to get alternative financing from Royal Bank of Canada before closing the deal, which was expected to provide a meager 3.6 percent rate of return. Many observers wondered whether the credit boom that had fueled the run-up in real estate prices was drawing to a close.

The Israeli investors, however, were betting that annual rents would rise further still, to $100 a square foot and beyond.

The Speyers were not just sellers in 2007, however. They had a role in the two mega-deals of 2007 that would mark the peak of the market, the $39 billion purchase of Equity Office Properties in February, and months later, the $22.2 billion takeover of Archstone-Smith Trust, a publicly traded company with 360 apartment complexes, mainly on the East and West Coasts. Those transactions checked in as the first- and second-largest privatizations ever of a public real estate company.

The bidding war for Equity Office Properties, the nation's largest office landlord, ignited in January 2007 when a group led by Steven Roth, the outspoken chairman of Vornado Realty Trust, offered $38 billion for the company, topping a $36 billion offer from the Blackstone Group. Sam Zell, the Chicago billionaire, had spent three decades assembling 590 buildings and over 105 million square feet of office space in virtually every major metropolitan market in the country. But the company's disappointing share price reflected that stock analysts never bought into Zell's strategy of creating a national brand for office space.

The Blackstone Group, the nation's largest private equity firm, had been on a shopping spree, buying one publicly traded real estate company after another and taking them private. Equity Office proved an irresistible target, and not just for Blackstone. The residential market showed signs of weakening, but office rents were expected to continue to rise. A gusher of capital from sovereign funds, domestic and foreign pension funds and wealthy individuals continued to pour into real estate. Roth, the sharp-tongued founder of Vornado Realty, a public company whose holdings include suburban strip malls, office buildings in Washington, DC, and New York and the retailer Toys"R"Us, wanted to create the largest commercial real estate company in the nation. But public real estate companies cannot assume a lot of debt without coming under fire from stock analysts. So Roth turned to two real estate titans for partners, Barry Sternlicht of Starwood Capital and Sternlicht's onetime mentor, Neil Bluhm, a Chicago real estate tycoon.

The parry-thrust between the rival bidders continued for weeks before Blackstone, headed by Stephen A. Schwarzman, won, with a $39 billion offer. Even as that drama came to a close, Blackstone was raising another $10 billion real estate fund. The company immediately flipped hundreds of EOP buildings for a premium to sixteen different buyers in record-breaking deals from Southern California to Austin, Texas; Chicago; and New York. Even as profit margins on the properties shrank, the buyers found lenders on Wall Street all too willing to finance as much as 90 percent of the price. Morgan Stanley, Wachovia, Goldman Sachs, Bear Stearns and Lehman Brothers, in turn, collected their fees as they packaged the loans and sold, or tried to sell, them to investors as commercial mortgage-backed securities.

In Los Angeles, Maguire Properties, one of the largest commercial landlords in Southern California, bought twenty-four Equity Office buildings. The developer Harry B. Macklowe took only ten days to buy seven EOP buildings in Manhattan for $7 billion with short-term high-interest debt. In one stroke,

Macklowe, a high-stakes gambler, doubled his real estate empire. Although rents in the buildings averaged less than $60 a square foot, the underwriting projected rents rising to $100 a square foot or more. Tishman Speyer paid $1.7 billion for six EOP buildings in downtown Chicago, solidifying its hold on that market. The company immediately put a "For Sale" sign on three of them, hoping to pay off some of the debt used to acquire the properties in the first place. "[It] taught everyone that no deal was too big," Scott Latham, then executive director of Cushman and Wakefield's capital markets group, told *Commercial Property News*, a trade paper.

Three months later, Tishman Speyer and Lehman Brothers did their own version of the EOP deal, announcing the $22.2 billion purchase of Archstone-Smith Trust and its 360 apartment complexes in cities from Phoenix to Fairfax, Virginia, and New York. The deal had an exotic financial structure and an interesting backstory. Top bankers at Lehman Brothers, one of the more aggressive real estate lenders, were upset at losing out on the $5.4 billion purchase of Stuyvesant Town-Peter Cooper Village. Lehman's ace commercial lender Mark A. Walsh had tied up with the Related Companies, the developer of the Time Warner Center in Manhattan, in that auction. But Jerry Speyer, a personal friend of Lehman's chairman, Richard S. Fuld, had won with financing from Wachovia. Taking a page from Blackstone's purchase of EOP, Walsh engineered a highly leveraged deal for Archstone in partnership with Tishman Speyer.

Tishman Speyer contributed $250 million, or about 5 percent of the $5.1 billion in equity in Archstone, with the potential to earn 13 percent of the profits. Archstone would survive as a corporate entity and key executives would remain in place. Walsh and Lehman Brothers matched them and led Bank of

America and Barclays in gathering $17.1 billion in debt plus $4.6 billion in bridge equity. Rob Speyer envisioned his company's investment as a hedge against the slowdown in the housing market. If people were not buying houses and condominiums, they would rent instead. But Speyer and Lehman Brothers also planned to retire some of the debt by unloading a block of Archstone's apartment complexes, starting with the sale of a 90 percent interest in sixteen properties in San Diego and Orange County, California, to Irvine Company for $1.4 billion. But by the time the deal closed in October 2007, Green Street Advisors estimated that the value of Archstone's assets had fallen by 8 percent as worries grew about subprime mortgages.

Rob Speyer seemed to be of two minds about the real estate market. He had sold a pile of trophy office buildings, making a fortune for his company and his partners. It was a signal, perhaps, that in his view real estate prices had topped out and would soon retreat. Yet, at the same time, he paid top dollar for a batch of Chicago office buildings and jumped into a highly leveraged acquisition of Archstone-Smith.

By the summer of 2007, the subprime mortgage industry that had flourished for years was threatening to pull down the national economy. The value of mortgage-backed securities held by banks, insurance companies, hedge funds and other investors was in free fall. They worried that they might not have sufficient capital to stay afloat. Many analysts and developers were still unsure whether the problem would ever swamp still-booming Manhattan. Still, advocates for low-income homeowners had been complaining for years that mortgage providers were issuing loans without regard to the borrower's ability to repay. But easy initial terms and rising housing prices had encouraged borrowers to assume oversize mortgages in the belief they would be able to quickly refinance at more favorable terms. Outright fraud by some lenders also contributed to the rise in the number of subprime mortgages. But once interest rates started to fall in 2006 and housing prices inched downward, refinancing became more difficult. Defaults by homeowners on subprime and adjustable-rate mortgages skyrocketed and subprime lenders in December 2006 started failing as more borrowers fell behind on their mortgage payments. Like a growing number of commercial loans, the subprime home loans had been combined with other mortgages, blessed by the rating agencies and sold to banks, insurance companies and other investors.

On February 8, 2007, HSBC, the large British bank, announced that it was setting aside an additional $1.76 billion because of expanding problems in its American subprime lending business. The bank indicated that the rate of subprime loan defaults was escalating faster than anticipated. HSBC said bad debt charges for the year would be about $10.56 billion, 20 percent higher than the average forecast by analysts. The bank's public statements triggered a sell-off of mortgage-linked securities.

On the same day, New Century Financial, the second-largest subprime mortgage lender, also warned of growing financial problems. Two months later, the publicly traded company filed in bankruptcy court for protection from creditors.

Over the following summer, the Federal Reserve cut the discount rate it charges banks to borrow money, a move that at least temporarily quelled fears in stock and credit markets and among investors and banks. The Fed reluctantly acknowledged that the credit crisis posed a threat to economic growth.

Bear Stearns later disclosed that two hedge funds it controlled were facing a wave of withdrawals by investors. In July,

Moody's and Standard & Poor's, which had given mortgage-backed bonds high ratings, suddenly downgraded more than $7 billion of them sold in late 2005 and 2006. The rating agencies also began cracking down on the lending practices in commercial real estate, where banks were issuing loans at generous terms while buyers put little or no equity into the deals. Office rents in New York and other major markets were still rising, but for the first time since 2004, the average vacancy rate for 58 metropolitan markets rose, albeit only slightly, to 12.6 percent from 12.5 percent, according to Torto Wheaton Research, a division of CB Richard Ellis. "Underwriting has gotten so frothy that we have to take a stand," Jim Duca, a group managing director at Moody's Investors Service told the *New York Times* in May 2007. "The industry was headed to Niagara Falls."[18]

At quitting time on Wednesday, May 23, 2007, an estimated seven thousand tenants and union members marched across Stuyvesant Town to highlight the need for new rent-stabilization laws to "preserve New York's dwindling stock of affordable housing." The "Hands Around Stuyvesant Town" march, which included more than fifty city and state elected officials and one hundred community organizations, marked the start of a campaign to overhaul the state's housing laws, which, organizers said, had swung in favor of landlords. "The price of housing in this city is effectively theft for working- and middle-class people," Ed Ott told the crowd. "Housing is hard to afford even with two incomes."

The median household income in Stuyvesant Town and Peter Cooper Village was close to $95,000. But the $5.4 billion sale of the complexes had served as a catalyst for both low-income and middle-class residents throughout the city who found it increasingly difficult to find housing they could afford. The housing crisis for poor and working-class New Yorkers was severe and more well-known, with many families paying more than half their income for shelter. Between 2002 and 2008, New York City lost more than two hundred thousand apartments affordable to tenants making less than $37,000, as median rents increased by almost 9 percent, according to the Furman Center for Real Estate and Urban Policy at New York University. At the same time, middle-income neighborhoods were disappearing. The problem was especially pronounced in Manhattan, where half the neighborhoods were identified in a study by the Brookings Institution as high income and 40 percent as low income.

City comptroller William Thompson focused on the continuing loss of apartments that were once in the state's middle-income Mitchell-Lama housing program. After twenty years in the program, developers were leaving in droves, paying off the government mortgages and pushing rents to market levels. "Forty thousand people are watching their homes change from affordable to no longer affordable," Thompson said at the rally. "We need to stand up to make sure all New Yorkers can stay."

It is hard to understand politics in New York without grasping the role of the real estate industry. Real estate is big business in a city whose economic health is often measured by the number of construction cranes swinging across the skyline. Property taxes account for the bulk of the city's operating budget. About 130,000 workers labored at construction jobs in the city in 2007. In this context, there is an intimate relationship between real estate tycoons and the city's 51 members of the city council. The council has little power relative to the mayor except in one area: land use. Most major projects and policies must get approval by the council. Therefore, real estate executives as a group are often the single biggest campaign contributors to council members, as well as state senators and assembly members from New York City whose votes could affect development policy.

But New York City is still primarily a city of renters, renters who vote, as elected officials well know. This dynamic can lend itself to peculiar maneuvers. City council president Christine Quinn, for instance, is a former tenant organizer who has fought to enlarge the city's affordable-housing program. She was an outspoken supporter of the tenant bid for Stuyvesant Town–Peter Cooper Village and a critic of the real estate speculators.

But few officials are willing to engage in a permanent state of war with the industry and risk losing its potential financial support. Nor are many developers willing to completely alienate a politician who can determine the fate of their next project. So, a few months after the sale of Stuyvesant Town, Rob Speyer emerged as one of the most generous supporters of Ms. Quinn's possible mayoral campaign, gathering up $22,275 in contributions from real estate executives.[19]

Still, the backlash against speculators who were buying tenements by the blockful in working-class neighborhoods was gathering steam. Activists had upended the sale of Starrett City, the sprawling Brooklyn complex, and were now pressuring state legislators to change the laws. "The large numbers being talked about drew people's attention," Neill Coleman, a spokesman for the city's housing agency, acknowledged to *The Real Deal*, a real estate magazine. "There's a renewed interest in what the city is doing from the press, from advocates and from elected officials."

Darcy Stacom, the broker who sold Stuyvesant Town-Peter Cooper Village, told executives at a real estate forum that she feared the "influence of politics on private transactions." Nevertheless, the speculative trend continued as Dawnay Day Group, a British real estate firm, bought a portfolio of 47 buildings in East Harlem for $225 million, and Stephen Siegel, a prominent commercial real estate broker, formed the SG2 group and acquired a large portfolio—1,137 apartments and 55 storefronts—in the Bronx for $300 million. In both cases, the buyers intended to exploit the gap between rent-stabilized and market rents.

At Stuyvesant Town-Peter Cooper Village, Tishman Speyer hiked the rents on deregulated apartments, renovated vacant units and ferreted out as many illegal tenants as they could find. Rob Speyer also sought to break down the institutional aura that surrounded the fifty-six (sometimes described as 110 buildings, because some structures have multiple addresses) nearly identical brick buildings. He established a green market inside the complexes on Thursdays and Fridays and, in a gesture of goodwill toward the tenants, brought former Mets star Keith Hernandez to Stuyvesant Town to toss out the first ball at a game sponsored by the Peter Stuyvesant Little League on Con Ed Field, near the East River. Rather than using pesticide, Tishman Speyer also released nearly 720,000 ladybugs in the fall of 2007 to eat the tiny mites and other insects destroying the extensive greenery. Some tenants welcomed the modern new health club that opened on Twentieth Street, the thoroughfare that separates Stuyvesant Town and Peter Cooper Village. But not the older residents, who were dependent on the supermarket that was ousted to make way for the health club, which they did not use.

Tishman Speyer's campaign to evict "illegal" tenants made a

far bigger impression on longtime residents of the two complexes than gyms and green markets. The company's lawyers and detectives identified tenants whose leases were up for renewal and who appeared to live elsewhere for at least 183 days a year. Ninety days before the leases expired, the law firms sent the so-called illegal tenants a "Golub notice," the equivalent of an eviction notice, because their Stuyvesant Town or Peter Cooper apartment did not appear to be their primary residence. "Tishman Speyer caused a lot of anxiety right from the beginning because we knew they wanted to get people out," said Richard Toes, a former narcotics detective who lived in Stuyvesant Town for more than thirty years.[20]

Under state law, a landlord can evict a tenant who is using a rent-regulated apartment as a pied-à-terre or subleasing the unit to another person at a higher rent. Tishman Speyer's lawyers and detectives culled information from property records and credit card databases. Hundreds of tenants were told that their lease would not be renewed unless they provided management with proof of employment and residency. Tishman Speyer discovered that one rent-stabilized tenant, Jeff Varner, actually lived in Kalamazoo, Michigan, where he worked as a news anchor for a local television station. He was not the only person who was unwilling to forgo a prized low-rent apartment after having moved away from New York City. "We want a community of people who actually live here," Rob Speyer said.

As word of the Golub notices coursed through the complexes, Al Doyle, the president of the tenants association, was inundated with calls from fearful rent-stabilized tenants who had received a notice or were afraid they would soon get a notice. The tenants association did not oppose evicting people who profited by subleasing rent-regulated apartments at a higher rent. But Tishman Speyer threw a much wider net, Doyle said. MetLife and Rose Associates had quietly issued nonrenewal notices to tenants who clearly were and were not entitled to a stabilized apartment. The widespread use of the notices generated a great deal of ill will among all residents, not just those who received the notices. Anxious residents were forced to produce pages and pages of documentation, and in some cases hire a lawyer, to prove their Stuyvesant Town apartment was their primary residence.

Agnes Lamy, a legal secretary who had lived in a one-bedroom apartment at Stuyvesant Town for a decade, initially ignored the nonrenewal notice she received in December 2007, thinking it was a mistake. But Tishman Speyer was intent on getting her out. The detectives had discovered that Lamy had signed a $60,000 loan for a studio apartment in Brooklyn. It was for her mother, she explained. Tishman Speyer demanded three years' worth of tax returns and bank statements to prove her residency. No sooner had she straightened out the matter, than she got another letter from the landlord wanting to know her connection to an apartment on East Thirty-Fourth Street, where she had lived with her now divorced husband fifteen years earlier. "They put me through the ringer, all the way," Lamy said of the four-month ordeal. "These were intimidation tactics."

Doyle asked the Urban Justice Center, which provides legal assistance to low- and moderate-income tenants, to hold an informational clinic for tenants at a junior high school near Stuyvesant Town. After more than a hundred residents showed up seeking advice, the Urban Justice Center turned it into a monthly event, consistently drawing fifty people per session.

Surfing through public records can also produce notoriously

unreliable or incomplete results. Dolores M. Shapiro, a sixty-two-year-old anthropologist and retired professor of nursing, was accused of living in Naperville, Illinois, a town, she said, that she had never even visited. She was forced to hire a lawyer, James B. Fishman, who discovered that a woman with the same name but a different middle initial appeared to be living in Naperville. Tishman Speyer dropped the case. "Their business model was fear," Fishman said. "It was all about scaring the crap out of people. Lots of tenants could not afford to fight back and hire a lawyer. Even when they won, it was a pyrrhic victory. It could cost thousands of dollars in legal fees."[21]

Suzanne Ryan was ordered to give up her Peter Cooper Village apartment after she got a notice claiming she and her husband lived in a beachfront home on Long Island. She too had to hire a lawyer to prove that Ryan's family used it as a summer beach house, while keeping their residence in the city, where her two children attended Catholic school. "It's a little Cape," Ryan explained. "We had fixed it up ourselves."

Jack Lester, a tenant lawyer, said he had represented dozens of tenants but lost only one case, a flight attendant who lived in Florida and used an apartment in Stuyvesant Town whenever she flew into New York.[22]

Rob Speyer vehemently denied accusations by residents and their lawyers that his company harassed tenants, saying Golub notices only went out when there was evidence of a second residence. Rob Speyer was bewildered by the tenant reaction. He had figured that legitimate tenants would feel no kinship with tenants who did not belong in a rent-regulated apartment. In the end, he said that one-third of the 1,099 tenants who received Golub notices in 2007, 2008 and 2009 left the complexes without a fight, a third proved that they were legitimate tenants and a third went to court. Ultimately, he said, half were illegal, although tenant advocates said that many tenants left rather than fight because they could not afford to hire a lawyer. "The numbers speak for themselves," Speyer concluded.[23]

But a climate of suspicion and distrust had set in, coloring much of what happened in the complexes, even efforts to beautify the grounds. In 2008, an army of workers armed with shovels, saws, tractors and backhoes swarmed across the eighty acres. Tishman Speyer expanded the lobbies of the buildings facing the grassy, tree-shaded oval at the center of Stuyvesant Town by knocking out some of the brick walls and adding glass boxes that housed new amenities, ranging from a day care center to a theater and a private event room. The transparent cubes contrasted nicely with the unrelenting brick of the complexes and lent a modern flair to the architecture. Although MetLife had spent $47 million refurbishing the complexes' fifteen playgrounds and installing new lighting and new landscaping throughout the grounds, Rob Speyer also brought in a new landscape architect, Peter Walker, and started all over again. He wanted a lush fantasia of colors and flowers worthy of the younger, wealthier tenants he was trying to attract. Eventually, he spent millions of dollars on an astounding array: 10,000 new dogwood, magnolia and cherry trees; 3,100 shrubs; 120,000 perennials; 40,000 annuals; and 100 hanging baskets. Every so often, the old plantings were yanked out and new ones put in their stead.

"We met with Rob every couple of weeks," said Walker, who is based in California. "It was his baby and he was interested in how it turned out. He wanted a show garden, something that would be spectacular, a transforming level of landscaping."[24]

Proud as he was, Rob Speyer could not help asking Doyle,

the tenant leader, what he thought of the results during a chance encounter at Stuyvesant Town. He was stunned when Doyle complained. Longtime tenants at apartment complexes are often wary of change, particularly one that turns the complexes into a construction site for extended periods. The new bushes at the base of the buildings offered some privacy for first-floor apartments, but Doyle said the older tenants complained that the plantings also obscured the views of the security cameras.

"What do they have against trees?" Rob Speyer said to me at the time. "I couldn't believe it. There's a group that will never be happy no matter what we do. That story sums it up."

Doyle acknowledged that "it sounds crazy." "But," he said, "the tenants were used to lush rolling green lawns. If you were a young mother, you could see your kids playing halfway across the property. The sight lines were blocked by the new trees."[25]

The landscaping and the glass cubes also proved to be rich fodder for a new blog, *Stuy Town Lux Living*, that premiered in April 2008. The blog dubbed the spots suddenly thick with bushes and young trees "Rape Forests," because of the impenetrable foliage. It got to the point that anything Tishman Speyer did at Stuyvesant Town was seen as a threat. Including the gardening.

The blogger behind *Lux Living* was a website designer and content provider living in a one-bedroom apartment, paying a rent-regulated $1,600 a month. A mix of *The Daily Show* and TMZ, *Lux Living*'s sharp-tongued parodies and fake news reports quickly found an audience, with thirty thousand unique visitors a month. The site linked to newspaper articles about the Stuyvesant Town deal and provided information concerning the latest doings. Faux reports highlighted the bare-breasted women at Tishman Speyer's Mardi Gras celebration and the high suicide rate among workers assigned to the nearly-always-empty Oval Lounge. The site was unsparing of Rob Speyer, who was described as a "real estate pirate," depicted in skimpy gym shorts and described as "reeking of alcohol and chain smoking." "It was a soap opera," the blogger told me. "The whole David-and-Goliath thing."[26]

The blogger of *Lux Living*, who was thirty when the blog started, also explored the tension between the recent college graduates and the established residents, be they originals who dated to the 1947 opening, their children now raising children themselves or young couples looking for a quiet corner of the city. Tishman Speyer's marketing aimed at a younger demographic to dispel the perception that Stuyvesant Town and Peter Cooper Village were more for the geriatric set. There were more than three hundred graduate students living in apartments rented by New York University, according to Tishman Speyer executives.

Many longtime tenants felt the students ignored their neighbors and played loud music when they got home at 3:00 A.M. on Saturday. Old-timers complained that the "kids" left garbage bags outside the garbage chute and neglected to sort their bottles and cans for the recycling bins.

"It changed from a stable community to a transient one," said Soni Fink, who has lived in her Peter Cooper apartment since 1961. "They were so eager to rent apartments at higher prices that the only people who could afford it were the kids, who put up dividing walls. Four or five of them would pile in. Young couples used to move in and settle down."[27]

In the late 1990s, MetLife removed the post-and-chain fences that protected every blade of grass inside the complexes. Appealing to young renters, Tishman Speyer took it a step farther, relaxing or even abandoning the pesky rules that once governed life in the complexes, including the prohibition on pets. Denis Delaney, whose parents moved to Stuyvesant Town in 1948, can still recall how the guards would chase after offenders who dared set foot on the lawns. So it was a shocking sight after Tishman Speyer took over to see young women lying out in the sun or people playing with their dogs on the grass. Soon there were footpaths crisscrossing Stuyvesant Oval's once-verboten lawn. "I used to jump over the chains and run on the grass because I was a kid," said Denis Delaney, fifty-eight. "But I liked it looking nice. Now there are cow paths."[28]

In 2007 and 2008, Tishman Speyer methodically went about renovating vacant apartments, raising rents and navigating the arcane system governing rent-regulated apartments in New York. The company spent more on apartment renovations than MetLife, about $53,000 per unit at Stuyvesant Town, installing maple cabinets, stone counters and higher-end appliances in the kitchens, refurbishing the bathrooms and laying down new parquet floors. At Peter Cooper Village, where the apartments were larger, the landlord spent $69,000, installing slightly better finishes.

Tishman Speyer diligently pushed the net effective rent for a one-bedroom at Stuyvesant Town to over $3,100 a month and over $4,000 for a two-bedroom. At Peter Cooper, one-bedroom apartments went for more than $3,200 and two-bedrooms for more than $4,700 a month.[29]

But a peculiar thing happened in the fall of 2007. Fewer and fewer people were renting apartments at Stuyvesant Town and Peter Cooper, where historically the vacancy rate was less than 2 percent. By the end of the year, Tishman Speyer had accumulated an inventory of 757 unrented apartments. The new owners discovered that they could in fact charge too much for an apartment in a sixty-year-old non-doorman building on the East Side. Renters found better deals elsewhere. Citi Habitats, a large rental broker, reported in 2007 that the average rent in the neighborhood west of Peter Cooper Village was $2,785 a month for a one-bedroom apartment and $3,846 for a two-bedroom unit.

Tishman Speyer was in a deep hole, considering that about 50 apartments a month turned over through normal attrition and now they had an additional backlog of 757 units, more than a year's worth of inventory. It was happening at complexes where traditionally there was a very low vacancy rate and a 10-year waiting list. Rob Speyer did everything to move product. The company dropped the rents and offered incentives to brokers who leased the most apartments: an all-inclusive trip to Cabo San Lucas for first prize; iPhones for the five runners-up. They offered tenants one month free rent and an American Express gift card loaded with $1,000. Rob Speyer later acknowledged that the company's effort to push rents to luxury levels had gone too far. "What happened, candidly, was we overstepped a bit," Rob Speyer told *New York* magazine. "In any business, you look at your inventory, you price your business to move your inventory."[30]

The rising vacancy rate was not just a concern of management. More than three hundred tenants showed up for an April 3, 2008, "town meeting" at the veterans' hospital on East Twenty-Third Street, sponsored by the tenants association and Manhattan borough president Scott Stringer. Speakers denounced the rising number of legal challenges launched against tenants, despite promises by Tishman Speyer that there would be "no radical changes." Garodnick, the councilman, told the crowd that Tishman Speyer had created a "landlord-versus-tenant culture" in which tenants lived in fear of getting an eviction notice. He also pointed out the suddenly high vacancy rate resulting from the new owners' relentless pursuit of higher rents. "Families moved to PCV/ST because it is renowned for its stability, its tranquil grounds and its sense of community," Garodnick wrote to Speyer. "Unfortunately, you are creating a culture of conflict that is having a negative impact. Everyone, from the original residents who moved into the complex in 1949 to the younger families who seek to settle down, is feeling the effects of these policies."

Tishman Speyer's financial model was also showing some signs of stress. Instead of net income rising as predicted, it had not really budged in a year. Expenses went up, what with three top law firms billing hundreds of hours to chase "illegal" tenants. Speyer's banker Rob Verrone of Wachovia called the trustee for the $3 billion first mortgage, suggesting that there was an inadvertent mistake, or what lawyers call a "scrivner's error," in the loan documents that prevented the new owners from shifting money from one reserve fund, say the one for repair and maintenance, to the interest reserve, which was used to plug the yawning $14-million-a-month gap between income and the actual loan payments. Their request to shift their reserve funds was denied. "They were looking to pull money from repair and maintenance to pay debt service," said Chuck Spetka, chief executive of CWCapital. "At that time, they weren't meeting projections so we could not and would not approve that. However, the magnitude of the problem was not yet evident."[31]

So early in 2008, Tishman Speyer elected to make a change in its payments for the $1.4 billion mezzanine loan, which was made up of eleven different segments. Under its loan documents, Tishman Speyer had the option to stop making payments and let the interest accrue for the tenth and eleventh segments, which totaled $500 million. That reduced the monthly debt service to $21 million from $23.7 million.[32] Speyer hoped that they had bought some time to reduce the inventory and boost revenues.

Whatever the issues at Stuyvesant Town, Rob Speyer was still in deal mode. They were not making more land in Manhattan, so the opportunity to snap up a rare undeveloped parcel was irresistible.

On March 21, 2008, Speyer vaulted to the head of a pack of prominent developers vying for the development rights to twenty-six acres of vacant land on Manhattan's west side, overlooking the Hudson River.[33] The competition for the billion-dollar deal had started months earlier when the economy was still on cruise control. But it now looked to be teetering at the edge of recession as lenders had all but shut the doors for large real estate deals because of the expanding credit crisis. Only a week earlier, Bear Stearns, a global Wall Street investment bank, had collapsed amid mounting losses on the huge amounts of mortgage-backed securities it had issued. The stock market tumbled as JPMorgan Chase bought Bear Stearns at a fire-sale price, ultimately, of $10 per share, a staggering loss as its stock had traded for $93 a share as late as February 2008. The deal was valued at about $1.2 billion, the worth of Bear Stearns' Madison Avenue headquarters.

Wachovia, the nation's fourth-largest bank and a leading lender for office buildings and multifamily properties, had announced in January that it would write down more than

$1 billion in commercial loans for the second half of 2007.[34] Morgan Stanley reported it was writing down $400 million in commercial loan losses. Unlike the borrowers for subprime residential mortgages, commercial landlords seemed unlikely to default. But investors suddenly refused to buy securities backed by commercial loans. That left banks like Wachovia, which packaged $24.2 billion worth of commercial loans as securities in 2007, stuck with loans that had dropped in value.

The shaky economic environment had already prompted one national developer, Brookfield Properties, to drop out of the competition for the twenty-six-acre parcel in Manhattan. But Rob Speyer and three rivals were not ready to give up the chase, at least not yet. After all, rents and occupancy rates remained fairly healthy. Maybe the markets would make a quick comeback from the credit crisis and the Bear Stearns debacle.

The billion-dollar deal offered an increasingly rare commodity: a large-scale development in Manhattan. The project was a political priority for Michael R. Bloomberg, whose administration had spent six years rezoning the once-industrial West Side for high-rise buildings, and a fiscal necessity for the Metropolitan Transportation Authority, which owned the land and hoped to reap a billion dollars from the sale. But while the deal presented a potentially lucrative opportunity, it came with enormous risks. A developer would have to spend an estimated $1.5 billion building platforms over active rail yards before starting the first tower in a roughly twelve-million-square-foot project that would take a decade to complete.

The Metropolitan Transportation Authority selected Tishman Speyer as the top bidder because of its blue-chip reputation and access to capital from around the world. The authority immediately entered into what turned out to be prolonged contract negotiations with Rob Speyer, whose company planned to erect four or five office towers and seven residential buildings with 3,053 apartments, a school and 13 acres of open space. Both Rob Speyer and his father, Jerry, saw a chance to do a project together that could have the same impact on New York as John D. Rockefeller Jr. had in the 1930s when he built Rockefeller Center.

Six weeks later, the negotiations foundered. Speyer insisted on delaying the closing and changing some of the economic terms. He did not want to start making payments for the development rights until the land was rezoned, a process that could drag on for eighteen months. In essence, Tishman Speyer wanted a free option on the development site. MTA officials did not want to wait that long for the first payment and risk Tishman Speyer's walking away from the project if the economy faltered or the zoning did not suit the developer's plans. Gary J. Dellaverson, the authority's chief financial officer, balked, telling Speyer in a series of tense phone calls that he had wasted the MTA's time and threatening to open talks with another bidder. Speyer, who was traveling in Europe, asked for more time. "Rob was just wracked with anxiety during that last week," Dellaverson said.[35]

On May 9, 2008, Mayor Bloomberg, desperate to salvage the project, invited the Speyers to his town house in London. Rob and his father flew in from Milan, where they had been meeting with investors. But the mayor had little leverage since he did not own the land. "The plan isn't dead by any means," Bloomberg declared in London. "Hudson Yards is the most exciting opportunity New York has." The Speyers issued a statement as well: "We still hope to complete this deal and reach an agreement that satisfies the needs of everyone."[36]

Back in New York on Monday, Rob Speyer met with Della-verson and nearly signed the contract. But at the last moment, he asked to postpone and raced back to Tishman Speyer head-quarters at Rockefeller Center to talk to his father. He seesawed between snatching up the headline-making deal and a paralyz-ing concern for the gathering financial storm. Sensing that the market had reached its peak, he and the company had started selling off some of their prime office buildings in January. As the sun set over Manhattan, Jerry and Rob went for a walk that stretched deep into the night before ending up at 3 Guys, an Upper East Side diner on Madison Avenue, between Seventy-Fifth and Seventy-Sixth Streets. Over tuna sandwiches, they weighed their desire to work together against the faltering econ-omy and the potential risks in their portfolio. They had run the company with an explicit understanding: Either one of them had veto power over any major undertaking by Tishman Speyer. But Jerry told his son, "You're going to be living with this proj-ect a lot longer than I. It needs to be your decision."

Rob paused for a moment before responding. "We're not do-ing it," he said.

"It was a great opportunity to develop a game-changing proj-ect in our hometown, something that we'd both dreamed of doing," Rob recalled five years later. "But we both had an ago-nizing feeling that the timing was wrong."[37]

The markets were jittery and Rob had a full plate of projects. Tishman Speyer and Lehman Brothers had already announced the $22.2 billion purchase of Archstone-Smith and now Stuyves-ant Town-Peter Cooper Village was demanding more and more attention. Investors like the California Public Employees' Retire-ment System, which had written a $500 million check, wanted to know why things were not going according to plan.

CHAPTER TEN

The Bubble Explodes

By the spring of 2008, Tishman Speyer had whittled down their huge inventory of unrented apartments to about four hundred units, by offering one month of free rent and other concessions to prospective tenants. Rob Speyer vowed once again that Tishman Speyer would be a longtime owner of Stuyvesant Town-Peter Cooper Village. Heckled by a tenant during a walk through Stuyvesant Town, he remained undaunted. Even if current residents did not always appreciate the lush landscaping, the health club and the amenities on Stuyvesant Oval, he said the new market-rate tenants did. "We've hit our stride," Speyer said at the time. "With all the positive changes at the property, interest is only going to grow from here."[1]

Yet, his business plan was even more out of whack with reality. Net effective rents—the rent after concessions, such as one month free rent—were slipping. The conversion of regulated apartments was moving even more slowly in 2008 than the year before. Moreover, Speyer and his partners had already burned through about two-thirds of their reserve funds.[2] On the political front, he was still getting angry letters from Councilman

Garodnick demanding that Tishman Speyer declare a moratorium on evictions and pay the legal expenses of residents who were able to prove that they were legal residents of Stuyvesant Town or Peter Cooper despite notices to the contrary.

"Tishman Speyer has launched a campaign against legal, legitimate tenants who have no business being pursued by their new landlord," Garodnick said. "This is a company that bills itself as a leader in New York and now they're using the cheapest of tactics against tenants who are clearly legitimate."

Beyond Stuyvesant Town, the Community Service Society, a nonprofit antipoverty group in New York, issued a study of the city's declining inventory of rent-regulated housing for poor, working-class and moderate-income New Yorkers. The group called for state and federal investigations of the loss of thousands of rent-regulated apartments that were once in a federal program for low-income tenants or the state's Mitchell-Lama program for moderate-income housing. "This was a combination of people trying to make fast bucks in a very overheated housing market and regulators taking the view 'anything goes,'" said David R. Jones, president of the society. "Someone should be held accountable for this kind of wrongdoing."

The mounting criticism of Tishman Speyer by tenants and housing activists, however, had no effect on the Speyers' reputation among New York's political, social and business elites. Jerry I. Speyer and Steven Rattner, a financier who managed the mayor's fortune, were instrumental in persuading Michael R. Bloomberg to run for a third term. But that required overturning the city's term-limits law, which would force Bloomberg to step down after eight years, on December 31, 2009. Speyer, Rattner and other business leaders appreciated the mayor's corporate approach to government and his friendliness to real estate development. Rattner served as an adviser to President Barack Obama on the auto industry and managed the mayor's personal fortune and philanthropic assets.

In their view, the middle of a financial crisis was the wrong time to replace the city's chief executive.[3] Bloomberg, who had previously been a staunch defender of term limits, agreed. Speyer and other business leaders aligned with Bloomberg then waged a campaign to convince the public that overturning term limits was a good idea, while running a bruising but ultimately successful lobbying effort to get the city council to extend term limits to twelve years. Bloomberg spent $105 million on his reelection campaign and won.

Still, Tishman Speyer had more than just Stuyvesant Town-Peter Cooper Village to contend with. Other highly leveraged assets purchased at the top of the market were showing signs of stress. Tishman Speyer and Lehman Brothers had planned to sell as many as half the 359 apartment complexes in the Archstone-Smith portfolio to reduce the debt on their $22.2 billion acquisition. The only problem was that prices were coming in a good deal lower than expected when they were even able to drum up bids for the properties. The partners sold the 948-unit Archstone San Jose complex in California for $192 million, $38 million, or 16.5 percent, less than the average price it paid per apartment. Another complex in Denver, Monterey Grove, sold for $56 million, $2 million below its allocated value. Despite those setbacks, Ian Lowitt, Lehman's chief financial officer, told analysts in June that Archstone was in serious discussions to unload $2 billion worth of property. Lehman and Tishman Speyer also wrote down their investment in Archstone by 25 percent.

Tishman Speyer was not alone. Record-breaking deals were suddenly unraveling from New York to California. The developer

Ian Bruce Eichner, who was building a high-end casino in Las Vegas called the Cosmopolitan, defaulted on a $768 million construction loan from Deutsche Bank, which took over the property. Centro Properties Group, an Australian mall operator, put itself up for sale after failing to refinance billions of dollars in short-term debt stemming from the acquisition of an American shopping center portfolio. In Los Angeles, Maguire Properties, one of the biggest commercial landlords in the region, was struggling with huge debts from buying a portfolio of buildings in Orange County whose tenants, it turned out, were imploding subprime mortgage companies.

Harry B. Macklowe, a prominent Manhattan developer with a willingness to double down as fierce as any riverboat gambler's, lost much of a vast real estate empire in May 2008 when he was unable to refinance $7 billion in high-interest, short-term loans. Macklowe, a ruthless, gravelly voiced negotiator, fended off his lenders for more than six months. But ultimately he was forced to sell his prized possession: the fifty-story General Motors Building on Fifth Avenue, and three other midtown towers, for a breathtaking $3.95 billion, to a group led by Mortimer B. Zuckerman, chief executive of Boston Properties.[4]

Only fifteen months earlier, Macklowe had been more successful than at any other point in his career. Son of a garment industry executive and a college dropout, Macklowe owned eight prime Manhattan office towers and a group of luxury apartment buildings. He also controlled two rare development sites in midtown. Macklowe wagered much of what he had to buy seven skyscrapers as part of the Equity Office Properties deal for $7 billion.

The market appeared to be booming and credit was easily available. He and his son put up only $50 million of their own money and borrowed $7 billion from Deutsche Bank and Fortress Investment Group to finance the rest of the purchase. The average annual rent from the seven midtown office buildings was $59 a square foot, William Macklowe, Harry's son, revealed during the crisis. But, he added, Deutsch Bank and Fortress underwrote the deal on the assumption that rents would soon soar to $100 a square foot. It was a remarkable illustration of the risks that Wall Street bankers and developers were willing to take. But William Macklowe also seemed to forget his symbiotic relationship with the bankers and the Macklowes' role in making the calculations on which the underwriting was based. Most of the loans were typical nonrecourse debt, meaning the lender could take the property in the event of default but not the borrower's other assets. Harry Macklowe, however, backed one loan with a $1 billion personal guarantee.

A year after the purchase, the senior Macklowe, seventy-one, found himself unable to refinance the debt and pay off the original loans. It was not the first time that Macklowe's back was to the wall. But in the midst of the crisis, he went sailing on his 112-foot racing yacht in the Caribbean, while his son stayed home to negotiate with the bankers. At least outwardly, Macklowe appeared to be stress free, oblivious to the possibility that his empire might once again slip through his fingers, much as it had in the early 1990s.

"Our lenders have supported us in the past to an extraordinary degree," Macklowe told me one evening in his office, shortly before he left for the Caribbean. "We're pretty confident that, going forward, we'll be able to achieve accommodations and extensions from our group of lenders."[5]

But after months of unsuccessful haggling and a journey to the Middle East in a fruitless search for partners, Macklowe was forced to relinquish not only the seven towers to his lenders but also the GM Building, across Fifth Avenue from the Plaza Hotel, where he'd bought a full-floor condominium.

The sale of the GM Building alone, for a record $2.8 billion, was an anomaly in this new era, made possible only in partnership with Zuckerman's partners—Goldman Sachs, Morgan Stanley and investment funds from Qatar and Kuwait. Otherwise, deal making was coming to a screeching halt as the bond market for mortgage-backed securities, the fuel for the rapid escalation of prices in 2005, 2006 and 2007, shut down amid concerns about defaults and delinquencies. The sales volume for office buildings plummeted by 74 percent nationally to $54.3 billion, from a $210.3 billion peak in 2007, according to Real Capital Analytics.

Multifamily housing was no different, with the volume of apartment properties dropping by 62 percent nationally and 64 percent in New York City. With office rents falling and vacancy rates hitting 10 percent in every metropolitan area in the country except New York, many of the buildings that had traded hands in recent years were in jeopardy as owners struggled to meet oversize debt payments with diminishing revenues. The underwriting for many of those loans was based on income projections rather than actual income. It didn't require a full-scale recession for the rickety financial architecture to collapse, only a slowdown in the rate of growth. Wachovia put the senior piece of the $3 billion mortgage on Stuyvesant Town-Peter Cooper Village on its watch list, because the net income from the property was so far below the debt service. Of course, that was also true the day that Wachovia closed on the loan.

Moody's Investors Service, the bond-rating agency, announced in the spring of 2007 that it planned to adjust how it rated commercial mortgage-backed securities (CMBS) to better reflect the risk. But the damage was done. Moody's, like Standard & Poor's and Fitch, had already stamped the loans with investment-grade ratings, based on what had quickly turned out to be fanciful projections. By then, Wall Street had repackaged hundreds of billions of dollars in loans as securities and sold them to investors.

"Loans with more aggressive terms that weren't available in '03 and '04 became the norm in '06, when suddenly lenders became very accommodating," said Mike Kirby, a principal at Green Street Advisors, a research company in Newport Beach, California, that tracks real estate investment trusts. "The attitude was, 'Gee, we're not going to own this stuff; we get terrific fees for underwriting these loans, and we can blow it out in a CMBS deal in three months."[6]

Analysts wondered if the credit crisis was about to swamp commercial real estate. Deutsche Bank had piled up $25.1 billion worth of commercial loans. Morgan Stanley had $22.1 billion and Citigroup held $19.1 billion. Lehman Brothers, the most aggressive of all, was actively trying to sell $40 billion worth of commercial real estate assets, a high-risk bridge equity loan for the Archstone-Smith acquisition. Lehman had not been as quick as others to package the loans as securities and get them off the company's balance sheet. More than half the assets were in the United States, with 26 percent in Europe and 17 percent in Asia.[7]

In August 2008, Laurence Gluck, a New York real estate investor, notified lenders that he was in imminent danger of defaulting on the mortgage for Riverton, the middle-class housing complex in Harlem that had been built by MetLife in 1947. Gluck had bought the property in 2005 for $132 million with a $105 million bank loan. A year later, Gluck and his partner, Rockpoint Group, refinanced the property with a $225 million senior loan from Deutsche Bank and a $25 million junior loan. Deutsche Bank combined the loan with other mortgages and sold it to investors. The refinancing enabled Gluck and Rockpoint to recoup their original investment, pay off the initial loan and set aside $53.3 million in reserves for renovating the complex and interest payments. They put the remaining $60 million in their pockets, without any legal obligation to give it back if the project went sour.[8]

Gluck planned, like Tishman Speyer and BlackRock at Stuyvesant Town-Peter Cooper Village, to dress up the sixty-year-old, middle-class complex and replace rent-regulated residents with tenants willing to pay market rents. The developer installed new elevators, upgraded the lobbies and landscaped a seven-hundred-foot interior courtyard at a complex whose residents once included jazz pianist Billy Taylor, former mayor David N. Dinkins and Clifford L. Alexander Jr., secretary of the army in the Carter administration. But Gluck's push to convert the apartments to market rents quickly fizzled. Rental income covered less than half his debt service. Less than two years after he refinanced the property, Gluck was on the verge of default. He ultimately walked away, turning the keys over to his lender.

Gluck, who has a Jimi Hendrix poster prominently displayed in his office, told me that the banks drank the "Kool-Aid" of the era by providing oversize loans based on "pro forma" underwriting. Asked if he hadn't had a sip of Kool-Aid himself and profited handsomely from the arrangement, he acknowledged that he had. In the meantime, the estimated value of Riverton had fallen to $170.3 million by October 2008, according to Realpoint, a research firm that assesses mortgage-backed securities.

Small wonder that some housing activists began describing Gluck and his bankers as "predatory equity."

Within a few weeks, Citigroup analysts issued a report in August entitled "Looking for Other Rivertons." They came up with a list of twenty-two properties—one in Chicago, two in San Francisco and nineteen in New York—in rent-regulated markets with CMBS loans based on projections of rapidly increasing revenues. In each example, the project revenues did not cover the debt service on day one of the deal. Stuyvesant Town-Peter Cooper Village figured prominently on the list, although Citi analysts were optimistic about its fate, given the complexes' desirable location and the fact that "cash flow [was] gradually improving."

In May 2008, Nori Gerardo Lietz, the adviser to the California Public Employees' Retirement System who had given the Stuyvesant Town investment a hearty thumbs-down, told her clients at CalPERS that they should demand a meeting with Tishman Speyer and BlackRock executives. She told them that the sponsors' rosy projections were not materializing. Revenues were not growing as quickly as predicted. Operating expenses were rising. The rental market in general was softening. Tenants were up in arms. As a result, Tishman Speyer was burning through the complexes' reserve funds at a faster rate than anyone anticipated. It might take a year or two, but eventually the reserves would fall to empty and the sponsors, Tishman Speyer and BlackRock, would be unable to make their mortgage payments.

"I kept harping," Lietz recalled, " 'This thing is going bankrupt.' "[9]

A meeting was finally set for May 22 at CalPERS's offices at

Lincoln Plaza in downtown Sacramento. Lietz drove out from her home in San Francisco. Rob Speyer flew out on a private jet with several other Tishman Speyer and BlackRock executives. Dale Gruen and Robert Lewis, the executive in charge of managing BlackRock Realty's relationship with CalPERS, also came in from the firm's San Francisco office. CalPERS and CalSTRS were major clients. Gruen had invested $2.75 billion in multifamily housing on behalf of CalPERS. In 2006, he declared that his firm viewed "New York as one of the nation's best apartment markets for investors." No more.

They were met at CalPERS by Judy Alexander, the soft-spoken real estate investment manager who was the primary contact at CalPERS for BlackRock, as well as her bosses, Ted Eliopoulos, CalPERS's newly installed senior investment officer, and Randy Pottle, a senior portfolio manager.

Given the enormity of CalPERS's investment, the pension fund had received periodic updates on the progress at Stuyvesant Town-Peter Cooper Village. But this was Speyer's first meeting with CalPERS and he quickly acknowledged that the property was "underperforming expectations."

He had e-mailed the group a mass of numbers. There was a detailed breakdown of how many one-, two- and three-bedroom apartments had been deregulated in Stuyvesant Town and Peter Cooper since they took over. The report showed how revenues had increased as a result. But operating costs were up too. The deregulation of units just was not happening fast enough. Speyer told them that the net operating income—the only number that really mattered to investors—was off by a stunning 33 percent from what they had projected.

It was no mere bump in the road. According to the private

placement memorandum that CalPERS and other investors had gotten eighteen months earlier, net income was supposed to top $211 million by the end of 2008. A $70 million shortfall was a big gap to fill.

Still, there were no fireworks. In the characteristic style of CalPERS's investment executives, Alexander and Pottle asked probing questions in a monotone that did not betray their concerns.

The BlackRock executives presented a thick overview of the residential market in New York, where rents still showed resiliency despite a slowing of condominium prices and the gathering wreckage from the subprime mortgage market. They conceded that the financial sector had become a drag on the economy. But Gruen did not foresee a severe slowdown.

Instead, Speyer offered hope to the CalPERS executives. Southern California was a mess. Entire subdivisions were defaulting on their mortgages. And the independent mortgage lenders who had popularized the sale of high-interest mortgages to buyers who could ill afford to pay them were tumbling into bankruptcy court, laying off thousands of employees and leaving their Orange County offices vacant. New York was different, or so it seemed.

"We had a plan for turning the situation around," Speyer recalled. "We had a capital program involving renovating units and upgrading the feel and look of the property."[10]

The CalPERS team expressed their disappointment, as well as their hope that a turnaround was in the offing. But Lietz, CalPERS's adviser, showed no such restraint. She snickered through much of the meeting, with an I-told-you-so tone that Speyer and Gruen found grating. Even the pessimistic Lietz, however, could not have imagined what would happen over the next couple months. Still, Lietz said, "They had a bunch of headaches. Everything was falling apart."

Many real estate investors in New York, the hottest market nationally throughout the boom, also held out hope that the credit crisis would pass quickly. The vacancy rate in midtown office buildings was still relatively healthy, even if deal making had slowed dramatically. Macklowe could be dismissed as an overeager gambler. The Stuyvesant Town-Peter Cooper Village deal had problems, but most analysts figured that Tishman Speyer would never let it slip into bankruptcy.

Then all hell broke loose in September as the crisis that began with the subprime mortgage market ballooned and the economy sank into a severe recession.

On September 15, 2008, Lehman Brothers, the fourth-largest investment bank in the United States, filed for bankruptcy protection, an event that shook the financial capitals of the world and led to a subsequent string of costly bailouts. It was the largest bankruptcy filing in U.S. history, and by the end of the day, the Dow Jones had fallen 504 points, the biggest drop in points since the 2001 terrorist attack on the World Trade Center.

Much like Bear Stearns four months earlier, Lehman's share price had been in a tailspin for weeks, but federal officials did not offer Lehman a lifeline. Lehman had borrowed heavily to fund its investments, principally in housing and mortgage-related assets. Lehman's ratio of assets to owners equity, an indicator of the bank's level of risk, jumped from about 24:1 in 2003 to 31:1 by 2007. The investment bank's bet generated handsome profits during the real estate boom. But once the housing market cooled and the subprime crisis unfolded, Lehman suffered unprecedented losses. Lehman also got stuck with huge positions in deals like Archstone-Smith and low-rated mortgage securities after the credit markets shut down. In the second quarter of 2008, Lehman reported losses of $2.8 billion and was forced to sell off $6 billion in assets, setting off fears that a fire sale would depress the value of commercial properties.

American International Group, the giant international insurance company, suffered a liquidity crisis on September 16, 2008, following the downgrade of its credit rating. At the opening bell of the stock market that morning, AIG's stock price plunged by 60 percent. Moody's and S & P downgraded AIG over continuing losses on mortgage-backed securities, which forced the company to deliver more than $10 billion in additional collateral to certain creditors. That evening the board of governors of the Federal Reserve Bank announced that the Federal Reserve Bank of New York had been authorized to create a twenty-four-month credit-liquidity facility from which AIG could draw up to $85 billion.

Merrill Lynch, fearing it was next to fall, agreed to a buyout by Bank of America. Panic spread. Investors lost confidence in financial institutions. Banks refused to lend to other banks. Hedge funds pulled out cash. Stocks fell by anywhere from 55 to 72 percent in once-booming Brazil, Russia, India and China. The International Monetary Fund estimated in October that banks and other investors would suffer $1.4 trillion in losses on loans and securities. The Bush administration devised a $700 billion bailout known as TARP, the Troubled Asset Relief Program, which was used to prop up banks and car companies. The Treasury pledged up to $200 billion to cover losses at Freddie Mac and Fannie Mae, the mortgage giants.

The crisis was not a natural disaster but the result of a poisonous stew of shoddy mortgage lending, the exorbitant pooling and sale of loans to investors who didn't know enough to ask the right questions about how risky they were and risky bets on securities backed by the loans, a federal inquiry led by the ten-member Financial Crisis Inquiry Commission concluded in its 2011 report.

The 633-page report highlighted the carelessness of the country's biggest banks, portraying Citigroup, AIG and Merrill Lynch as essentially asleep at the wheel. The report cited testimony showing how executives at AIG were oblivious to the company's $79 billion exposure to credit-default swaps, a quasi-insurance policy sold to investors seeking protection against a drop in value of securities backed by home loans. Merrill Lynch managers, in turn, were surprised when seemingly secure mortgage investments suddenly suffered huge losses, while Citigroup executives conceded that they paid little attention to mortgage-related risks. Both Citi and Merrill had portrayed mortgage-related investments to investors as safer than they really were. The commission noted that "Goldman Sachs has been criticized—and sued—for selling its subprime mortgage securities to clients while simultaneously betting against those securities."

"When the housing and mortgage markets cratered, the lack of transparency, the extraordinary debt loads, the short-term loans and the risky assets all came home to roost," the report found. "What resulted was panic. We had reaped what we had sown."

The same could be said of the commercial mortgage markets, where Tishman Speyer and BlackRock raised the debt and equity for the Stuyvesant Town deal. "The seeds of the default were present in the initial structure of the debt," said Sam

Chandan, president of Chandan Economics, an adviser to real estate investors and lenders, and an adjunct professor at the University of Pennsylvania. "We had a situation where three or four key assumptions were required to make the debt marketable. But those assumptions were made without any observable underpinnings."[11]

One key assumption at Stuyvesant Town was that the sponsors would be able to deregulate 12 to 15 percent of the apartments a year. "It was unprecedented," Chandan said. "There's no empirical basis for that projection in a project this size."

Further, the data presented to investors was often opaque, requiring someone with the diligence of a bloodhound to get to the bottom of it. In granting the Stuyvesant Town-Peter Cooper senior mortgage an investment-grade rating, Moody's stated that a critical indicator, the "actual" ratio of the complexes' cash flow to debt service, was a healthy 1.3. That meant that there was more than enough cash flowing from the property to make the debt payments. Deeper in the report, a reader could discover that the "actual" cash flow was based on estimates for 2011, not the actual cash flow from the property when the loan was written in November 2006. Moody's ultimately did raise a concern that the "current" cash flow only covered 40 percent of the debt payments.

Perhaps some of the fundamental shortcomings got overlooked by investors and lenders because the market was moving at top speed, leaving little time to scrutinize the numbers. There were only thirty days between the date Tishman Speyer signed the contract to buy the complexes and the day they closed on the deal, a process that customarily lasted three months. The bankers then raced to pool the mortgages in a security that could be rated investment grade and sold to investors. In 2007, for instance, there were $230 billion in commercial mortgage-backed securities, the equivalent of $4 billion to $5 billion in bonds being issued every week. "For some investors the speed of the market precluded the laborious analysis of any individual deal," Chandan said.

The commission found that the credit rating agencies—Standard & Poor's, Fitch and Moody's—were "cogs in the wheels of financial destruction." But the crisis could have been avoided, the report said, if not for widespread failures in government regulation, corporate mismanagement and heedless risks taken by Wall Street. The commission excoriated regulators—the Securities and Exchange Commission, the Office of the Comptroller of the Currency, the Office of Thrift Supervision—that "lacked the political will" to scrutinize and hold accountable the institutions they were supposed to oversee.

Low interest rates instituted by the Fed after the 2001 recession played a role in the crisis, along with the "aggressive home ownership goals" set by government and the government-controlled mortgage giants, Fannie Mae and Freddie Mac. It also pointed out how Fannie and Freddie, eager to stanch the loss of market share to Wall Street investment banks, had loosened underwriting standards, bought and guaranteed riskier loans and blithely increased their purchases of mortgage-backed securities. But Fannie and Freddie were not major factors in the crisis, the commission concluded.

A deep current of anger over Wall Street's heads-I-win, tails-you-lose culture poured into the public debate. Although Goldman Sachs denied it, newspaper columnists heaped vitriol on the investment bank for continuing to sell mortgage-backed securities while Goldman was purging them from its own accounts. E. Stanley O'Neal, chief executive of Merrill Lynch, left the firm in 2007 with a severance package worth $161.5 million, despite crippling losses from mortgage securities. In March 2009, AIG announced it was paying $165 million in executive bonuses. During a federal hearing, Representative Henry Waxman, Democrat from California, grilled Richard S. Fuld, the former Lehman chairman, over executive compensation. "Your company is now bankrupt, and our country is in a state of crisis, but you get to keep $480 million. I have a very basic question: Is this fair?"[12]

Fuld demurred, saying that he had in fact taken $300 million in pay and bonuses over eight years.

In November, the once-invincible Blackstone Group, one of the world's largest private equity firms, reported a third-quarter loss of $500 million.[13] The damage showed up in nearly every industry. Over the course of 2008, the S & P 500 stock index tumbled 39.5 percent, the steepest drop since the Depression. Blue-chip corporations from Bank of America to Citigroup and Alcoa lost more than 65 percent of their value.

Real Capital Analytics, a research firm, cataloged $106 billion in distressed and potentially troubled commercial properties by the end of 2008. The real estate market had deteriorated over the first nine months of the year, but foreclosures were still rare. The widening scope of the problem was startlingly evident, however, in the wave of defaults and foreclosures that followed Lehman's collapse. At least twenty metropolitan areas faced $1 billion or more in distressed or potentially troubled commercial property, Real Capital reported. New York and Los Angeles, ground zero for many highly levered transactions in 2006 and 2007, accounted for $23 billion in troubled or distressed properties. Phoenix, Houston and Atlanta had the most properties. Retail had the largest pipeline of potentially troubled properties, with shopping mall companies such as Centro and General Growth Properties struggling under enormous debts and a growing number of retail tenants filing for bankruptcy protection. The hotel sector was already seeing its fair share of distress.

The Urban Land Institute predicted that 2009 would be the worst year for commercial real estate "since the wrenching 1991–1992 industry recession." The downturn in the economy and the frozen state of the credit markets posed a danger even for property owners current on their loan payments but unable to refinance a maturing mortgage, especially when the value of commercial real estate dropped by 25 to 35 percent.

The much-celebrated 2007 deal for Equity Office Properties, with a portfolio of 573 commercial properties, had turned into a sterling example of the excesses of the real estate boom, with the wreckage strewn across the country, from Southern California to Austin, Texas; Chicago; New York; and Stamford, Connecticut. The Blackstone Group paid $39 billion for the portfolio and simultaneously flipped hundreds of buildings in it to sixteen different companies for $27 billion and a quick profit. The resale triggered record-breaking deals in Stamford, San Francisco, Portland, Chicago and Austin. Lenders provided lavish financing on the unrealistic expectation that rents and demand would continue to rise without pause. The mortgages were pooled and converted to commercial mortgage-backed securities.

Instead, the buyers were crippled financially by a recession, corporate layoffs and drops in both occupancy and rents. The new owners' inability to make their mortgage payments became a crisis for the pension funds, regional banks and insurance companies that held the asset-backed securities. Tishman

Speyer bought six EOP buildings in downtown Chicago and immediately tried to sell three in order to pay down its debt. But only one building brought an acceptable offer. So like many of the other buyers, Tishman Speyer teetered at the edge of default. Even Blackstone was hurt by the roughly one hundred EOP properties it held on to as their value skidded by 20 percent. "These were aggressive acquisitions under the best of circumstances," said Paul E. Adornato, a senior real estate analyst at BMO Capital Markets.

The New York office market's immunity to the downturn that was plaguing most American cities finally ended. "We have fallen further faster than any time in the last 20 years," Mitchell S. Steir, chief executive of Studley, a national real estate broker, told the *New York Times* in December 2008. "There has been more damage to real estate values in the last four months than in any other four-month period. The pace with which it has occurred is astonishing."

Long after the credit crisis began in 2007, many investors and real estate executives expected a "correction" to the rapid escalation in property values. The collapse of the bond market for mortgage-backed securities had served as a brake on deal making. But after the fall of Lehman Brothers, which was widely regarded as the "real estate ATM," it was clear that something more catastrophic was taking place. Tishman Speyer abruptly pulled out of a deal to buy the former Mobil Building, a 45-story, 1.6-million-square-foot tower on Forty-Second Street near Grand Central Terminal, for $400 million. Then Standard & Poor's dropped its rating on the bonds for the $5.4 billion purchase of Stuyvesant Town-Peter Cooper Village, citing an estimated 10 percent decline in the properties' value and the rapid depletion of $650 million in reserve funds.[14]

The rating cut had little impact financially on Stuyvesant Town tenants, Tishman Speyer or BlackRock. Bondholders, however, now held paper that was worth less than what they had paid for it. It would be difficult to resell the bonds except at a steep discount. But the announcement also generated yet another headline and a grim reminder to the public that Tishman Speyer's stewardship at Stuyvesant Town was not going well.

For Speyer, his relationship with Garodnick, the councilman who lived in a market-rate apartment in Peter Cooper Village, was a source of endless frustration as criticism of Tishman Speyer mounted in the city council, in the city's tabloids and on the blogs. The two men were about the same age, smart and well educated. They seemed to get along when they met at Tishman Speyer world headquarters. But it got to the point where Garodnick was calling Tishman Speyer every week or so to complain, about the landscaping, the high vacancy rate or the legal costs of tenants having to defend themselves against eviction. After reading the latest newspaper article in which Garodnick blasted Tishman Speyer for harassing tenants, Speyer would turn angrily to Martin J. McLaughlin, a longtime lobbyist and political fixer who worked for him, demanding, "Why can't we work together?"

"Rob," McLaughlin would explain as he outlined the Kabuki theater that accompanies tenant-landlord relations in New York, "he lives there. He gets up to go to work in the morning and five people complain to him. This tenant shit is normal. This is what happens when you're a landlord."[15]

McLaughlin would go on to say, "Rob couldn't quite wrap his

head around his role as a landlord and Dan's role as a tenant. Rob felt it had to do with his outbidding the tenants for the property. Rob took it personally. Dan did not."

In 2008, the lives of Garodnick and Speyer seemed to be on parallel tracks. On May 10, Garodnick, then thirty-six, married Zoe Segal-Reichlin, twenty-nine, a talented lawyer he had met on a blind date just as Stuyvesant Town-Peter Cooper Village was put in play by MetLife. She recalls little of their first encounter, at an East Village restaurant, which came only hours after she completed the bar exam. Their second date was the night before Garodnick's inaugural press conference, announcing a tenant bid for the complexes. She graduated magna cum laude from Brown University and received a law degree from Harvard Law. Their budding romance survived her move to Washington to work for the Lawyers' Committee for Civil Rights. After their marriage, she returned to New York and became associate general counsel for Planned Parenthood. The couple had a son in January 2011.

Rob Speyer, then thirty-nine, married Anne-Cecilie Engell six months later on November 12. They had met quite by accident at a friend's birthday party. For Speyer it was love at first sight, he said. For his wife, he added, "it wasn't."[16] Engell, a marketing director at Iconix Brand Group in New York, was from Denmark. She had graduated from Cornell and received an MBA from New York University. Marriage was a bit of a logistical problem. He is Jewish, while Engell is Lutheran. They resolved the dilemma by having Matthew A. Mitchell, her best friend from college and a Universal Life minister, preside over a small private ceremony at their apartment. Three days later, they flew to Copenhagen for another nondenominational

ceremony in front of two dozen friends and family. His father
was his best man. During the summer of 2010, the couple had
twins.

Despite the similarities in their lives, there was no bridging
the gap between Speyer's plan to displace tenants and transform
Stuyvesant Town-Peter Cooper Village into a yuppie haven and
Garodnick's effort to preserve the complexes as the last affordable harbor for middle-class tenants trying to raise families in
an increasingly expensive Manhattan. "I would sit with Dan and
I couldn't understand why there was such a gulf between our
point of view and his point of view," Rob Speyer said. "He was
a rational, decent guy. There was just a basic gulf between the
way he saw things and the way I saw things."

Garodnick was equally puzzled by the real estate tycoon.
"He never seemed to understand how I could criticize Tishman
Speyer for how poorly they were treating the tenants at Stuyvesant Town," Garodnick said. "I was surprised how someone who
seemed so nice was trying to push people out of their apartments."

Speyer and Engell spent their honeymoon in Copenhagen and
later in the French Alps, hoping to get in some cross-country
skiing. The rugged Alps are more known for downhill skiing.
Mont Blanc, the highest mountain in Europe west of Russia,
rises to 15,771 feet. Speyer retained his connection to high
school wrestling with a secret passion for the soap opera
matches of World Wrestling Entertainment. Other than that,
he was not very interested in sports. Engell, the better athlete
of the two, had grown up traversing the countryside in Denmark. As it turned out, Speyer spent less time on the slopes

than on the telephone talking to bankers, investors and advisers about the deteriorating financial situation at Stuyvesant Town and Peter Cooper Village.

There were calls to lawyers and Morgan Stanley, the bank that Tishman Speyer and BlackRock hired to advise them on a restructuring plan, as well as the investors and the advisory committee comprised of equity partners. The complex was not meeting the numbers set out in their business plan. At the end of 2008, net income at the complexes was up almost 30 percent to $138 million from the prior year, but was still well shy of the $211.7 million projected in their business plan, and the $252 million in annual debt service.

There was no question that they needed an infusion of fresh capital and a restructuring of their debt stack if they wanted to salvage the asset. The property had lost as much as $2 billion in value in the downturn, if it was ever worth $5.4 billion. It appeared that the $3 billion first mortgage was safe. But Rob Speyer and his partners figured that the fourteen firms—ranging from Hartford Financial to the Government of Singapore's GIC, SL Green and Allied Irish Banks—that had lent the partners a total of $1.4 billion in junior loans would have to agree to major concessions. As for the hundreds of millions of dollars poured into the deal two years earlier by the Church of England, GIC, CalPERS, and the other pension funds, it was gone. All gone.

For CalPERS, Stuyvesant Town was one of a handful of speculative real estate deals into which the pension fund had plowed hundreds of millions of dollars. Instead of generating double-digit returns, the properties were losing value by the hour. "We took some very tough medicine in real estate," Clark McKinley of CalPERS would later say.[17]

Tishman Speyer and BlackRock, however, told their lenders that they would not inject additional capital into the asset unless their new money jumped ahead of the junior loans in priority. The question was whether the junior lenders would be accommodating or refuse to take a backseat to Tishman Speyer and BlackRock. Speyer figured that he still had twelve months to work out an arrangement with the junior lenders, since they did not expect to exhaust their reserve funds until January 2010. "She sat through a lot of conversations," Speyer said of his wife. "We were joined at the hip."[18]

The situation in New York had not improved for the complexes or the broader economy by the time they returned in January. Speyer's days were spent tending to Stuyvesant Town and other troubled assets, as well as their projects in Asia and South America, where the economy was still in relatively good shape. At night, Speyer and his wife went for long walks along the esplanade that skirts the Hudson River waterfront near their apartment in Greenwich Village. Huddled against the fierce winds blowing off the river, Speyer described the inner emotions that he rarely revealed in business meetings. "For some reason it hit me in that moment that all the equity that had been invested was likely lost," Speyer said. "We hoped to restructure, but the premise was that $1.9 billion in equity had been wiped out. I thought about the different investors who'd signed up for the deal. It really shook me. Cecile said to me, 'What's going to define you is how you react to this. It's not the failure. It's how you deal with the failure. You have decades to do other deals. You have to focus now on standing up to the failure.'"

But things were about to go from bad to worse.

Both sides in the Stuyvesant Town litigation, the so-called Roberts case, were expecting a decision from the appellate division of the state supreme court in the first quarter of 2009 on the tenants' appeal of the lower-court decision tossing out their case. They had made their arguments to the appellate division on September 28, 2008.

The choices were simple. The court could deny the appeal, handing a second victory to the complexes' owners, or rule in favor of the tenants by declaring that the owners had illegally deregulated more than four thousand apartments at Stuyvesant Town while taking tax breaks from the city. Either way, the case would almost certainly advance to the court of appeals for a final decision.

Tishman Speyer, BlackRock and MetLife still felt confident that they would prevail. But the stakes were high. If the decision went against them, the entire premise of Tishman Speyer's business plan—the rapid deregulation of apartments in order to charge higher, market-rate rents—would be gutted.

The plaintiffs, however, had a new litigator, if not a new law firm. Stuart Saft and Michael Fleiss, who had originally brought the tenants' challenge, left the law firm Wolf Haldenstein Adler Freeman & Herz after the case was dismissed in state supreme court on August 23, 2007. Wolf Haldenstein had taken the case on a contingency. After the case went up on appeal, the firm's senior class-action litigation partner, Daniel W. Krasner, turned it over to Alexander H. Schmidt, a jack-of-all-trades litigator whose résumé included contract disputes, antitrust litigation, derivative shareholder suits and real-estate-related litigation. But this was his first exposure to the wacky world of rent stabilization.

He had little time to waste in learning the thirty-year history and the mind-numbing nomenclature of rent-stabilization laws, and state and city housing codes. He also needed to familiarize himself with the periodic battles in Albany between landlords and tenants, Republicans and Democrats, that resulted in new and sometimes contradictory laws. "It was a steep learning curve," Schmidt conceded.

The Rent Stabilization Law was enacted by the city council in 1969 in response to a continuing housing shortage and the need to regulate rental buildings that were not covered by stricter rent-control laws. (Rent control covers apartments built prior to 1947 that have had no tenancy turnover since 1971.) Stabilization applied to apartment buildings completed after 1947 and before 1974, with the twin goals of allowing landlords to implement reasonable rent increases and to prevent profiteering and "unjust, unreasonable and oppressive rents," while ensuring that there was an adequate supply of stable and affordable housing in New York.

In 1993, there was a showdown in the state legislature over efforts to "reform" rent regulations. The real estate industry had long complained about the inequities of the rent-stabilization system, where rents for tenants were kept low regardless of their income. Republicans in the state senate who sought to eliminate regulation from apartments of higher-income New Yorkers were opposed by members of the Democratic-controlled assembly and tenant advocates, who cast the Republicans as advocates for the landlord class. The Republicans said it made no sense to regulate rents for the rich, but opponents feared that "luxury decontrol" was the first step toward the elimination of all rent regulation. The Republican-dominated senate threatened to let the rent law expire altogether unless it was revised.

Albany, the state capital, swarmed with tenant rallies, while lobbyists plied the halls of the legislature in what has become a ritual every time the stabilization law comes up for renewal.

In the end, the legislature compromised, with the Republicans getting a form of "luxury decontrol." Under the change, the owners of apartments that rent for $2,000 or more a month would be allowed to raise rents to market levels when the apartments were vacated. Rent protection would also be lifted from apartments with rents of $2,000 or more per month that were leased to tenants who made $250,000 a year or more. In exchange, the Republicans agreed to extend rent laws for four more years, twice as long as they had previously allowed.

Tenant advocates like Michael McKee, chairman of the New York State Tenant and Neighborhood Coalition, acknowledged that luxury decontrol would affect less than 2 percent of the one million rent-stabilized apartments. But the new law also contained provisions that would hurt all tenants with what they said were "hidden grabs for landlords."

The most important preserved the landlord's right to charge tenants each month a percentage, one-fortieth, of the cost of refurbishing an apartment. The increase did not expire at the end of forty months; it became a permanent addition to the legal rent for that unit. At the time, the state housing agency regarded the one-fortieth payback period as overly generous and had sought unsuccessfully to extend it to seventy-two months.

"So generous a rate of return provides a great incentive for owners to provide extensive and sometimes unnecessary renovations, especially on vacant apartments, when tenant consent is not necessary, thus reducing the supply of affordable housing," the agency said in a 1993 memorandum.

The legislature reduced the income threshold in 1997 for

so-called high-rent, or luxury, decontrol to $175,000 for two succeeding years. But the housing laws also established some exceptions to decontrol, and the exceptions were what was at the crux of the Stuyvesant Town lawsuit.

In December 1995, the state housing agency issued an operational bulletin stating that high-rent decontrol "shall not apply to housing accommodations which are subject to rent regulation by virtue of receiving tax benefits" from housing programs such as J-51, which was designed to encourage landlords of rent-stabilized or rent-controlled apartments to invest in their property in return for tax breaks. In other words, apartments whose rent was $2,000 a month or higher at a complex like Stuyvesant Town that was receiving J-51 tax benefits could not be decontrolled until after the benefits expired.

But Sherwin Belkin, a young landlord attorney at the time, and other lawyers from his firm wrote a series of letters to the housing agency in 1995 arguing that it had wrongly interpreted the law. Belkin focused on the three-word phrase "by virtue of." He argued that properties that were regulated "by virtue of" receiving J-51 tax benefits could not be decontrolled. But other properties, like Stuyvesant Town, which were subject to regulation prior to receiving the benefits, could be decontrolled.

The housing agency twice dismissed Belkin's interpretation. But in a January 16, 1996, letter, Assistant Commissioner Darryl J. Seavey of the state housing agency seemed to reconsider, telling Belkin he might have a point. Seavey said that Belkin offered a "feasible alternative" to the standard way of interpreting the statute. Since the sponsoring memorandum by the state senator who introduced the bill was "silent" on the meaning of "by virtue of," Seavey said he applied a lexicographical definition of the words to arrive at Belkin's interpretation. Seavey cautioned that if a landlord deregulated an apartment before the J-51 tax benefit period had expired, the tax abatement would be reduced proportionately.

Seavey concluded, however, by saying that his "opinion letter" was "not a substitute for a formal agency order issued upon prior notice to all parties and after having afforded all parties an opportunity to be heard." None of that happened. The letter was issued solely to Belkin.[19] The housing agency did not release an advisory opinion on the matter. But landlords throughout the city did use the letter as the starting point for what Tishman Speyer, the Real Estate Board and others from the real estate industry said was "15 years of practice" in which apartments were deregulated while receiving tax breaks.

In 2000, the housing agency did formally adopt the position embodied in Seavey's letter, in part by inserting the word "solely" before "by virtue of," thus reinforcing the real estate industry's interpretation. At the very least, it was odd that a housing policy reversal with enormous implications would take place based on a dizzying argument over the meaning of an ambiguous three-word phrase.

But it also amounted to a break in logic. Many landlords with rent-stabilized apartments complained that they did not make enough money to upgrade boilers, point the brick facades or replace roofs. The J-51 program was designed to entice those landlords to invest in their own aging properties by providing modest tax breaks. It is hard to imagine why legislators would then allow landlords receiving those benefits to bail out of the rent-stabilization system.

The net effect of the housing agency's adopting the landlords' "alternative" interpretation of the law is that it enabled New York City landlords to deregulate thousands of apartments in buildings that were receiving J-51 tax benefits. Just adding the single word "solely" to the statutory language led to the deregulation of over four thousand apartments at Stuyvesant Town-Peter Cooper Village and thousands of other apartments in an estimated nine thousand buildings in Manhattan and elsewhere over the span of fourteen years.

More than six years later, nine former and current tenants at Stuyvesant Town challenged the interpretation, contending that the complex had received J-51 tax benefits since 1992 worth $24.5 million, which precluded the owners from decontrolling so-called high-rent apartments. Belkin, now acting on behalf of Tishman Speyer, argued that the "plain language" of the statute had been applied by the state housing agency for fifteen years, permitting landlords to deregulate units.

"To me," Schmidt countered, "it seemed crystal-clear that the intent of the statute was to prevent deregulation so long as taxpayer funds were being accepted by the landlord. The housing agency in December 2000 violated all the rules by adding the word 'solely' to the statute in a way that completely changed the meaning of the statute. I thought landlords must've been laughing all the way to the bank."[20]

On March 6, 2009, Rob Speyer's car was just pulling up to the curb at Chhatrapati Shivaji International Airport in Mumbai, India, when his cell phone buzzed. He was exhausted. He had been in India for a week looking at what would become his company's first foray into the world's second-most-populated nation, behind China. The proposed project was a joint venture with one of India's largest banks to build a $100 million office complex in Hyderabad, a fast-growing technology center. It was

2:00 A.M. and the airport, South Asia's busiest in terms of international passenger traffic, was a mad whirl of private cars, black-and-mustard taxis and white buses funneling through a series of narrow, high-security checkpoints. There were seemingly thousands of people there in the middle of the night trying to make their flights at the international terminal.

George Hatzmann, Tishman Speyer's associate general counsel, was on the phone in New York, where it was still March 5. The New York State appellate division of the state supreme court had just handed down a stunning decision: The owners of Stuyvesant Town-Peter Cooper Village had wrongfully raised rents and deregulated thousands of apartments after receiving special tax breaks from the city's J-51 housing program. Tishman Speyer, and practically the entire real estate industry, had expected the appellate division to dismiss the case, upholding a lower-court decision in favor of the landlord. No one thought it was even possible that this would be reversed. The reversal could ultimately cost Tishman Speyer, BlackRock and MetLife hundreds of millions of dollars more, if they were required to repay residents of roughly 4,400 apartments for improper rent increases over the preceding four years.

"We lost the J-51 case," said Hatzmann, his voice clear and sharp despite the thousands of miles between them.

Speyer's response was a roar: "Shiiittttt!"[21]

Speyer felt like he had been punched in the stomach. His lawyers had assured him that the tenants' case was certain to be dismissed. They would appeal to the state's highest court, of course. But if this ruling was upheld, he knew not only that the partnership would be liable for rent rebates and damages, but it had also just gotten infinitely more difficult to restructure the financing and stave off bankruptcy. The starting point for a restructuring was determining the current value of the asset. He figured that the worth of the complexes had dropped to $3.2 billion since the meltdown on Wall Street and the resulting recession. But this ruling could take it down another billion because rents would be re-regulated, limiting their ability to exploit the gap between regulated and market rents. "It was not on the radar screen of possibilities," Speyer later recalled. "That ruling was a severe blow. It put the asset in free fall."

Judge Eugene Nardelli of the appellate division ruled on behalf of the tenants, saying that "the broader interpretation of the phrase 'by virtue of' urged by the plaintiffs was more consistent with the overall statutory scheme, which makes no distinction based on whether a J-51 property was already subject to regulation prior to the receipt of such benefit." The court customarily defers to the judgment of the appropriate state agency in applying the law. But Judge Nardelli declared that the state housing agency was not entitled to deference since a "legal interpretation" is the court's responsibility. Moreover, the court said, by inserting the word "solely," the housing agency had violated a legal principle. Citing precedents, Nardelli wrote that the "new language cannot be imported into a statute to give it meaning not otherwise found therein."[22]

On the same day, one of the law firms representing Tishman Speyer, Belkin Burden Wenig & Goldman, was set to celebrate its twentieth anniversary at its office on Madison Avenue near Fortieth Street when they learned of the decision. Sherwin Belkin, the name partner who played a historical role in the case, raised his glass of champagne before what turned out to be a somber group of partners and associates. "Here's to the worst decision in the history of the firm," Belkin said glumly.

Andrew Mathias, the president and chief investment officer of SL Green Realty, a real estate investment trust that had made a $200 million junior loan in the deal, told analysts during an earnings call a couple weeks later that the decision "had such negative implications for the property and the $2 billion of common equity that [sat] subordinate to [their] position" that they decided to write down 75 percent of the interest-only loan.

David Schonbraun, a senior executive at SL Green, told analysts that the company did not believe in 2006 that the Stuyvesant Town deal was "overly aggressive," particularly because it had "$2 billion in newly invested cash from a deep-pocketed sponsorship group," Tishman Speyer and BlackRock. "However," he continued, "the deal was doomed by a combination of the recession, poor execution by the sponsor, and most importantly, an adverse J-51 tax ruling, which is contrary to legal opinions we've received and the opinion by the DHCR. This ruling was a shock to the real estate industry and irreparably harmed the value of the asset and has generally wreaked havoc in that space."[23]

Many in the real estate industry, including the Rent Stabilization Association, a landlord lobbyist, predicted chaos, claiming that some eighty thousand deregulated apartments throughout the city were now subject to re-regulation. They said that building values would fall sharply, along with property tax revenues, which account for the bulk of the city's operating budget. "They've basically re-regulated tens of thousands of apartments overnight," said Joseph Strasburg, president of the RSA, who had once lived in Stuyvesant Town and helped revive the dormant tenants association. "Every single tenant living in a decontrolled apartment can file for overcharges. What's the incentive for landlords to do these kind of major renovations if at the end of the day the apartments will continue to be regulated?"

Contrary to Strasburg's hyperbolic "tens of thousands" estimate, the ruling mainly affected thousands of apartments in Manhattan, where rents were more likely to be over $2,000 a month and candidates for deregulation. Harold Shultz, a former city housing commissioner, put the number closer to thirty thousand. Tenants nonetheless were ecstatic.

The residents of Stuyvesant Town and Peter Cooper Village, where Tishman Speyer was deeply unpopular, cheered the ruling. It was vindication for those who believed that the landlord had conspired to purge the complexes of middle-class tenants. But no matter which side of the barricades you stood on, all the residents wondered when their rent would be rolled back and by how much. And that's good news any day of the week in Manhattan.

Privately, many tenant advocates and lawyers had been pessimistic about the lawsuit's chances of success. Now the appellate division had handed tenants a unanimous decision. "It's a good thing for the tenants and for affordable housing," said Al Doyle, president of the tenants association, who together with Councilman Garodnick, Manhattan borough president Scott Stringer, Congresswoman Carolyn Maloney, state senator Tom Duane, Assemblyman Brian Kavanagh, tenant advocate Michael McKee and Harvey Epstein of the Urban Justice Center held a celebratory press conference the day after the decision.

Stringer called on Tishman Speyer and BlackRock to surrender, rather than try to appeal the decision. "It is time for the owners of Stuyvesant Town and Peter Cooper Village to sit down with residents of the complex to resolve this dispute over rent overcharges in a fair and equitable manner," said Stringer, who had filed an amicus brief on behalf of the tenants.

Annemarie Hunter, a plaintiff in the case who attended the press conference, explained that she had not joined the lawsuit "to make a political stand for rent stabilization," although it was "a noble side effect." It was more a cry of survival for the middle class. She said she believed that MetLife and Tishman Speyer had acted improperly by deregulating apartments and collecting luxury rents to the point where she and her family could no longer live in Manhattan. She and her husband, David Hunter, and their two young boys moved to a market-rate, two-bedroom apartment in Stuyvesant Town in 2003. They enjoyed the Norman Rockwell ambiance of the complex; her sons were enrolled in local schools. Despite the perception among some residents that market-rate tenants are rich, she said, most are not.

"Rent and childcare quickly eat up two incomes in this city," she said. Expecting a 25 percent jump in her monthly rent of $2,995, Hunter and her family reluctantly packed up in 2007 and moved. The monthly mortgage and maintenance payments for the small apartment they bought in the Riverdale section of the Bronx came to $2,865, less than the rent at Stuy Town.[24]

The unanimous decision by the appellate division left Tishman Speyer little legal room, although their lawyers hoped that the state's highest court, the court of appeals, would overrule the more liberal appellate division of the state supreme court. But if the decision was upheld, it would have a devastating effect on the investors who put in $1.9 billion in equity and, at least, the junior lenders. The investment memorandum Tishman Speyer and BlackRock gave to potential equity partners listed the litigation as one of two dozen risk factors associated with the Stuyvesant Town-Peter Cooper Village deal. The memorandum stated that the plaintiff's claims were "without merit." But it warned that if the plaintiffs did prevail, "the Partnership would suffer an immediate and very substantial loss of revenues and would be unable to carry out a significant part of its plan to convert rent-stabilized units to market-rate units. The loss of revenues, as well as any money damages that the court might award against the Partnership, would have a material adverse effect on the Partnership's financial results and the Investor Limited Partners' investments."

CHAPTER ELEVEN

How to Lose $3.6 Billion
in Two Years

In the six months after Rob Speyer's soul-searching walks along the Hudson River with his wife Anne-Cecile, the situation at Stuyvesant Town-Peter Cooper Village grew more bleak. No matter how many times Tishman Speyer revised its budget to account for changing market conditions, they could not keep up with the deteriorating financial performance. Revenues in the first six months of 2009 fell 6 percent, or $9.5 million, behind current budget projections, according to a quarterly internal analysis sent to lenders. At the same time, operating expenses ballooned by 16 percent, or $7.8 million over budget. Legal fees from the J-51 case, as well as bank consulting fees, gobbled up millions of dollars. The grim bottom line showed that the property lost $84.6 million after debt service in the first six months of the year and would top $174 million by the end of the year.[1] Tishman Speyer continued to "recapture" vacant apartments but the company had ceased renovating the units at the end of 2008 and waived its asset management fee starting in the fourth quarter of 2008, Speyer said, as part of a desperate effort to "preserve capital."[2]

No matter what happened with their appeal of the J-51, or Roberts, case, there were no signs of relief. The unemployment rate swelled to 8.5 percent nationally, the highest level in a quarter century. More than five million jobs had evaporated since the start of the recession in December 2007. Real estate values had fallen by as much as half since the CMBS-induced high of 2007. Even in once-robust New York City, corporations slashed payrolls and dumped suddenly unnecessary and expensive office space, sending vacancy rates upward and rents down. The price of apartments also retreated from an average of $1.3 million, but now even apartment rents in Manhattan were falling. The average monthly rent for a two-bedroom apartment slid 7.8 percent between 2008 and 2009 to $3,826, while the average for three bedrooms fell 8.2 percent, from $5,589 to $5,126, according to Citi Habitats, a residential real estate broker.

At the 2006 closing party for the Stuyvesant Town deal at Rockefeller Center, Rob Speyer and MetLife's Robert Merck had exchanged pleasantries over the relentless upward march of apartment rentals and sales. But it turned out that their deal marked the high point of the market. Now Rob Speyer was hoping that rents would not plunge any lower.

But the challenges faced by Tishman Speyer and its partner BlackRock at Stuyvesant Town were similar to those of other highly leveraged deals and companies from that era. On April 16, General Growth Properties, the country's second-largest mall operator, with two hundred shopping centers in forty-four states, filed for bankruptcy protection. Founded by the Bucksbaum family, General Growth had a reputation for innovation and a well-regarded portfolio, which included Ala Moana Center in Honolulu, the Glendale Galleria in Los Angeles and Water Tower Place in Chicago. But the company struggled during the recession because of an inability to refinance its debt, much of it piled up during a shopping spree at the peak of the market. In the largest retail real estate deal in history, General Growth paid $12.6 billion in 2004 to acquire the Rouse Company, another mall operator, which owned Faneuil Hall Marketplace in Boston and South Street Seaport in Manhattan. But when the credit markets shut down, the mall operator was caught with $27 billion in short-term debt and no ability to refinance. General Growth filed for bankruptcy after months of fruitless negotiations with its creditors.

Two months later, a national hotel operating company, Extended Stay, filed for bankruptcy protection with a story nearly identical to General Growth's. The hotel industry had been hammered by a drop in corporate and leisure travel during the recession, which cut property values in half. Extended Stay, which owned 680 properties in 44 states, also had to contend with a crushing load of debt. The filing came only two years after the Lightstone Group, a real estate firm based in New Jersey, bought the company at the market peak for $8 billion, including $7.4 billion in financing. The seller was Blackstone Group, the ubiquitous private equity firm that had acquired Extended Stay in 2004, when it had 425 properties, for $2 billion and the assumption of $1.1 billion in debt. Blackstone moved quickly to bulk up by adding to the company's stable of hotels using all manner of credit and then sold the company to Lighthouse in a leveraged buyout. Blackstone, and two partners, reacquired Extended Stay in 2010 for $3.9 billion as the company left bankruptcy protection. A group of creditors subsequently sued Blackstone in federal court claiming that it had grossly inflated the original $8 billion sale price and siphoned off $2.1 billion from the transaction.

A group led by Tishman Speyer defaulted on loans related to its $2.8 billion purchase in 2006 of twenty-eight office buildings in Washington, DC, once owned by CarrAmerica Realty. The other partners in the deal included Lehman Brothers and SITQ, the real estate subsidiary of a Canadian pension fund. It was a solid portfolio with a tenant list that included prominent lobbyists and prestigious corporations. In those heady days, buyers like Tishman Speyer were willing to pay a premium for office properties with vacant space on the assumption that new tenants would pay higher rents than existing tenants already locked into long leases. But empty space became a gaping problem in the recession as demand weakened and rents declined. Tishman Speyer and its partners were forced to suspend payments on junior loans totaling about $570 million. "It's great real estate," said Rob Speyer. "We're in discussions with our lenders to reach a compromise."[3]

The problems ran even deeper at Archstone-Smith, the national apartment complex operator purchased by Tishman Speyer and Lehman Brothers for $22.2 billion just after what turned out to be the peak of the market, in the fall of 2007. The value of the 88,000 apartments owned by Archstone stumbled badly with the recession. With the company in danger of default, Lehman Brothers and Bank of America put up another $500 million to keep Archstone afloat. But Tishman Speyer, which had invested $250 million in the initial deal expecting to get 13 percent of the profits, decided not to participate.

Despite the glaring problems at Archstone, Carr and Stuyvesant Town-Peter Cooper Village, Rob Speyer insisted that the sour deals represented only a fraction of the $35 billion in real estate assets that his company owned or managed around the world. Jerry Speyer sat next to him during an interview in Tishman Speyer's offices at Rockefeller Center. They insisted that the Tishman Speyer machine was still running full-throttle. The elder Speyer added that the company was still providing investors with "20 percent returns." "You show me anybody who measured up to that standard," he said. "None of us are good enough to have a 1,000 batting average. It doesn't exist."

Meanwhile, the backlash against predatory capital and speculative, debt-laden deals like the one at Stuyvesant Town, Delano Village or Riverton was in full swing in New York's state capital, where tenant advocates pressed legislators for a complete overhaul of the state's rent regulations. They argued that the new owners had defaulted on their loans after having overpaid for tens of thousands of apartments occupied by working- and middle-class New Yorkers. That housing, they said, was now in danger of falling into disrepair as the owners or lenders deferred maintenance on the buildings. Urban planners and housing experts like Harold Shultz of the Citizens Housing and Planning Council warned that the effect on surrounding neighborhoods, many of which were far more modest than Stuyvesant Town's, could be catastrophic.

The Democratic-controlled assembly passed and sent to the Senate for approval ten bills in the spring of 2009 that would severely undercut the ability of landlords, particularly those who paid extraordinarily high prices at the height of the real estate boom, to rapidly raise rents, re-regulate apartments and reap profits. For the first time in decades, Democrats controlled the Senate, albeit by a slim margin, prompting hopes of a quick coup. "The tenant movement has never been more united," said

Michael McKee, then treasurer of the Tenants Political Action Committee. "We're working hard to repeal vacancy decontrol and reform the rent laws."

The real estate industry launched a counterattack, lobbying Republicans and some select Democrats in the Senate to block the bills, saying that the measures would bring to a halt refurbishment and investment in older residential properties. "Everybody's worried," said Steven Spinola, president of the Real Estate Board of New York, the industry's powerful lobbying arm. "This is legislation that'll ruin housing and ruin investment."[4]

But tenant advocates and Democratic legislators countered that the new laws were aimed at speculators, whose financial plans were shaky to begin with. They said that the overhaul of state rent laws was necessary to curb abusive landlords and the loss of housing for working- and middle-class tenants on the Lower East Side and in Harlem, Queens, East New York and the South Bronx. Unscrupulous operators armed with "predatory equity" from the banks had saddled properties with unsustainable debts and showered tenants with eviction notices in an attempt to replace rent-regulated residents with market-rate tenants. Sheldon Silver, the assembly speaker, said, "We cannot sit back and allow the lifeblood of our communities—teachers, firefighters, police and everyday working people—to be priced out of where they live."

Edward Kalikow, a third-generation real estate operator whose company, Kaled Management Corporation, controls 6,500 apartments, mostly in Queens and Manhattan, blamed the Stuyvesant Town deal and others like it for igniting the tenant backlash in the legislature. He said new owners acquired properties with unrealistic plans for quick profits and debt amounting to 80 percent of the purchase price. "They were underwriting deals assuming that they'd relocate thousands of rent-stabilized tenants at a ferocious speed," Kalikow said. "Given the dynamics of the system, there was no way that could happen. Most of us understand that real estate is not a get-in, get-out business. Life has gotten a lot more difficult for us as a result of these abuses to the system. More tenants vote than landlords. I accept that."[5]

Kalikow said there were upward of sixty thousand rent-stabilized units in various stages of financial distress, most bought with easy money. "Now you have an overreaction in the legislature," lamented Kalikow, who opposed changes to the rent laws. In the past, the real estate industry had depended on the Republican leadership in the Senate—which Democrats then controlled, by thirty-two to thirty members—or a sympathetic Republican governor to block such bills. The top priority of the Real Estate Board and the Rent Stabilization Association was stopping the overhaul. The two groups implored members to send extra contributions and hired a Bronx political operative, Stanley Schlein, to make their case in Albany.

In the chaotic closing days of the legislative session, the real estate industry gained the upper hand, persuading a handful of Democrats in the Senate to join the Republicans in scuttling the pro-tenant bills. McKee and other tenant advocates vowed to continue the battle during the next legislative session.

But the Real Estate Board, the Rent Stabilization Association, the Community Housing Improvement Program and other real estate groups also moved to protect their interests in the courts, by backing Tishman Speyer's appeal of the J-51 decision. If the decision stands, said Joseph Strasburg of the RSA, chaos would ensue: landlords who took J-51 benefits would have great difficulty determining the legal rent for the re-regulated apartments since the court was silent on the issue. If the court decision stands, they said, apartments that had been improperly deregulated would again be subject to rent regulations and landlords would have to repay tenants for rent hikes that exceeded the annual increases set by the Rent Guidelines Board over the past four years. A landlord could be subject to triple damages if he was found to have knowingly exceeded the numbers set by the board.

Fearful owners, they said, would stop all renovations and improvements because of the uncertainty of recovering the costs. Strasburg appealed to contractors and construction unions who would, in turn, lose work. "All of a sudden, people who had dropped off the face of our earth have re-emerged and seen the seriousness of this," said Mr. Strasburg. "This would be disastrous."

Despite the appellate court ruling in March, Tishman Speyer was optimistic that the state's highest court, the court of appeals, would set the record straight. The firm sent a memo in October to lawyers who filed amicus briefs for the Real Estate Board of New York, the Rent Stabilization Association and other supporters suggesting that they keep a low profile in the event of a victory. "If we win, we don't want you to say anything in the press," the memo advised, said one lawyer. "We don't want to rub their noses in it."

But Tishman Speyer's equity partners were much less sanguine about the fate of their investment. As they waited for the court of appeals to issue its decision, Larry Fink, chairman of BlackRock, flew to California in July 2009 to personally apologize to the board of the California Public Employees' Retirement System for endorsing a $500 million investment in the

Stuyvesant Town-Peter Cooper Village deal, according to Bloomberg News. The value of the property had declined by more than half to $2.13 billion, according to the Realpoint credit rating agency. Now the junior lenders, along with CalPERS and all the other equity partners, were deeply underwater. CalPERS was also taking hits on a number of its more adventurous real estate deals, including LandSource Holding Company, which went bankrupt seventeen months after the pension fund invested $970 million. At the top of the bubble, the pension fund had poured billions into speculative, highly leveraged deals, hoping to recoup a return of 13 percent, rather than a customary 7 or 8 percent.

After topping out at $260 billion in October 2007, the value of CalPERS's assets, real estate included, plummeted by $100 billion over the following eighteen months. BlackRock, which wrote down its own $112.5 million investment in Stuyvesant Town-Peter Cooper Village, was among a network of real estate advisers for the pension fund that received $2.8 billion in fees between 2004 and 2009.

But CalPERS, which wrote off its $500 million investment in Stuyvesant Town, was now reconsidering its relationship with BlackRock. "We took our profits elsewhere and plowed them into these highly leveraged, in retrospect, too highly leveraged properties like this one in New York," said Clark McKinley of CalPERS. "When the market tanked, we got caught."[6]

The CalPERS board of administration and its staff held their annual weekend retreat July 27 through July 29, 2009, at the Lake Natoma Inn in Folsom, California, a suburb of Sacramento known for its famous Folsom State Prison. The point of the meeting was to make a strategic assessment of investment opportunities going forward for the nation's largest pool of investment capital. But the gloomy market and CalPERS's struggle to make up for its losses over the prior year was not far from anyone's mind. Nevertheless, someone had placed a cheerful quote from Albert Einstein atop the weekend agenda: "In the middle of difficulty lies opportunity."

CalPERS serves 1.6 million active and retired state workers, municipal employees, judges and school bus drivers. It is funded by billions of dollars in annual contributions from taxpayers and employees. But the level of contribution depends on how well CalPERS's investments perform. In the fiscal year that had just ended, CalPERS posted a record loss of $56 billion, or a 23.57 percent drop in the fund's performance, the greatest single-year decline in its seventy-seven-year history. The implications were enormous for municipalities that could be asked for larger annual contributions to make up the difference at a time when unemployment was climbing and property values falling.

Beginning in the late 1990s, the CalPERS board increasingly gave outside advisers like BlackRock more control over decision making on real estate investments. Like many pension funds, its liabilities were swelling as increasing numbers of members retired, while its assets shrank. In the hunt for better returns, the fund gradually shifted from conservative, income-oriented investments like malls and office buildings to more risky ventures, ranging from pinot noir vineyards in Oregon to LandSource Holding in Los Angeles and Stuyvesant Town–Peter Cooper Village. CalPERS often borrowed money to make the investments, a strategy that worked in a rising market but ended disastrously when the Great Recession set in.

The featured speaker on the first day was actually an outsider—Larry Fink, the chairman of BlackRock. In the course of an hour-long presentation, Fink acknowledged that the Stuyvesant Town investment had been unsuccessful and expressed his regret that CalPERS had lost so much money. Oddly, few in the audience focused on Fink's apology, recalled Joseph Dear, CalPERS's new chief investment officer.

What got everyone's attention was Fink's warning that the fund's newly established target for a return on investments was way too optimistic given the circumstances. The exuberant optimist had turned into a Cassandra. CalPERS figured it needed an annual return of 7.6 percent in order to be fully funded to meet its pension obligations in 2024.

"You're not going to get a seven point six percent return when the U.S. is seeing a subpar growth rate of two to three percent," Fink said. "You'll be lucky to get six percent . . . maybe five percent."

Fink's prediction found an echo in newspaper articles, which raised the possibility that taxpayers would have to bail out the fund. As it turned out, CalPERS's investments grew by 11 percent in 2010. But ultimately, all of the people responsible for the fund's crushing losses were pushed out or fired, including BlackRock.

Three thousand miles to the east, in Florida, executives at the State Board of Administration exchanged e-mails acknowledging that their entire investment had been "wiped out." On July 28, 2009, the SBA's senior investment officer, Doug Bennett, authorized the accounting department to write off the entire investment, $266,780,948, which included $16.8 million in fees associated with the deal. The board later blamed the loss on the recession, leverage and slow income growth. They did not share CalPERS's 20-20 hindsight that the Stuyvesant Town deal had been fatally flawed from the beginning.

The Government of Singapore Investment Corporation, which manages more than $100 billion of the city-state's reserves, recognized its losses on the deal, $100 million in equity and $575 million in junior loans backed by the property. The value of GIC's assets had fallen more than 20 percent following the collapse of the global financial markets.

Ben Thypin, an analyst at Real Capital Analytics, put the deal on a death watch, saying it was only a matter of months before the owners of Stuyvesant Town-Peter Cooper Village ran out of money and defaulted on their loans. The much-ballyhooed transaction was a metaphor for an era of easy credit, greed and highly speculative deals. "When we look back on this deal, it may be seen as the poster child for everything that was wrong and right with an era that we may never see again," Thypin predicted. "The assumptions used to underwrite the deal were fantastical at the time and now appear delusional, if not dishonest. Even the most seasoned apartment operator could not have turned these units to market rate fast enough to meet the assumptions, putting aside the risk of market rents decreasing."[7]

But if Rob Speyer held out any hope of salvaging Stuyvesant Town-Peter Cooper Village by forcing lenders to write down the debt, it was all but extinguished on October 22, 2009, when the New York court of appeals ruled in a four-to-two decision that MetLife and the Tishman Speyer–BlackRock partnership had improperly charged market rents for thousands of apartments at the adjoining complexes while taking special tax breaks from a city housing program. The ruling left the owners liable for an estimated $200 million in rent overcharges and damages owed to tenants of 4,400 apartments. Tishman Speyer might also have to roll back rents for the 4,400 apartments to some as-yet-undetermined level, further undermining the market value of the complex. More important, in its negotiations with lenders, Tishman Speyer could no longer hold out the promise of rising revenues as vacant apartments were converted to market rents. Tishman Speyer released a statement saying the decision was "an unfortunate outcome for New York."

Given the flip-flop by the state housing agency on the issue and the debate over the meaning of the statute, the court focused on the state legislature's "intent" in 1993 when it revised the rent laws and gave landlords the ability to deregulate apartments under certain circumstances. Lawyers for the owners said that Stuyvesant Town-Peter Cooper Village became subject to rent stabilization in 1974, eighteen years before receiving J-51 benefits. Therefore, under the "plain language" of the 1993 statute, the lawyers argued that the landlords were permitted to deregulate apartments while receiving J-51 benefits.

The judges, however, cited the legislative history of the law, including transcripts of the debate in the state senate before the statute was adopted. The judges wanted to understand the intent of the legislators in passing the bill, rather than the dictionary definition of a single word. The hard-to-find material had been excavated by Alexander H. Schmidt, the lead lawyer for the tenant-plaintiffs, and kept under wraps until he submitted his final brief to the court of appeals. The brief quoted remarks by state senator Kemp Hannon, the Republican sponsor of the bill, who in response to a question from another legislator said, "At no point do you have the decontrol provisions applying to the buildings which have received the tax exemptions." Asked for further clarification, Hannon reiterated his point: luxury decontrol was unavailable to building owners who "enjoy another system of general public assistance, such as J-51 benefits."

Schmidt believed that the legislative history, in particular the transcript of the debate in the legislature over the bill, was the proverbial smoking gun for the case. In federal court, it is easy to locate these kinds of materials, along with accounts of the congressional debates. But the New York courts were an entirely different matter. Indeed, he eventually located a private data service and paid "thousands of dollars" for the materials. Senator Hannon's statement was in response to a question from Senator Olga Mendez, who, he said, "was clearly concerned that public money should not go to the owners who want to deregulate."

"We believed we had the right interpretation of the law, the right arguments," Schmidt said. "But finding the legislative history was a real boon. The court of appeals cited the debate in its opinion."[8]

As it turned out, he added, "The real estate industry had the documents all along."

Schmidt was in the lobby of the Port Authority Bus Terminal on Eighth Avenue in midtown Manhattan on October 22 when he checked the court of appeals website on his Black-Berry to see whether a decision had been posted. The court normally posted decisions on Tuesdays and expectations were high that this was the day. At 9:05 A.M., the decision popped up on the tiny screen. Suddenly, he could feel and hear the blood rushing through his veins. They had won. He insisted that he had always expected this outcome. But his pulse was racing, just the same. He quickly e-mailed his office and the plaintiffs with the news. Everyone was elated. By 10:15, the *New York Times* was reporting the decision on its website.

Garodnick and Doyle pulled together an impromptu press conference underneath the oak tree at First Avenue and Sixteenth Street, just inside the boundaries of Stuyvesant Town. The small group of activists had goofy smiles stretched across their faces as they shook hands again and again.

"This is a huge win for tenants," Garodnick said. "The court made it clear that you cannot pocket millions in taxpayer dollars while pushing rent-stabilized tenants out of their homes."

But there were still a number of thorny and immensely complicated issues left undecided by the court. Were the owners required to refund any rent overcharges to current and former tenants of the 4,400 apartments in question? How many years do you go back in calculating the baseline for the legal rent of the apartments in light of the decision? Whatever that date is, what rent increases, if any, could the landlord impose if the apartment was renovated or became vacant during that period? Every one of the 4,400 apartments had its own rent history and required a separate calculation to determine the legal rent going forward.

The real estate industry warned of the dire consequences of the decision, which could affect tens of thousands of apartments in the city, and the likelihood of years of litigation over the issues. Strasburg, president of the Rent Stabilization Association, said the ruling had the "potential to force some buildings into bankruptcy or foreclosure if they're required to roll back rents, but it would also have a direct impact on the city budget."

There was no uncertainty that the decision was a coup de grace for Tishman Speyer and BlackRock at Stuyvesant Town.

"It's the final nail in the coffin," Daniel Alpert, managing partner of Westwood Capital, said on the day the court ruled. "It's
been doomed for a while, but it's a spectacular way to go
down."[9]

On November 6, 2009, CWCapital Asset Management, the
country's second-largest "special servicer" of troubled mortgages, took control of the $3 billion first mortgage on Stuyves-
ant Town-Peter Cooper Village. With $650 million in reserve
funds nearly exhausted, Rob Speyer and his partners at Black-
Rock asked the loan trustees for a forbearance agreement, to
stave off foreclosure and allow time for a possible restructuring
of the loan. CWCapital's job was to administer the loans on
behalf of bondholders, oversee the property and determine
whether to foreclose in the event of a default. The first mortgage initially provided by Wachovia and Merrill Lynch had been
carved into five pieces. Each piece was pooled with other commercial loans in a securitized trust and sold on the bond market. Fannie Mae and Freddie Mac, the government-owned
mortgage companies, bought the senior-most tranches, or seg-
ments, of the five bonds, but under the terms of the securitiza-
tion, they had no right to intervene in a restructuring.

CWCapital came with several interesting connections. It
was owned by Caisse de Dépôt et Placement du Québec, Canada's largest pension fund. A division of the pension fund had
made a $90 million junior loan—part of the $1.4 billion in secondary loans—for the Tishman Speyer–BlackRock purchase of
Stuyvesant Town and Peter Cooper Village. Later, it would re-
hire Adam Rose and Rose Associates to manage the complexes
and put Andrew MacArthur, a key member of the second-place

bidding team in the 2006 auction of Stuyvesant Town, in charge of the eighty-acre campus.

But no one was surprised by the turn of events at the two complexes. Monthly reports on the gloomy financial status of the property were public documents. The $190 million general reserve was exhausted, the $400 million interest reserve had dwindled to $6.75 million and there was a mere $3.74 million left in the $60 million replacement reserve fund. Fitch Ratings, a credit service, estimated that the worth of the property had plummeted to $1.8 billion, or one-third of the purchase price three years earlier. They had lost $3.6 billion on this one deal within two years of taking over the complexes. Astonishingly, rents were still falling along with property values. The drop in value meant that the senior loan could lose more than $1 billion, while $1.9 billion in equity and $1.4 billion in junior loans were essentially wiped out.

Investors in scores of other commercial mortgage-backed securities were also facing losses. Moody's Investor Service reported that 113 multifamily CMBS loans totaling $1.1 billion tipped into delinquency in December. The delinquency rate for all CMBS loans reached 4.9 percent, up 500 percent from a year earlier.

In the end, any one of the 2006 bidders for Stuyvesant Town-Peter Cooper Village would have run into a financial typhoon, whether it was the tenants or Richard LeFrak, who offered $4.5 billion, or Apollo–ING Clarion–Dermot, which put up $5.33 billion. For different reasons, perhaps, they all got caught up in what one Wachovia banker called "market momentum." In return for sizable fees that provided the banks with hundreds of millions of dollars and made the bankers themselves into swaggering millionaires, Wall Street provided the financing based on numbers and projections that never made sense.

CalPERS, CalSTRS, the government of Singapore, the Church of England and the other funds from around the world that threw billions of dollars at Stuyvesant Town saw their investment disappear in a puff of smoke. It is worth recalling that Wachovia and Merrill Lynch cleared an estimated $210 million on the Stuyvesant Town deal, although it did not enable either institution to survive the ensuing Great Recession.

Stuyvesant Town-Peter Cooper Village tenants and their supporters were not going to sit by quietly while CWCapital and Tishman Speyer negotiated the fate of the two complexes. By very publicly asserting themselves, Councilman Garodnick and Al Doyle, the longtime president of the tenant association, warned all parties, including, perhaps, a new buyer, that they were an unavoidable part of the solution. Four days after the appeals court ruling, Garodnick and other elected officials wrote to Fannie Mae and Freddie Mac urging them to protect the tenants' interest in any loan workout. Any new financing plan "must preserve" the property for middle-class residents and retain the two complexes as a single community, said the letter signed by Assemblyman Brian Kavanagh, state senator Thomas Duane, Congresswoman Carolyn B. Maloney, Manhattan borough president Scott M. Stringer and Garodnick. Some of them worried that a resolution might entail separating Peter Cooper Village from Stuyvesant Town so that it could be turned into a luxury condominium complex, with its larger apartments and renovated lobbies.

The two mortgage agencies, which had been placed in a conservatorship under the Federal Housing Finance Agency because of billions of dollars in bad loans, had their own problems and wanted no part of the political imbroglio in New York. In separate letters, Fannie and Freddie responded, telling the officials that they did not hold the mortgage, but rather a security that contained the senior portions of the Stuyvesant Town–Peter Cooper mortgage as well as debt from other properties. Therefore, they told the tenants, Fannie and Freddie had no "legal authority to dictate a restructuring of the mortgage." Typically, they advised, the investors in the most junior tranches of the security (those who get paid only after the investors in the senior certificates have been paid) are given the sole right to certain decisions with respect to management.[10]

Doyle was amazed at the sudden notoriety of the two complexes. He overheard people discussing the matter on a downtown bus and in his doctor's office. But he was primarily concerned about what a default meant for the twenty-five thousand residents of the complexes. "We're worried about what we may face going forward if Tishman defaults," Doyle said. "We're worried about maintenance, security and other things that might be affected by a lack of money coming into the complex."[11]

Rob Speyer sought to open talks with Charles Spetka, CWCapital's chief executive, to discuss some kind of workout that would involve retaining control of the complexes and investing fresh capital. Speyer asked Christopher A. Milner, a managing director at BlackRock who knew Spetka, to set up a meeting. Eventually, Speyer and Paul Galiano, co-director of acquisitions at Tishman Speyer, got together in New York with Spetka; Gregory A. Cross, CWCapital's lawyer; and Andrew J. Hundertmark, CWCapital's asset manager. Speyer described how the partners had been squeezed by the vagaries of the market and a devastating court decision. Later that afternoon, the group walked the grounds of Stuyvesant Town and Peter Cooper Village.

Speyer and his partners figured that they really had only three options. The first was a consensual restructuring in which each side put in something to make it work. Failing that, they could go for the nuclear option by taking the property into bankruptcy protection and trying to force the lenders to write down the mortgage. Finally, they could turn over the property to CWCapital and walk away.

In the meantime, Michael Ashner, a pugnacious and supremely self-confident investor, and a few of the other junior lenders were growing increasingly vocal about their unhappiness with Tishman Speyer. Ashner's company, Winthrop Realty Trust, had made a $25 million junior loan. It was most certainly underwater, but he did not want to walk away empty-handed. His demand for specific financial information about the property went largely unsatisfied by either Tishman Speyer or CWCapital. For his part, Rob Speyer concluded that there was little point to haggling with the junior, or mezzanine, lenders because they were so far out of the money.[12] If he could not reach an agreement with Spetka and CWCapital over the senior mortgage, there was no point in talking. "In our view," Speyer said, "the value fell within the senior loan. We were either going to make a deal with CW, or we were out. The mezz guys were not the critical path."

Ashner said he found Tishman Speyer's approach "arrogant." He said he also bluntly refused to sign a confidentiality agreement with the borrower.[13]

On January 8, 2009, the money essentially ran out, as everyone at that point knew it would. Tishman Speyer and Black-Rock failed to make the required $16.3 million interest payment on the first mortgage and the $4.7 million due on the mezzanine loans. Their default triggered a blizzard of legal notices required under the loan documents, but Speyer was also hoping that the restructuring talks would finally begin in earnest.

CWCapital's lawyer Gregory A. Cross, chairman of the bankruptcy department at the Venable firm in Baltimore, sent a default notice to Tishman Speyer and BlackRock and notified Wachovia, Merrill Lynch and the lowest-ranked junior lender, Gramercy Capital Corporation, an affiliate of SL Green, that the default had occurred.

Three days later, on January 11, Wachovia and four of the twelve other mezzanine lenders notified Tishman Speyer that it had ten days to cure the default, or they would pursue their rights and remedies, including foreclosure.[14] The group—Wachovia, Allied Irish, Deutsche Genossenschafts-Hypothekenbank, Hartford Investment Management Company and Concord Capital—collectively accounted for $300 million in loans, the most senior tranche of the $1.4 billion in mezzanine financing. They were prodded, in part, by a very vocal Ashner, who urged a more aggressive approach with Tishman Speyer and BlackRock in a bid to recapture at least some of what they had put into the deal. Other junior lenders had signed a prenegotiation letter indicating their willingness to participate in a workout.

"I thought Stuyvesant Town had value, long term," Ashner said. "It was worth fighting over, as opposed to some one-hundred-thousand-square-foot building in Kansas."[15]

Ten days later, on January 21, Gramercy Capital announced its intention to replace Tishman Speyer with the Related Companies as the manager of the complexes, a move rejected by Spetka at CWCapital. Gramercy's executives, like Ashner, were still upset. Tishman Speyer refused to bargain with them

or to provide the junior lenders with detailed financial information.

Speyer called Spetka the next day with a proposal. If CW-
Capital would agree to write down the mortgage to $1.8 billion,
he and his partners would invest a quarter of a billion dollars in
new money. But Speyer wanted a preferred return of, say, 12 percent. The ladder of payments under this scenario would begin
with the monthly debt service for the newly reduced mortgage
and then a payment on the fresh $250 million in capital. Every-
thing after that would be split between the lenders and Tishman Speyer–BlackRock. Spetka, a taciturn man who rarely
betrays his emotions, said he would consider it and get back to
Speyer. But he saw little benefit to the arrangement. The upside
for the bondholders he represented was reduced to zero, in
Spetka's judgment, while he would have to pay an exorbitant
12 percent interest for the additional funding. He could get
cheaper money elsewhere.

"The only thing that they [Tishman Speyer] brought to the
table as a partner was a faster resolution than foreclosure and a
continuity of management, which we didn't view as particularly
valuable," Spetka said. "Their capital was expensive and not
needed."[16]

The following day, Spetka called Speyer with his answer:
No, thank you. But Spetka dangled what he thought was an
inducement to let go of the property without a bruising battle
in court. He offered Speyer a long-term contract to manage the
two complexes. Speyer immediately rejected the offer. "Our
investors had experienced a tremendous amount of pain,"
Speyer said. "It's not appropriate for Tishman Speyer Properties
to create a new profit center out of their pain."[17]

Speyer and his company were juggling a number of sour real

estate deals at the same time, including Archstone-Smith, a $22 billion acquisition, and the CarrAmerica office buildings in Washington, DC, a $2.8 billion purchase. The Speyers were also in tough negotiations with a representative of the Federal Reserve Bank of New York to restructure their company's loans on five Chicago office buildings, including the Chicago Mercantile Exchange and the stately Civic Opera House, a pair of buildings purchased in 2007. Not long afterward, the vacancy rate in Chicago shot up to 15 percent and property values plunged.

The Fed inherited the debt in 2008 when JPMorgan Chase bought the original lender, Bear Stearns, and the government took on many of its troubled assets. Jerry Speyer had been a director of the New York Fed from 2001 through 2007. The Fed brought in his partner in the Stuyvesant Town-Peter Cooper Village deal, BlackRock, to handle negotiations over the Chicago buildings. They were being tougher, not easier, Jerry Speyer said ruefully. But none of Tishman Speyer's problems had generated as many headlines as Stuyvesant Town.

On Sunday, January 24, Speyer and Galiano gathered with a small group of lawyers and advisers at the offices of Fried Frank at 1 New York Plaza, a fifty-story tower at the south end of Manhattan, overlooking the ferry terminal and New York Harbor. Paintings of big sailing vessels lined the hallways, as at many downtown law firms. The mood was tense, solemn and resigned.

The chairman of the firm's real estate group, Jonathan L. Mechanic, handled a lot of work for Tishman Speyer, including the original purchase. He and Speyer debated the wisdom of filing for bankruptcy protection. But Tishman Speyer characteristically avoided legal slugfests that play out in open court. The economics of the deal were in shambles. CWCapital was uninterested in a restructuring. Unless they wanted to battle with the lenders over control of the property while the media recorded every move in tabloid headlines, there was little else to do but give the property back to the lenders and let their investors know that it was over.

"Those were tough calls," Speyer recalled in 2011. "It's always easy to call investors when you've generated a three-times or seven-times return for them. Try calling an investor when you've lost their capital and there's no more hope."[18]

It was already dark when Speyer left Fried Frank, jumped into a cab and headed home. He made one final call, to Spetka, who was home with his wife and daughter on the Upper East Side watching television. The conversation as the cab rolled toward Greenwich Village was brief and without rancor. "We want to give the property back to the lender," Speyer said. "A protracted legal fight is not good for us, the tenants, New York City or the bondholders."

Spetka exhaled slowly. He had dodged what could have been a very messy bankruptcy court battle conducted in the center of an international media spotlight. "It was exactly the right thing to do," Spetka said of Tishman Speyer. "When I hung up, I felt like I'd won the lottery.

"It was important to Tishman to maintain their reputation in the investment market and in the city," Spetka continued. "They could've put up a battle, but it wasn't worth the cost. The attorney bills would've been astronomical and the press would have been brutal. External factors, coupled with this asset being outside of their core competency, really doomed the investment."[19]

The next day the *New York Times* and the *Wall Street Journal* carried prominent stories about the demise of what MetLife had called "the largest real estate transaction in world history."[20] The ensuing deluge of wire service reports and radio and television coverage was comparable to the deal's announcement in October 2006. Tishman Speyer issued a brief statement: "It has become clear to us through this process that the only viable alternative to bankruptcy would be to transfer control and operation of the property, in an orderly manner, to the lenders and their representatives. We make this decision as we feel a battle over the property or a contested bankruptcy proceeding is not in the long-term interest of the property, its residents, our partnership or the city."

The Speyers simultaneously sent out a second message: Despite the recent setback, all was well with the Tishman Speyer empire, which spanned four continents and included a $33.5 billion portfolio of seventy-two million square feet of office space, the rough equivalent of all the office space in Los Angeles and Houston combined. They had sold $12 billion worth of property in 2006 and 2007 for enormous profits. "After writing off the equity in a handful of distressed deals," said Rob Speyer, "our annual returns on both a 10-year and a 30-year basis are over 20 percent on average." His father added, "We've done a lot of deals. We've had some fantastic results. We've also had some bad results. I'd argue that there's nobody that does what we do that has a better record."[21]

Asked about the events at Stuyvesant Town, Mayor Michael R. Bloomberg continued his cheerleading for Tishman Speyer. "It's not clear that the tenants of Stuyvesant Town are any worse off or better off," he said. "I can tell you, from what I know, Tishman Speyer's been a very reputable company. The way they manage buildings, the tenants are pretty happy in them."

The billionaire mayor then offered cold comfort to the

tenants. The deal, he said, had "generated a lot of tax revenues, which went to pay our cops and firefighters and teachers, and if you want to question that deal, go back and ask them would they like to give back part of their salaries which was paid by that."

Untangling Stuyvesant Town took the better part of 2010, as CWCapital worked through a thicket of legal issues. Until those matters could be settled, Tishman Speyer continued to manage the complexes, although it lowered its profile as much as possible and began reassigning senior executives. The fact that the mortgage was spread among five trusts rather than a single bank did not help either. But the two Manhattan complexes, with their plain brick facades, proved to be an enduring piece of catnip for hedge fund investors, old-line real estate families and other investors. Where else could you find 11,232 apartments and 80 acres of valuable land in Manhattan?

Two former bidders, Stephen Ross of the Related Companies and Richard LeFrak, the billionaire real estate developer, had already contacted CWCapital to talk about a possible sale. Douglas Durst of the Durst real estate family also called on CWCapital, as did Daniel Alpert of Westwood Capital. "Despite the turbulence surrounding this property in recent years," Ben Thypin, the senior analyst at Real Capital Analytics, said, "Stuyvesant Town remains an irreplaceable asset that many deep-pocketed players will be interested in."[22]

Spetka and his lawyers moved quickly to foreclose on the property. He hired Adam Rose, co-president of Rose Associates, the company that managed Stuyvesant Town-Peter Cooper Village for MetLife, as an adviser and ultimately as the property manager. Spetka also brought in Andrew MacArthur to oversee the complex, as well as other distressed properties. MacArthur was no stranger either. In 2006, he was part of a bidding group that narrowly lost out to Tishman Speyer in the Stuyvesant Town-Peter Cooper Village auction.

CWCapital met with Garodnick and the tenants association, promising to work closely with them and put the acrimony of the past behind them. But Doyle, Garodnick and their supporters had every intention of reviving their own effort to buy the adjoining complexes. They hired Moelis and Company, a real estate advisory firm, and Meredith Kane, a well-respected real estate attorney at Paul, Weiss, Rifkind, Wharton & Garrison. They also opened talks with city comptroller John Liu about a possible partnership with the big pension fund the New York City Employees' Retirement System. A March 13 forum sponsored by the tenant association drew an overflow crowd to the 1,100-seat auditorium at nearby Baruch College, where Doyle spoke of the necessity for tenants to speak with "a single voice." Volunteers from all 56 buildings at the two complexes circulated unity pledges, eventually signed by more than 7,100 residents. Soon, Related, LeFrak and others came calling on the tenants association as well.

Tacitly, all the suitors recognized that they could not execute a deal without, or in spite of, the tenants. The political opposition would be too fierce and no lender would want to step into the middle of that mess. "We don't think the politics are such that anybody can do a deal over the objections of the tenants," said Wilbur Ross, an investor specializing in distressed properties who had teamed up with Richard LeFrak after Tishman Speyer's default.[23]

Doyle listened patiently to their entreaties and promises. In a quiet voice, he delivered the same message to each and every one: "We would like the entire place to remain affordable, and we would like to own it."

In late February 2010, a billionaire hedge fund operator jumped into the fray, complicating the already byzantine political and financial picture at Stuyvesant Town and sending a nervous shudder through the tenants of the complexes. David Tepper, the founder of Appaloosa Management, a New Jersey hedge fund specializing in distressed properties, had quietly bought up nearly $800 million worth of bonds in the five trusts that held the $3 billion at Stuyvesant Town-Peter Cooper Village. He picked them up at a sometimes-steep discount, because of the property's well-publicized financial woes. Tepper filed a lawsuit in the U.S. district court in Manhattan seeking to block the Stuyvesant Town foreclosure, claiming that CWCapital had acted "irrationally and imprudently" in pursuing a course that could cost debt holders hundreds of millions of dollars. A foreclosure, the suit argued, could cost as much as $200 million in transfer taxes, which would cut into the amount of money bondholders ultimately received. Appaloosa said that CWCapital should have pushed the owners into bankruptcy, thereby avoiding the taxes and maximizing returns for investors.

Tepper asked the court to replace CWCapital, saying the company had "irreconcilable conflicts of interest" because it was both a "servicer" and a debt holder. "We're not trying to take control," Tepper told me at the time. "We're trying to prevent CW from acting in a reckless manner. We want a voice in the process." As for the tenants, he stressed that he was not an adversary. "We recognize that there needs to be some degree of rent-controlled apartments there," he said.

Tepper was a shrewd investor. His company had made $7 billion in 2009, including $2.5 billion for Tepper himself, by buying low-priced shares of Bank of America and Citigroup and betting that the Obama administration would not take over the financial system. But the tenants wanted no part of an opportunistic hedge fund. "The tenants are not in favor of prolonged legal wrangling," said Garodnick. "We don't think it will be helpful to extend the process here by fighting among the creditor parties."[24]

More broadly, housing advocates worried that meat-and-potatoes housing complexes that had been saddled with enormous mortgages during the real estate boom would fall into disrepair or be resold for an unsustainable price. "The fact that these investors so grossly overleveraged these buildings is a symptom of the larger economic crisis that we're dealing with now," Benjamin Dulchin, executive director of the nonprofit Association for Neighborhood and Housing Development, said at the time. "The fact that some of these players are trying to further maximize their profit, again at the expense of affordable housing in the city, is pretty horrifying."

At a hearing on April 29, CWCapital's lawyer Gregory Cross asked the court to dismiss Tepper's complaint, saying Appaloosa had no standing to intervene. Appaloosa owned certificates issued by five separate trusts that held the Stuyvesant Town mortgage and other commercial loans totaling $24 billion. The trusts typically selected a "special servicer" to maximize the recovery on behalf of all the certificate holders. Cross argued that there would be total chaos if every certificate holder was allowed to intervene, each pulling in a different direction. At the end of the hour-long hearing, Judge Alvin Hellerstein concluded, "Appaloosa's interests are not likely to be impaired or impeded," and dismissed the case.

Afterward, Judge Hellerstein's decision was cited again and

again in similar disputes that involved commercial mortgage-backed securities.

Councilman Garodnick and the tenants association were moving to revive their own plan for purchasing the complexes. They wanted to act quickly, before the lenders planted a new For Sale sign on First Avenue. There was a buzz about it on the blogs, in the tenant board meetings and at larger gatherings. "I think the people want stability," Garodnick said. "They want to get out of this model where the property is changing hands every three to five years, and where owners have a business plan designed to push people out."[25]

The tumult over Appaloosa had barely died down when two other creditors tried to seize control of Stuyvesant Town-Peter Cooper Village, before CWCapital could go through with its planned foreclosure in September of the Tishman Speyer–BlackRock partnership. Armed with a $45 million investment, Michael Ashner's Winthrop Realty Trust and Pershing Square Capital Management, a hedge fund, announced in August that they planned to foreclose on the property and convert the 11,232 rental apartments at the complexes into an "affordable cooperative" and reap a windfall.

Ashner, who was a junior lender in the Stuyvesant Town deal, took his long-standing interest in the complexes to Pershing's leader, William A. Ackman, who had much deeper pockets and a reputation as an activist investor. At one point, Ackman predicted there was a "$2 billion potential profit opportunity," which he eventually offered to split with tenants.[26]

By now, every potential buyer circling the property had concluded that the complexes were worth more than $1.8 billion.

The suitors also recognized that they needed the tenant association as an ally, given the broad public interest in the complexes from the public and from politicians ranging from Councilman Garodnick to U.S. senator Charles E. Schumer. It would be impossible to obtain a $3 billion mortgage in the still-frozen credit markets, but they would not need that much anyway if a large block of residents bought their apartments, at a discount to market. The profits would come with the sale of another block of units at market prices.

Ashner and Ackman had a plan that they said would please the tenants and the mortgage lenders, while making a tidy profit for themselves. "The unique circumstances of Stuyvesant Town today create the opportunity for us to make an attractive investment, for tenants to buy their apartments at below market prices and for the first mortgage lender to get back its money," said Ackman, the tall, trim chief executive of Pershing Square.

But CWCapital, which represented the bondholders who had a $3 billion first mortgage on the property, was not about to yield to an interloper with a relatively tiny $45 million investment. CWCapital had tried weeks earlier to buy out Ashner and a top swath of four junior lenders, who collectively had $300 million in secondary loans on the property. After initially offering $15 million, CW raised its offer to $45 million, hoping the lenders would take it, figuring something was better than nothing. But Ashner refused to go along with what had to be a unanimous decision. Instead, he bought the entire tranche for $45 million, or fifteen cents on the dollar, and enlisted Ackman in his quest to take over this iconic property. Ackman, whose company managed over $6 billion in capital, was a powerful partner.

"There was a lot of risk," Ackman explained during an interview in 2011, "but it was a relatively small amount of money for the opportunity to make multiples of our investment. I wouldn't have done it for $500 million, but for $45 million it was an interesting risk-reward."

Ackman, who at forty-five exuded boyish charm and intelligence, was in the midst of a $28 billion restructuring of General Growth Properties, the second-largest mall operator in the country. He had bought a 25 percent stake in the company during the financial crisis with the idea that the company was worth more than its flagging stock price. He lent the company $375 million after it fell into bankruptcy protection in 2009 so it could continue operating and then pushed the company to split into two, a move that ultimately generated enormous profits for himself and benefits for shareholders, lenders and employees.

The ever-brash Ashner trumpeted his own claim to fame. "I'm the reason Tishman Speyer threw in the towel in January," he told me. "They were so arrogant that they thought they'd tell everyone what to do. I got my group to send a default notice."

Although Speyer viewed Ashner as an obstructionist in the final weeks that he controlled the complexes, it is unlikely that Ashner's move figured prominently in the final decision to walk away from what had been a disastrous investment.

Many Stuyvesant Town-Peter Cooper Village residents viewed the Ashner-Ackman duo as Dracula preying on their embattled village. Certainly Doyle and Garodnick were wary. The most obvious question was, did Ackman and Ashner mean the same thing as the tenants when they used the word "affordable"? "These are profit-motivated investors," said James Sullivan, a managing director of Green Street Advisors. "That's their starting point. It's hard to envision any scenario in which they could accomplish that without alienating the residents of Stuyvesant Town."[27]

Garodnick, who met with Ackman and Carolyn B. Tiffany, Winthrop's president, said that he was disappointed but not surprised that the complexes were being treated as a "pawn in a financial chess game." He warned them in a letter that "tenants can only support a proposal that puts home ownership within reach" and allows existing, rent-regulated tenants to remain in place. Tenants would oppose a plan, he added, that involved an oversize mortgage that created financial pressure on the landlord to oust existing rent-regulated tenants. "It is of the utmost importance that this property remain accessible to New Yorkers of moderate means who aspire to live there in the future."[28]

There was also sniping from potential rivals for the complexes. Wilbur L. Ross, an investor in distressed assets who was working with the developer Richard LeFrak on a plan to buy Stuyvesant Town, was dismissive of the Ackman-Ashner gambit, as was Gerald Guterman, who also wanted to do a co-op conversion at the two complexes.

CWCapital went to court asking for a temporary injunction to block the Pershing-Winthrop auction scheduled for August 25. Its lawyer Gregory Cross argued that under the terms of the "inter-creditor agreement" that governed all lenders in the deal, Winthrop and Pershing had to pay off the first mortgage, which now totaled $3.7 billion with accumulated fees and penalties, before it could foreclose. CWCapital reckoned that Winthrop and Pershing would not be able to raise enough money to pay off the senior mortgage.

But CWCapital also paid homage to the tenant association and the concept of an affordable co-op, without spelling out any details. "We think that we have a plan that ultimately will be supported by tenants and will provide an affordable housing solution for this project," said Joseph R. Ryan, an attorney for CWCapital at an August 19 hearing before Judge Richard B. Lowe III. "That is a project now that is adrift without any new equity capital. What our people bring to the table is new equity capital and a plan to revitalize this project."

The battle was now swinging back and forth between the courtroom and the streets, for the hearts and minds of the residents. Ashner and Ackman fired off a letter to Doyle and the tenants association proposing an alliance in which the tenants would get a "substantial equity" stake in the 80-acre property, the ability to set apartment prices and the power to veto major decisions made in the course of converting the 11,232 apartments to a co-op. "Working together," the letter said, "we believe that we will be able to effectuate an affordable non-eviction conversion while protecting the long-term affordability of the property for current and future tenants and ensuring that those who wish to remain rent-stabilized renters can do so."

Subsequently, Ackman and Ashner offered the tenants "full veto rights with respect to all major decisions" and said the tenants association "will not be required to contribute any capital to obtain its ownership position."[29]

It was an extraordinary offer for a pair of financial swashbucklers and it got the tenants' attention. "We're intrigued," Doyle quipped. Garodnick added warily that he looked forward to digging deeper into the offer to see how it measured up against the tenant goals.

This maneuvering showed "that this time around people are paying attention to what the 25,000 people at Stuyvesant Town want," said former city housing commissioner Rafael E.

Cestero. "You have two big players reaching out to the tenants and saying, 'We want to work with you.'"[30]

In court, Ackman and Ashner's lawyers cited a different section of the intercreditor agreement than the one CWCapital relied on, saying that it gave them the right to foreclose and cure the default "following its acquisition of equity collateral." The two investors also conceded that they would put the complexes in bankruptcy protection if CWCapital refused to write down the senior loan, which would have almost certainly resulted in a forced write-down of the senior mortgage.

Ackman and Ashner's lawyers told the court that foreclosure would reduce the existing debt on the property by $1.4 billion, by formally wiping out the junior loans. They said nothing about the senior mortgage. CWCapital's foreclosure action would also have formally wiped out the junior lenders. Gregory Cross, CWCapital's lawyer, countered that Ackman and Ashner, as junior lenders, could have paid off the $3 billion senior loan and taken control of the property after the owners defaulted in January. But they lost the opportunity after CWCapital accelerated the loan three weeks later.

On September 16, Judge Lowe ruled against Ashner and Ackman, saying that the "intercreditor agreement prohibits junior lenders from acquiring ownership and control of the Equity Collateral unless they pay any outstanding indebtedness."

Moreover, he said, "the public interest is best served by maintaining stability in what [Pershing Square] concedes is 'the largest residential property in Manhattan and home to a significant portion of the city's moderate income housing.'"

Cross, whose law firm was based in Baltimore and was the subject of disparaging mutterings from his opponents about the quality of out-of-town lawyers, was elated. An angry Ashner vowed to appeal the decision and attempt to stop CWCapital's foreclosure sale.

But ultimately, Ashner and Ackman sold their interests in October to CWCapital for $45 million, their initial cost, and dropped the litigation. Ackman, who still insists that the judge got it wrong, likened the outcome to returning a lottery ticket to the store after you've lost for a full refund. "I have learned from prior experience," Ackman told his investors in a letter, "that sometimes the better part of valor in an investment situation is to move on. Onward."

CWCapital formally took control of Stuyvesant Town and Peter Cooper Village in October 2010, restoring Rose Associates as the manager of the complexes. It did not, however, foreclose on the loans, preferring to take over the entity that owned the complexes and avoid an estimated $100 million in transfer taxes. Technically, that meant that the junior lenders and the equity investors still had a stake in the property, but it was highly unlikely they would ever recover a dime.

One thing was sure: Tishman Speyer's forty-seven-month reign at Stuyvesant Town-Peter Cooper Village was now over.

CHAPTER TWELVE

Reckoning

The public can be forgiven if it expected Tishman Speyer and the BlackRock Group to suffer huge financial setbacks or tarnished reputations from the spectacular debacle at Stuyvesant Town and Peter Cooper Village. After all, an international array of investors, pension funds and lenders lost over $3 billion, which reverberated in state and city government budgets from California to Florida. Some twenty-five thousand tenants were left anxious and uncertain about the fate of their homes.

But the truth is that the well-oiled machine that is Tishman Speyer chugged along after the default, extending its development prowess to new markets. BlackRock, if anything, got bigger and more powerful. It is the nature of a business in which the principal players are using other people's money and the Wall Street casino supplied the markers for risky bets that investors or taxpayers would ultimately have to pay, while its croupiers collected enormous fees whether the players won or lost. The two companies came out of it relatively unscathed, belying industry lore that New York is one of the most unforgiving markets in the country. Indeed, those at the intersection of high finance and real estate are more often exonerated.

Tishman Speyer and BlackRock did lose a combined $225 million, the 4 percent of the $5.4 billion purchase price that they put into the deal. In the Speyers' case, the firm provided $56.25 million and their closest partner, the Crown family, put up an equal sum. But those losses were offset by a gusher of at least $48 million in acquisition, equity, asset and property management fees in 2007, 2008 and 2009 that flowed to Tishman Speyer, as the operating partner. Tishman Speyer and Black Rock also charged their equity partners multimillion-dollar fees to get into the Stuyvesant Town-Peter Cooper Village deal.

The Speyers received an additional fee based on the dollar volume of construction work at the property, which totaled $21.8 million for the landscaping, refurbished storefronts and new signage at the complex. But given the property's dismal financial performance, Rob Speyer elected to waive the asset management fee beginning in the fourth quarter of 2008 in a bid to "share the pain" and avoid antagonizing investors and lenders.

Before Rob Speyer formally turned over the keys to Stuyvesant Town-Peter Cooper Village in October 2010, he and his company moved rapidly to clean up a trove of troubled properties within their vast international portfolio, none of which were as deeply underwater as Stuyvesant Town-Peter Cooper Village.

Tishman Speyer raised $2 billion in equity to recapitalize the buildings in DC and to look for bargains among the office buildings and development deals now in trouble with their lenders. In June 2010, Tishman Speyer and a partner invested

$50 million each and restructured a $1.4 billion loan package covering the five Chicago office buildings it bought at the top of the market, including the Civic Opera House and 10 and 30 South Wacker Drive. Later in the year, the Speyers even added to their Chicago holdings, buying a newly erected forty-five-story office tower at 353 North Clark in Chicago for $385 million.

In Washington, DC, the Speyers and their partner SITQ paid off a $600 million junior loan, extended the term of the senior loan and invested $100 million in the twenty-eight Carr-America office buildings. SITQ, a real estate company with a $17 billion portfolio of office buildings, hotels and apartment buildings in Canada, the United States, France, Germany, the United Kingdom and India, was well acquainted with Tishman Speyer's debacle at Stuyvesant Town. SITQ then owned CW-Capital, the special servicer that took over the complexes after Tishman Speyer defaulted. But that did little to tarnish the firm's reputation.

In some cases, Tishman Speyer simply cut its losses. Rob Speyer had to stabilize a troubled office complex in Seattle that he bought at the top of the market in 2007 for $234 million. He put up $59 million in equity and financed the deal for the complex, known as Second and Seneca, with a $175 million mortgage from Bank of America. But the occupancy dropped to 60 percent during the recession. In 2010, he negotiated a loan modification and paid down a portion of the principal, reducing the debt to a $153.3 million senior loan and $16.7 million subordinate note, whose repayment was tied to the performance of the property. Finally in 2011, Speyer sold the building for $186 million, 20 percent less than he paid for it four years earlier.

But they were not licking their wounds. Rob Speyer was

particularly proud in August 2011 of selling a twenty-two-story office tower his company had just completed in Queens for $415.5 million, enabling Tishman Speyer to reap a $75 million profit on an initial investment of $28 million. Rob and his father were in constant motion. Their company completed 10 million square feet of new projects in the United States, Brazil, China and India, including the 2.2-million-square-foot WaveRock office complex in Hyderabad.

At the same time, the Speyers made $4 billion worth of new acquisitions and development deals in 2010 and 2011 in Los Angeles, San Francisco, Chicago, Paris, London, Brazil, India and China. As Stuyvesant Town faded from their corporate memory, Tishman Speyer had an impressive thirty-five million square feet of projects in their development pipeline, the largest being a sixty-six-acre mixed-use development in Shanghai called Jiang Wan (the Springs) New Town.

A long year after leaving Stuyvesant Town-Peter Cooper Village for good, Rob Speyer tried to describe what had gone wrong with their plans for the complexes. He was clearly tense and uncomfortable, as if the dentist had just told him he would need root canal work. He sat in a small conference room at Tishman Speyer headquarters with his friend and adviser Steven Rubenstein, president of Rubenstein Communications, a media-relations firm. Like Speyer, Rubenstein is an heir apparent, the son of Howard J. Rubenstein, a legendary figure who over the course of a fifty-year career advised mayors, governors, media titans and just about every real estate mogul in New York. Even if the clients hated each other, they all sought Howard's counsel.

Steven, who attended Dalton prep school with Speyer, has many of his father's qualities, including an ability to defuse a client's angry first reaction to a crisis and map out a strategic response that takes into account both the political and economic constraints in New York City. Tishman Speyer's decision to walk away from Stuyvesant Town–Peter Cooper Village, for instance, was described as stemming from the company's desire to do what was in the best interests of the tenants.

Speyer acknowledged the magnitude of the disaster, although both he and his father did not want the demise of the deal to become Tishman Speyer's epitaph. They expressed a conviction that this one deal would not affect the reputation of an honorable company that had year in and year out provided 20 and 30 percent returns for its investors. Indeed, the billionaire Lester Crown told friends that Stuyvesant Town–Peter Cooper Village was the only deal on which he lost money in five decades of investing with Tishman Speyer.

"We paid the ultimate penalty," Rob Speyer said. "We lost our investors' capital and our capital. [But] a company is not judged by a single transaction. A company is judged by the overall body of its work."[1]

Some of the Speyers' rivals gleefully put the blame for the outcome on Rob's shoulders. They depicted him as a privileged prince whose youthful arrogance blinded him to the obvious pitfalls. But this scenario only works if his father, Jerry Speyer, went into hibernation during the boom, like Rip Van Winkle, suddenly waking up years later to discover that his son had run the family business into the ground. The truth is that Jerry was the chairman of Tishman Speyer and had to approve every deal. "The two of us have a simple arrangement," Rob Speyer said. "Either of us can veto any decision the company makes. We work closely together. We both are invested in any decision the company makes anywhere."

The decisions they made were not that different from those made by other real estate tycoons who took advantage of fee-grabbing bankers and loose underwriting standards to borrow billions of dollars. Even if the deal did not work out, there were few downside consequences and little risk.

The potential upside was breathtaking. Jerry and Rob Speyer described Stuyvesant Town at the time of the sale as an asset they intended to hold on to for generations to come. At first glance, this might seem out of whack with the exit strategy outlined in the investor memorandum, which was to gentrify the complexes, more than double revenues, and then sell in seven years at a handy profit.

But at the time, the Speyers intended to be the ultimate buyer, following the same path they took with another landmark.

Jerry Speyer was a minority owner (he and billionaire Lester Crown owned a five percent stake) and the operating partner when he first bought Rockefeller Center in 1996 for $900 million, with partners David Rockefeller, the Agnelli of Italy, the Stavros Niarchos family of Greece, and Goldman Sachs. He carefully restored the landmark complex's luster as the real estate market soared. Speyer and Crown bought the complex for $1.85 billion five years later in 2001, when the partners put it on the auction block. But the strategy that worked so well at Rockefeller Center failed completely at Stuyvesant Town.

Rob Speyer, other real estate executives and even some pension fund executives who invested in these highly leveraged projects blamed their ultimate collapse on the vagaries of the market and the surprising J-51 court ruling that re-regulated thousands of apartments, cutting deeply into residential revenues. "The biggest driver in the underperformance of the investment was the deterioration of rents," Rob Speyer said. "We were a victim of our own bad timing. It couldn't have been worse timing."

But the catastrophic failure was not simply a matter of bad timing. The reality is that nearly every single assumption in their business plan for Stuyvesant Town-Peter Cooper Village was wrong, dead wrong. The company that seemed to have the golden touch when it came to overseas development or iconic commercial properties like Rockefeller Center or the Chrysler Building completely overestimated its ability to turn Stuyvesant Town-Peter Cooper Village into a luxury complex.

Their plan to deregulate and renovate apartments at a faster pace than most landlords have ever imagined was a failure. Within the first year, before the recession and the collapse of Lehman Brothers, Tishman Speyer discovered that its projections for market rents were higher than anyone was willing to pay for an apartment in a sixty-year-old complex without doormen and modern amenities. So they accumulated a backlog of hundreds of unrented, overpriced apartments. That set off a downward spiral as the company reduced the market rents to attract tenants, and reduced them again as the market softened and demand slackened.

They were no more prescient with their plan to evict 1,600 "illegal tenants" as a quick way to boost rents. They spent a fortune hiring investigators and three different law firms to ferret out illegals, only to discover that they had alienated virtually the entire population and come up far short of their goal. The bulk of the "illegals" had been culled by MetLife and Rose Associates prior to Tishman Speyer's purchase.

Their miscalculations could not withstand a slowdown in rent increases, let alone a full-blown recession. Small wonder that net income for the complexes in 2008 was $138 million, 35 percent less than the $211.7 million forecast in the "confidential private placement memorandum" given to investors two years earlier.

Between October of 2008 and August of 2009, Speyer said that net effective rents at Stuyvesant Town-Peter Cooper Village fell by 27 percent or more. There is no question that the market was getting soft, but the steep drop at Stuyvesant Town-Peter Cooper Village was one more example of just how badly Tishman Speyer miscalculated.

The average rent for a Manhattan apartment fell by only 8.7 percent to $3,399 between 2007 and 2009, according to one of Manhattan's largest rental brokers, Citi Habitats. But from the beginning of its tenure, Tishman Speyer pushed the rents for market-rate units so high that many potential renters sought better deals elsewhere. As a result, the vacancy rate climbed to more than 6 percent from 2 percent the year before Tishman Speyer took over. Small wonder then that the net effective rent plummeted from a peak of $4,250 a month at Peter Cooper to $3,050 in August 2009, and from $3,750 a month in Stuyvesant Town to $2,750 during the same period, according to Tishman Speyer's own figures.

Tishman Speyer had stopped renovating vacant apartments at Stuyvesant Town and Peter Cooper Village at the end of 2008, three months before the appellate division of the state supreme court ruled that Tishman Speyer and MetLife had wrongfully deregulated 4,400 apartments while taking special tax breaks from the city.

"The default at Stuyvesant Town really had nothing to do with the Roberts case," said Stuart M. Saft, the real estate lawyer who analyzed the deal for two potential bidders and for an investor after the collapse. "There was no economic basis in the first place," Saft said. "It's great middle-income housing. But people who pay top dollar won't rent there. It's never going to be considered luxury housing."

Saft had also devised the original tenant lawsuit challenging the deregulation of apartments at Stuyvesant Town and Peter Cooper Village. Having assessed the property from so many angles, he was hired by one investor after the default to determine whether there were grounds for a lawsuit against Tishman Speyer and BlackRock. There were not. But Saft concluded in a June 2010 report for the investor that the fundamental flaw in Tishman Speyer's analysis was that it ignored "the age, nature and reputation of the property and the determination of the residents and local elected officials to fight gentrification of the property or the fact that a newly constructed property would not have these disadvantages."

After he was no longer involved with the property, Speyer conceded that he had completely misunderstood the political complexity of buying and managing rent-regulated housing in New York, and the historical and cultural significance of Stuyvesant Town-Peter Cooper Village as a middle-class bastion in Manhattan. The hostility from residents, tenants in general and the elected officials took him by surprise.

"In retrospect," he said, "I realized I'd lived a bit of a charmed life, both professionally and otherwise. This was a failure and a failure on a pretty epic scale. I did not appreciate the political and social dynamics that came along with the real estate in this deal," he added. "I thought if we abided by the law and behaved honorably that everything would be okay on the civic front. It seems obvious now, but it didn't occur to me that people hated the law and therefore they hated us. We weren't used to being portrayed as the guys in the black hats.

"There was a connection between my single-minded focus on business and how I missed the bigger picture on this deal."[2]

At the urging of Rubenstein, Speyer hired Michele Adams, who ran a business and civic association founded by the Rudin real estate family, the Association for a Better New York, to keep him apprised of the political currents in the city and to build a portfolio of civic and philanthropic activities. In late 2010, Rob also took on a more high-profile role in the political sphere, establishing the Committee to Save New York to support the newly elected Democratic governor, his friend Andrew M. Cuomo. The group sponsored television and radio ads supporting the governor in his ultimately successful battles with public-sector unions over pensions, teacher tenure and government spending.

Speyer initially took responsibility for raising a treasure chest of more than $10 million for an ad campaign backing the governor's conservative approach to the state budget. He pledged to contribute $1 million on behalf of his firm. The campaign was designed to counterbalance the annual media offensive from state-employee unions during the legislative debate over the budget.

Some developers balked at turning over their checks to Speyer, as if he was the only executive who knew the governor. Not wanting to "feather Rob's nest," as one executive put it, they gave their money to the Real Estate Board or some other entity, rather than Speyer or Adams. As a result, there was friction with his cofounders, Kathy Wylde, president of the Partnership for New York City, and Steven Spinola, president of the Real Estate Board of New York. Still, in 2011, the group raised $17 million, according to public records, much of it from wealthy and powerful executives giving $250,000 or more. The group steadfastly declined to disclose the names of the donors and was not legally bound to do so.

But in keeping with Speyer's newfound sensitivity to city and state politics, Rob insisted that he sought to temper the animosity toward unions among some developers and business leaders, which could have undercut the we're-all-in-this-together message of the committee.

A full-on attack on unions, similar to Tea Party–inspired campaigns in Wisconsin or Ohio, could have provoked a backlash among liberals, Democrats and others in the most unionized state in the country. The committee included several private-sector union leaders from the construction industry, exacerbating tensions within the labor movement and providing political cover for a Democratic governor who did not want to be portrayed as antiunion. The group hewed closely to Cuomo's fiscal agenda: cutting state spending, capping local property taxes and cutting pension benefits for public employees.

In 2011, the committee was the single biggest spender in the state on lobbying, pouring nearly $12 million into ad campaigns in support of the governor. "All the messaging was positive, about bringing people together," Speyer said. "Many people had predicted that the committee would be much more divisive toward the other side."

Speyer also moved on another front, lobbying hard to follow in his father's footsteps at the real estate industry's powerful lobbying arm, the Real Estate Board of New York, or REBNY. In the summer of 2012, the group announced that Speyer would be its new chairman come January.

But the Speyers and others on the committee were the same people in 2008 who persuaded the billionaire Michael Bloomberg to jettison his support for term limits and overturn the city's election law so he could run for a third term as mayor. With the Committee to Save New York, some of the city's wealthiest citizens were seeking to exert more influence and control over a political process in which tenants and labor unions, in their view, had too much clout. The committee's members and agenda showed, as Bill Mahoney, research coordinator for the New York Public Interest Research Group, put it, "a small number of New Yorkers continue to play a disproportionate role in the state's political discourse."

The heads-I-win, tails-you-lose scenario played out in equal measure for BlackRock. The company's founder and chairman, Larry Fink, was depicted in an April 2010 *Vanity Fair* profile as possibly "the most powerful man in the post-bailout economy." His company, which controlled or managed a jaw-dropping $12 trillion in assets worldwide, emerged as the largest asset management firm in the world. His views were so highly valued that he served as a consigliere for Jamie Dimon at JPMorgan Chase, John Mack at Morgan Stanley, AIG's Robert Willumstad and even the U.S. Treasury. Fink, one of the highest-paid chief executives in the country, told *Vanity Fair* that the public's rage at Wall Street was misplaced. "I feel it was the culture of America that was guilty," he said. "We were living fat and happy and the whole system was one of excess speculation and leverage."

But few profited from that culture as handsomely as Fink. Certainly, the pensioners at BlackRock's clients might not feel the same way. CalPERS, CalSTRS and the Dutch PKA lost a combined $669.7 million on the deal, six times as much as BlackRock. Fink declined to be interviewed for this book, but in the *Vanity Fair* profile, he echoed Jerry Speyer's sentiment in saying that a money manager could not be "100 percent perfect." "Our real estate division is struggling because of bad performance, and we're making changes," he told the magazine. "I don't care if the whole industry blew up, our job is to do better than the industry, and we didn't in real estate. I am not making excuses. I lose sleep over these problems."

The Stuyvesant Town-Peter Cooper Village loss was "an embarrassment," he added. The reporter recounted that Fink's voice then dropped to a whisper. "I mean, my mother gets her pension from CalPERS."

In a rare public rebuke of Fink's company, CalPERS dumped BlackRock in October 2010 as manager of its $1 billion portfolio of apartment complexes. BlackRock had managed the portfolio since 1998. The value of the pension fund's total assets had plummeted 24.8 percent—while the real estate portfolio alone took a 48 percent hit—in the year ending June 30, 2009, the largest single-year decline in CalPERS's history. The investment losses could have triggered a substantial increase in annual payments from the municipalities and school districts that belonged to the fund to enable CalPERS to meet its projected obligations to retirees. But the pension fund adopted a "rate smoothing plan" that phased the losses over three years so as not to require one jolting increase at a time when many cities and towns were struggling to make ends meet in the face of a sharp recession and a steep drop in property values.

It wasn't all BlackRock's fault. Other outside managers were responsible for CalPERS's having to write off a $100 million equity investment in Page Mill Properties, a Palo Alto, California, complex where tenants had complained that rent hikes of as much as 33 percent had forced out residents who could no longer afford to live there. The fund also lost nearly $1 billion on LandSource Holding, which held fifteen thousand acres in Los Angeles County and would tumble into bankruptcy only seventeen months after the investment. But the debacle at Stuyvesant Town-Peter Cooper Village was a double whammy for what had been a renowned pension fund.

"It was a significant disappointment," Joseph A. Dear, chief investment officer of CalPERS, said of the $500 million investment in Stuyvesant Town. "We transferred about $7 billion from managers that let us down in the crash to others who performed better."

"The entire catastrophe with the CalPERS real estate portfolio was enormously painful," Dear added in an interview in 2011. "Stuyvesant Town was an acute source of that pain. I say that because it involved not only an enormous amount of capital, but it was also a source of embarrassment that appeared to be in contradiction of our good governance, responsible investor policies."

The pension fund purged many of the executives who promoted the Stuyvesant Town investment over the objections of CalPERS's adviser Nori Gerardo Lietz, who had warned that it was doomed from the start.

In 2011, CalPERS's board revamped its investment criteria, emphasizing income-producing core assets providing a 7 percent return, rather than devoting so much capital to chasing the ephemeral 13.5 percent return promised by more high-risk ventures like Stuyvesant Town. At the same time, the board pivoted away from raw land and residential properties to office buildings. After coming under intensive criticism for a deal that involved displacing rent-regulated tenants who were very much like the fund's pensioners, CalPERS also adopted a policy effectively prohibiting investments in deals that use excessive rent hikes to oust low- and moderate-income families from rent-regulated housing.

"This policy will help us ensure that external managers who deploy CalPERS capital won't inappropriately displace households in rent-regulated units as a result of their investment strategies," said Rob Feckner, CalPERS's board president, after announcing the policy change in April 2010. "Such strategies have exposed CalPERS to risks and have caused adverse impacts to renters that must not happen again."

BlackRock went through its own internal purge. Fink replaced BlackRock Realty's chief Fred Lieblich in 2008, although Lieblich remained at the firm until his retirement in March 2010. Lieblich turned to meditation and yoga to regain his bearings. Even so, Lieblich declined several times to discuss what he said was a still-painful period in his life.

However, Rob Friedberg, a former managing director of BlackRock Realty who worked on the Stuyvesant Town deal, was remarkably frank in his assessment of the winners and losers. Friedberg left BlackRock in 2008 amid the upheaval in the real estate department. "There are two winners: the borrowers who used this non-recourse, securitized debt [and] who cashed out are giant winners," said Friedberg, who now runs his own investment firm, Capstone Realty, in Englewood, New Jersey. "The property went down, they give the property back, no recourse to them personally. The other winners are all the investment bankers who made these loans. There are a lot of fees when you borrow $4.5 billion."[3]

In 2009, BlackRock paid $13.5 billion for Barclays Global Investors, the ailing British bank's investment management unit. Jittery banks and governments ranging from the Federal Reserve to the Bank of Ireland to Greece sought the company's advice. Whatever the smudges on BlackRock's reputation because of Stuyvesant Town and the dismissal by CalPERS, the world's largest asset manager regained its footing quickly, reporting in the spring of 2011 that its first-quarter profit soared 34 percent to $568 million over the same period a year earlier. BlackRock's assets under management, a key indicator of the company's financial health, rose 8 percent to $3.65 trillion, making it, by that measure, the largest financial institution in the world.

"We're very excited about the future of BlackRock," Fink told analysts in a conference call. "We believe this is principally over. We can look forward to growth now."

Rob Verrone, the banker who earned an estimated $140 million in fees for Wachovia by erecting the financial structure for the Stuyvesant Town–Peter Cooper Village deal, does not like to dwell on the past. Verrone, who once courted reporters, is now reluctant to do interviews, especially if they dredge up his Italian background and the *Godfather* movie poster that once decorated his office. But he couldn't help himself. He wanted to make clear that Wachovia and Merrill Lynch suffered no pain when it came to the largest real estate transaction in history. He and his colleagues got an investment-grade rating for the $3 billion mortgage and quickly pushed it off the banks' balance sheets.

"From a financial standpoint," he said, "everything went right for Wachovia and Merrill."[4]

He made no mention of the junior lenders he and his colleagues pulled into the deal, or the pension funds and other investors who ponied up over $1.8 billion and then lost it.

Besides, he added, far more "outlandish" deals were done after Stuyvesant Town-Peter Cooper Village, including Lehman Brothers and Tishman Speyer's $22.2 billion acquisition of Archstone-Smith's 359 apartment complexes in 2007 and Blackstone's $26 million all-cash buyout of Hilton Hotels Group. The value of the apartment complexes dropped swiftly before the deal even closed. And Hilton Hotels groaned under the weight of $20 billion in debt during the recession and the decline in business travel.

But any list of outlandish deals would have to include the Lightstone Group's $8 billion purchase of Extended Stay Hotels by Lighthouse, which put up only 7.5 percent of the purchase price. Verrone and Wachovia underwrote the financing along with Merrill Lynch, Bear Stearns and Bank of America. It wasn't long before Extended Stay tumbled into bankruptcy court. "We lost a lot of money on that one," Verrone conceded.

Verrone left Wachovia in 2008, before the bank was swallowed by Wells Fargo and before Bank of America absorbed what was left of Merrill Lynch. Verrone and his new firm, Iron Hound Management, now represent debtors in their negotiations with lenders for extensions, interest reductions and discounts for payoffs, sometimes for his old clients.

Manus Clancy, an analyst at Trepp, a credit rating agency that follows the market for commercial mortgage-backed securities, estimated that Stuyvesant Town-Peter Cooper Village was one among fifteen thousand "pro forma" mortgages for apartment complexes, office buildings, hotels and other real estate based on often wildly optimistic estimates of what the property would be in years to come, rather than actual income. The Kushner real estate family's $1.6 billion purchase of the skyscraper at 666 Fifth Avenue in 2006 from Tishman Speyer is a prime example of the phenomenon in commercial real estate, while the $8 billion sale of the Extended Stay chain stands in for the hotel industry.

The financial industry has resisted the reforms spelled out in the Dodd-Frank legislation that might inhibit indiscriminate lending by bankers who were only too willing to take the enormous fees and unload the loans and the risk on investors in the form of mortgage-backed securities. The legislation calls for institutions issuing those kinds of securities to retain a 5 percent stake in any offering, ensuring that the banks have skin in the game and an interest in prudent terms and the outcome of the deal.

"There's a real difference between what a conduit lender thinks and a bank executive who will hold the loan through maturity," said Sam Chandan, president and chief economist for Chandan Economics and a professor at the University of Pennsylvania.[5]

Otherwise, there have been few structural changes to the way the market for commercial mortgage-backed securities functions, whether it is the oversight of the rating agencies or the relationship of the different parties in the transaction to one another. The volume of lending today is simmering at only a fraction of the hundreds of billions of dollars issued during the real estate boom. But prices for multifamily housing in 2012 were once again on the rise, even as profit margins thinned as properties changed hands. That led some analysts to wonder whether another minibubble was in the offing.

"Participants in the market will point out that deals are of higher quality now and are more conservatively underwritten than a few years ago," Chandan said. "However, that's a cyclical feature of the market. We know from previous cycles that the loan quality deteriorates as the market picks up. The potential for problematic loans remains."

In the fall of 2011, Steven A. Kandarian assessed the winners and losers of the deal for Stuyvesant Town-Peter Cooper Village that he helped engineer as MetLife's chief investment officer. The complexes remain intact and most of the tenants, he said, "still have rent stabilization protecting them." The losers, he said, were the lenders and pension funds.

"The primary losers are the people involved in financing the transaction," said Kandarian, sitting in a boardroom on the forty-first floor of MetLife's corporate offices at Forty-Second Street and Avenue of the Americas, in Manhattan. "That's where the risk should be."

The outcome, however, could have easily gone the other way, he said. "The bubble could have kept on going." Rents could have continued to soar along with real estate prices. But they didn't.

It's unclear where the sponsors—Tishman Speyer and BlackRock—fit into Mr. Kandarian's evaluation.

MetLife, of course, came out a big winner. Kandarian, now chairman of the board, president and chief executive officer, is understandably proud that he picked the top of the market for the sale and got a record-setting price, $5.4 billion. It produced a one-time net gain of $3 billion for the insurance company and, he pointed out, generated $262 million in taxes for the city and the state.

But more than one long-term tenant at Stuyvesant Town-Peter Cooper Village said that MetLife's responsibility extended beyond the company's profit margins. John Marsh, the activist who succeeded Doyle as president of the tenant association in

2012, quoted a line from the commemorative plaque in Stuyvesant Oval that honored Frederick W. Ecker, the MetLife chairman. The plaque described Ecker as the man "who conceived and brought into being this project, and others like it, that families of moderate means might live in health, comfort and dignity in parklike communities, and that a pattern might be set of private enterprise productively devoted to public service."

In Marsh's judgment, the decision to sell the complexes set in motion the very forces that are destroying Ecker's noble intentions and devotion to public service, leaving aside for a moment his approach to racial discrimination. In the relentless pursuit of profit, Marsh said, Stuyvesant Town and Peter Cooper Village are becoming home to the well-heeled and a highly commercialized venture.

Kandarian dismissed the notion that he and the company have betrayed Ecker's vision. MetLife honored its promises and commitments well beyond the twenty-five years required by the deal with the city, he said. Ultimately, their obligation was to the company's financial well-being. And the company was now responsible to shareholders and Wall Street.

"We spent six decades owning and managing that property in a very responsible way," he said. "But the quote on the statue didn't say, 'in perpetuity.' Selling our interest to a high-quality New York real estate investor doesn't denigrate those words at all."

Even after Tishman Speyer's default and the continuing recession, Stuyvesant Town-Peter Cooper Village remained an alluring prize for the Related Companies, AREA Property Partners, the Durst real estate family in partnership with City University of New York, Gerald Guterman and Westwood Partners, and especially the tenants themselves.

One year after Tishman Speyer and BlackRock left Stuyvesant Town-Peter Cooper Village for good, Dan Garodnick, the councilman, and Al Doyle, the tenant leader, announced in November 2011 that they were once again seeking to buy the two complexes in order to preserve them as a leafy refuge for middle-class families in high-priced Manhattan. This time, however, they had a deep-pocketed partner.

They hoped that the lenders who controlled the property through CWCapital would sell it to them in a deal that would enable tenants to purchase their apartments or remain in rent-regulated units. The idea was to preempt another overheated auction that would put the property in the hands of a heavily leveraged owner who might try to oust residents in favor of higher-paying tenants.

"This is the beginning," Doyle told me in November 2011. "We're trying to take control of the destiny of Stuyvesant Town-Peter Cooper Village in order to keep it an affordable property."

They hoped that they could cobble together a financial deal that would not leave the tenants with the kind of outsize debts that drowned Tishman Speyer and BlackRock. It would almost certainly include some kind of city, state and federal subsidies, as well as property tax breaks.

Senators Charles E. Schumer and Kirsten Gillibrand, Congresswoman Carolyn Maloney, Assemblyman Brian Kavanagh, city council speaker Christine Quinn and other elected officials immediately endorsed the effort. "If tenants have an ownership piece of these complexes it will be good not only for them," Schumer said, "but will also help secure their affordability for future generations of middle-class New Yorkers."

The tenant association formed an alliance with Brookfield Asset Management, a real estate company that managed $150 billion worth of assets, including fifty thousand apartments. In 2006, Brookfield had made a relatively small junior loan, $25 million, to the Tishman Speyer–BlackRock joint venture. Like all the other junior lenders, they had written off their loan in 2009. Now the company wanted to get involved in the tenant buyout.

Barry S. Blattman, a senior managing director at Brookfield, said his company was eager to help the tenant association "take matters into their own hands." Brookfield was not interested in becoming the landlord. But given the difficulty in obtaining financing for large real estate deals, Blattman said a condominium structure, in which tenants buy their apartments, might be the best way for CWCapital to get the highest possible price for the property now.

At a standing-room-only community meeting at Baruch College a few days later, on Saturday, December 3, Blattman was described by tenant leaders and their advisers in glowing terms as a white knight for the beleaguered tenants. No one mentioned that Blattman's company, Brookfield, owned the private park downtown that had been taken over by the Occupy Wall Street movement. Brookfield and city officials had been trying for weeks to evict the group, whose daily forays against the banks and the wealthiest 1 percent of Americans were disrupting the city's financial district.

There were well over 1,200 Stuyvesant Town and Peter Cooper Village residents in attendance at the Baruch College auditorium, with 150 yellow-shirted volunteers from the tenant association circulating through the crowd with flyers and sign-up sheets. "The entire city is watching what you do here and they're cheering you on," said an ebullient Garodnick.

"This bid is not geared for quickly flipping apartments at a huge profit or any other actions that will undercut the character of our community," Garodnick told the crowd. "Our bid is motivated by a desire for stability and an affordable home-ownership option for those who want it with gradual appreciation over time."

You could have heard the pipes clanging in Stuyvesant Town, it was so quiet when Meredith Kane spoke. A real estate lawyer and an adviser to the tenant association, Kane described in general terms what a tenant-led condominium conversion would look like. She said the plan was to preserve the open space at the complexes from new development, improve the maintenance at the buildings and create permanently affordable rental units with government help. She was short on details, in part because there had been no negotiations yet over price or structure.

The idea was that the tenants would purchase Stuyvesant Town-Peter Cooper Village and convert the complexes to a single condominium, under a plan in which no tenant would be evicted. An unspecified number of units would be set aside for residents who wished to remain in a rent-regulated apartment. A second category would be comprised of tenants who believed in Stuyvesant Town-Peter Cooper Village as a middle-class enclave. They could purchase their units at a steep discount to market. But there would be restrictions on any subsequent sales so that the units would remain affordable to families earning the median income of those living in the complexes. Finally, tenants who wanted the relatively unfettered right to sell their apartment for the highest possible price could buy their units at a modest discount to market.

It was an attempt to provide something for everyone. Still, the auditorium rang with hundreds of questions that could not be answered at the time: What would the apartments cost? Would apartments on higher floors have a higher price tag? Could a resident swap for a larger or smaller apartment? Why a condominium rather than a cooperative?

Under a tenant-led conversion, Brookfield would provide a down payment on the purchase price and obtain a mortgage through either the lenders or an independent bank. This scenario presumed that a large block of tenants, perhaps 50 or 60 percent, would buy their units early on, allowing the condominium association to pay off a portion of the mortgage and lower their costs. Sales of apartments at market rates would subsidize the stabilized rental units.

Brookfield would earn a hefty fee for its role and arrange for individual apartment loans. Brookfield might also retain ownership of the complexes' garages and retail space.

Although Al Doyle declined to identify a potential price, most analysts figured that the tenants could afford to pay about $3 billion, or roughly $300 a square foot. It would be difficult to go higher. To make this complicated process work, the net monthly cost of owning an apartment had to be roughly equal to the current cost of renting one, otherwise there would be little incentive to purchase a unit. At the same time, the tenants were betting that a profit-driven real estate company would be unable to obtain the financing in tight credit markets that would allow them to pay a higher price for that eighty-acre set of complexes in Manhattan.

Eugene Costiglio, who has lived in the complexes for a

quarter century, found the prospect of ownership intriguing, but he was not ready to commit. Costiglio, who works at an investment bank, moved to Stuyvesant Town from Queens in 1987 after languishing for six years on the waiting list. Later, he moved to Peter Cooper Village. During the reign of Tishman-Speyer, he said he spent twenty-two months and $22,000 successfully fending off Tishman Speyer's attempt to evict him. They claimed that his small bungalow on Long Island was his actual home and sought to evict him, saying he was not entitled to a rent-stabilized unit by law. But he ultimately proved that his primary residence was in Peter Cooper Village.

For him, a condominium conversion came down to one issue: "I think it's a wonderful idea if the price is right."[6]

Linda Ayache, a semiretired tenant and an ardent tenant activist, said she probably could not afford to buy her apartment. Her parents were some of the first residents of Stuyvesant Town in 1947. She got her own apartment when she married in 1970. Now divorced, she is a self-confessed sports fanatic and the unofficial neighborhood watch commander on her floor. Her regulated rent is over $1,300 a month, up from $161.65 in 1970. She said she favored "anything that gets it under tenant rule, whether we buy or not."[7]

But CWCapital, the special servicer representing the bondholders who controlled the complexes, was not as eager to embrace the tenants as it had been during the wrestling match with Ackman and Ashner.

The official response to the proposal from the tenant association and Brookfield was simple: We cannot begin to discuss a sale before we resolve the Roberts litigation. Chuck Spetka and Andrew MacArthur from CWCapital argued that they could not calculate the value of the property without knowing the legal rents for the 4,400 apartments—nearly 40 percent of all the units—that had been improperly deregulated.

The court decision did not determine the legal rents going forward, nor the extent of the rent overcharges made to potentially thousands of tenants over an unspecified number of years. But Spetka and MacArthur, whose fiduciary responsibilities were to the lenders, not the tenants, estimated that the complexes were worth far more than the tenant group could pay.

Spetka and MacArthur suspected that Brookfield and the tenant association were trying to buy the complexes on the cheap. Privately, they dismissed Garodnick's press conferences as the tactics of a politician on the make. They knew that some of the city's largest real estate companies were still salivating over the prospect of owning the complexes, including the Related Companies, the Durst real estate family and others. Michael Ashner, who was now allied with Richard Mack from AREA Property Partners (formerly Apollo Real Estate), was still interested after having lost out to Brookfield in the competition to partner with the tenants. And Jerry Guterman directly challenged the tenant association with his own plan for a co-op conversion after they rebuffed his entreaties.

After all, the real estate market, especially the market for apartment rentals, was surging once again.

Spetka and MacArthur, the vice president who oversaw the two complexes, set out to purge the complexes of what they viewed as Tishman Speyer's legacy, establish at least a détente with Garodnick and the tenant association, and, like Tishman Speyer, renovate vacant apartments, push rents higher and enhance net income.

As the new landlord, CWCapital and Rose Associates tried to assure tenants that it was not on a wholesale campaign to oust longtime residents. But that does not mean that all twenty-five thousand tenants universally viewed them as a benevolent force. There were tenants who complained to their neighbors and in the blogs about Rose's decision to continue the weekly green market and allow noisy food trucks to pull up around Stuyvesant Oval, offering grilled meat, tacos, juice drinks and other items to residents.

Margaret Salacan and other tenants found what they called the commercialization of the complexes appalling. "The food trucks don't belong on the property," she said over coffee at a shop on Twentieth Street. "They bring noise, fumes and garbage. The original purpose of the oval was to create an oasis in the middle of the city."[8]

The opposition was by no means unanimous, as many residents liked the convenience. One of the biggest uproars came in the winter of 2011 when MacArthur, who has children who skate, decided to install a temporary ice rink atop one of the playgrounds. A vocal group of tenants, though by no means all, rained criticism on the rink in the blogs and in letters to the tenant association and the local newspaper, saying it was an illegal, profit-making enterprise that drew nonresidents to the complexes. In a meeting with Garodnick, MacArthur told him, "You're caught between cranky tenants and gleeful kids. Anywhere else, this would be considered an amenity."

The rink opened anyway, attracting more than double the number of anticipated skaters on the first weekend.

In a telling move that had both symbolic and practical meaning, CWCapital tore out the extensive landscaping installed by Rob Speyer soon after he took over the complexes. Speyer had spent $21.8 million on new signs, a facelift for storefronts on First Avenue and truckloads of trees, bushes, flowers. Workers planted ten thousand trees in two months, cramming thick copses of young ornamental trees beneath a canopy formed by mature London plane and pin oak trees. They stocked the flower beds with seasonal and ornamental flowers requiring periodic replacement and hung flowerpots from lampposts, which needed constant watering in the summer.

Early in 2011, Adam Rose, the property manager hired by CWCapital, gleefully yanked out five hundred trees, donating two hundred to city parks and disposing of the remaining three hundred. Rose, who never forgave Speyer for firing his firm when he took over, donated five thousand ornamental cabbages to the parks department. "They so overplanted," Rose said of the prior owners. "The landscaping didn't raise the rents one cent. Why? They're still non-doorman buildings with only one bath."[9]

Raising the rents to improve cash flow was foremost on the agenda of Rose and CWCapital. In that respect, CWCapital was no different from Tishman Speyer. They just did not have to carry as much debt or move as swiftly to try to make ends meet. After the 2009 court of appeals ruling, Tishman Speyer struck a deal with the tenant-plaintiffs in the court case, temporarily rolling back rents by hundreds of dollars for the 4,400 apartments covered by the decision. But that agreement expired in December 2010, and when CWCapital was unable to reach a permanent accord with the plaintiffs, the company took an aggressive position, unilaterally raising the rents as leases expired and throwing the issue back into the courts.

The rents for all 11,232 apartments at Stuyvesant Town and Peter Cooper Village were regulated, but over 2010, 2011 and 2012 two distinct classes of units emerged. Roughly 60 percent of the units were the traditional rent-stabilized apartments whose rents averaged about $1,500 a month. The rents for the other 40 percent, all of them renovated and modernized, were at or near market rates, although annual increases were restricted by the city's Rent Guidelines Board.

By the fall of 2012, rent for a two-bedroom apartment in Stuyvesant Town, for instance, was $4,385 a month, up from $3,850 a year earlier. One-bedroom units were going for $3,200 a month. A two-bedroom apartment at Peter Cooper Village cost even more, about $4,600 per month.

It is worth noting that CWCapital steadily increased the net income at the two complexes, but seven years after the original sale they still did not generate enough income to cover the debt service on the $3 billion mortgage. The property needed about $195.6 million in net income or cash flow to break even. But Manus Clancy, a senior managing director at the Trepp credit rating agency, estimated that the net cash flow for 2011 was only $130 million, up from $122.9 million in 2010. A $65 million shortfall.

But they are gaining ground. CWCapital has steadily increased the number of units renting at or near market rates from 4,300 to 5,331 by spending lavishly—$85,000 to $120,000 per unit—on the renovation of every vacant apartment. They installed wood cabinets, new wood floors, European bath fixtures, granite countertops and high-end appliances.

Under new rent regulations adopted by the state legislature in 2011, landlords can recover their investment by raising the rent by one-sixtieth of the renovation cost. In other words, the rent for an apartment that once went for $1,500 a month could be hiked by $2,000 after a $120,000 renovation, to $3,500. Plus, regulations permitted a 20 percent bump in rent for vacant apartments. It hardly mattered that the apartments were rent regulated.

The marketing of Stuyvesant Town-Peter Cooper Village today says a lot about the new tenants. The ads in 2012 are pitched to a younger, more well-heeled, and most likely, single tenant than the striving families typical in the past. The ads highlight a "sophisticated selection of services, amenities and events" and conclude with a tagline that many longtime residents find infuriating: "Stuyvesant Town. Live and Live It Up."

Judging from the young college students and recent college graduates who jammed into the leasing office on two separate days in July 2011, the incoming tenants are young, fashionable and single. Many were accompanied by their mothers. That month, 2,000 prospective renters visited the leasing office; 360 signed leases. Middle-class families can hardly afford the renovated units. Federal guidelines suggest that housing costs should not exceed 30 percent of the household income. With apartments renting for $4,000 or more a month, or $48,000 a year, a family would need to earn more than $160,000 a year.

Very often the young people crowding the leasing office are willing to double and triple up in order to pay the rent. Katie Schloer, a New York University student from Philadelphia, lived in a one-bedroom apartment with two friends, both students. Noah Nielsen moved to a two-bedroom apartment in Stuyvesant Town after graduating from the University of Vermont. He had two roommates. They built a wall in the center of the living room to make three bedrooms and split the rent, $3,500 a month.

But Nielsen, like Schloer, had no intention of setting down roots. He left after a year. "I didn't want to be surrounded by older people and families," Nielsen said. "I wanted to feel like I'm in Manhattan."[10]

The cultural differences between the newcomers and their dormitory lifestyle and the more established, family-oriented tenants created some tension. Complaints abounded about the young people who stayed up late, played their music loud at night or caroused drunkenly in the playgrounds. "They're filling apartments beyond their capacity, in many cases with people who have no regard for the community as a long-term home," Garodnick said.

But there is more at work here than simply the gulf between the twentysomethings and the families and retirees. People no longer work for the same company or institution for their entire lives, be it MetLife, the New York City public school system or Beth Israel hospital. Nor do they tend to live in the same apartment or house for decades at a time. We live in a more rootless era, where careers can change several times in the course of a lifetime, companies go in and out of business and personal addresses change periodically. The golden age of Stuyvesant Town-Peter Cooper Village as a stable redoubt where parents raise their children and retire may have passed.

"To me, this place was about family," said Margaret Salacan, who has lived in Stuyvesant Town since 1988. "Now it's about transients."[11]

At 5:00 P.M. on November 29, 2012, the tenant-plaintiffs and CWCapital, the company that controlled Stuyvesant Town-Peter Cooper Village, announced that they had reached a $68.75 million agreement to settle the class-action claims arising from the

Roberts case. The settlement, which had the preliminary approval of Justice Richard B. Lowe III, would put to rest all rent
overcharge claims and set the legal rents for the 4,311 apartments that were illegally deregulated while the complex received city tax breaks. Judge Lowe set a hearing on final
approval for April 9, 2013.

Thousands of current and former tenants would get anywhere from $150 to six figures, with the nine original plaintiffs
receiving at least $25,000 each for the time and effort spent on
the case since it was filed in 2007.

Rumors had swept across the complexes for more than a year
that a settlement was near. But that was only after CWCapital's
attempt to go around the plaintiffs by lobbying the state legislature for a "legislative solution" ended in total failure. They had
persuaded a Republican state senator whose district was closer
to Cleveland than Manhattan to submit a bill that would have
allowed the owners of Stuyvesant Town-Peter Cooper Village
to repay the $24 million in tax breaks it received at 9 percent
interest, a total of at least $26.16 million. But the bondholders
would not have to roll back rents or repay what tenant advocates
once estimated were $200 million in rent overcharges. Al-
though the bill had the support of the real estate industry, it had
no chance of passage in the Democratic-controlled Assembly, so
the bill died that summer without a vote by the legislature.

Months later, the two sides—three if you count MetLife—
did get close to a deal. But what proved to be impossibly complicated was trying to cobble together a general agreement that
covered the rent history for 4,311 separate apartments and, ultimately, a potential 21,250 tenants who at one time or another
had lived in the affected units since January 2003. Some units

had had multiple tenants over the seven years covered by the proposed settlement. The negotiations were covered by a strict confidentiality agreement, but one participant groused that MetLife had quibbled over a couple hundred thousands of dollars, delaying the announcement by several weeks.

The bondholders will pay $58.25 million toward the settlement, and MetLife, which had deregulated three-quarters of the 4,311 apartments and made a $3 billion profit on the sale, will pay the remaining $10.5 million.

In the immediate aftermath of the announcement, Garodnick was wary. He said he would withhold judgment as to the fairness of the agreement. "Tenants had overpaid for years as a result of illegal rent reregulation, and they have been waiting a long time for relief," he said. "I am concerned that a significant number of tenants may be subject to rent increases under this agreement."

He called on CWCapital to start meeting with the tenant association to discuss the conversion proposal.

Alexander Schmidt, the lead lawyer for the tenant-plaintiffs, provided a far more optimistic view of the settlement, saying that the agreement, combined with past rent rollbacks by Tishman Speyer, brought the total recover to $146.85 million. Just as important, he said, the settlement eliminated what CWCapital had described as an impediment to their sitting down with Garodnick and the tenant association to discuss a tenant-led purchase and condominium conversion.

Schmidt's firm, Wolf Haldenstein, and a second firm, Bernstein Liebhard—will receive 27.5 percent of the settlement, a total of $18.9 million.

CWCapital had expressed a willingness to discuss a tenant

conversion in 2010 when it was trying to fend off a takeover attempt by Ashner and Ackman. But two years later, the special servicer was in no hurry to sit down with the tenants or any other potential buyer. Andrew MacArthur from CWCapital said that it would take another year to sort through any potential legal challenges from disgruntled tenants. Besides, he said, the company would put the property up for sale only when it would enable bondholders to get maximum recovery.

"There's no change in our posture and we expect that will continue well into 2014," said Gregory Cross, the Venable lawyer who handled the case for CWCapital. "We have an appeal period and a lot of stuff to implement. We're not committing to any timeframe."

Since Tishman Speyer's default in 2010, the bondholders had made about $360 million in advances, for apartment renovations, legal fees, and other costs related to managing the property. Another $600 million in fees and penalties had also piled up. In other words, CWCapital would eventually be looking for about $4 billion so that bondholders "could be made whole."

In the meantime, the settlement also establishes the legal rents for the apartments under rent stabilization laws. A block of tenants in the affected apartments are facing the prospect of rent hikes. The "legal" rents for thousands of apartments are now above market, more than CWCapital could reasonably charge. Instead, management offers a lower, preferential rent.

The ultimate fate of Stuyvesant Town-Peter Cooper Village is not going to play out quickly, but there are clear trend lines that are working against its historic role as a middle-class bastion. This once stable and affordable refuge for firefighters, nurses, municipal workers and small business owners has increasingly become home to more well-heeled students and professionals who pay as much as $4,385 a month—or $52,620 a year—for a two-bedroom apartment with only one bathroom and no doorman.

At the time of the sale in 2006, less than 30 percent of the units were getting at or near market rents. Today, it is 48 percent, even if all those apartments are now regulated by rent stabilization laws. Every month, long-term residents vacate another 15 to 20 truly affordable apartments. The units are quickly renovated and re-rented at much higher rates.

Michael McKee, the long-time tenant activist, says that the reason this is happening in Stuyvesant Town-Peter Cooper Village and across the city is because of a "dramatic weakening of the rent laws" over the past 20 years. "A huge amount of damage has been done to affordability," he said.

As a result, the traditional middle-class families who live in Stuyvesant Town-Peter Cooper Village have become a shrinking minority, replaced by nomadic young professionals who have no intention of setting down roots.

Those tenants are unlikely to buy in to a tenant-led scheme whose goal is the preservation of Stuyvesant Town-Peter Cooper Village's legacy as a middle-class refuge.

In many respects the trend at the complexes reflects broader changes taking place in American society. The recession coupled with the housing bust has accelerated and cut deeply into the net wealth and income of the kind of families who typically lived in Peter Cooper Village or worked in Detroit's auto factories. "The middle class has shrunk in size, fallen backward in income and wealth, and shed some—by no means all—of its characteristic faith in the future" since 2000, according to a 2012 Pew Research Center study called "The Lost Decade of the Middle Class."

The Related Companies and other large real estate companies continue to argue that the complexes remain valuable as
rental properties. To outbid them, Garodnick, Doyle and the
other leaders of the tenants association will have the formida-
ble, perhaps insurmountable, task of demonstrating that a significant block of tenants are ready, willing and able to purchase
their units. A substantial number of tenants are also going to
have to set aside their desire to cash in on any appreciation in
favor of an ideal Stuyvesant Town-Peter Cooper Village that is
forever home to the city's middle class. They would also need
to obtain public subsidies and prove that it would be politically
costly for CWCapital to pursue a sale to the highest bidder.

"We want to acquire the property and adhere to our principles of affordable housing with no changes to the configuration
of the complexes," Doyle said shortly before stepping down as
president of the tenants association. "We're trying to create an
affordable condominium. It's not going to be where you buy an
apartment and flip it for your own profit."

In the end, Tishman Speyer and BlackRock's ambitions for
Stuyvesant Town-Peter Cooper Village blew up amid their hu-
bris and greed. But the dynamic they set in motion is changing
the historical, cultural and social significance of the complexes
to New York City and the nation forever.

Acknowledgments

I have been locked on to Stuyvesant Town ever since I learned in August 2006 that Manhattan's largest complex was going up on the auction block. Like many New Yorkers, I knew *of* Stuyvesant Town. A friend and colleague, Terry Golway, had lived in that brickyard and described its special history and culture. Another friend, Dennis O'Neil, had even brought me over there to hear Black 47 in a bar on First Avenue. But I didn't *know* Stuyvesant Town. Nor did I realize that my first story for the *New York Times* in 2006 would lead to a string of stories that would extend for another six years.

When this project began, I thought I already knew all about the history of Stuyvesant Town, the intricacies of the sale and the subsequent collapse of the biggest deal in real estate history. Little did I know. Even after I completed the first draft, I continued to discover new and surprising information and anecdotes that left me wondering, "How did I miss that?"

I should start by thanking Brian Tart, the president and publisher of Dutton, who believed in this book and encouraged me all along the way. I also want to give a shout-out to the graphic artist who came up with the book jacket. Brilliant. Certainly a lot better than my idea.

I have a newfound admiration for the keepers of the records, letters, memos and photographs of the past—in short, the archivists, who often instantly put their hands on the perfect item in response to my endless queries. Douglas Di Carlo and his colleagues at the La Guardia and Wagner Archives at LaGuardia Community College dug up a favorite of mine: the transcript of La Guardia's announcement that Metropolitan would build Stuyvesant Town. The librarians at the New York Public Library were also quietly diligent on my behalf. Eric Wakin, the Lehman curator for American history in the Rare Book and Manuscript Library at Columbia University, was a big help early on. Daniel B. May, the company archivist at MetLife, was also helpful in guiding me through Metropolitan's voluminous files and photo library.

At the *New York Times*, Jeffrey P. Roth, a photo specialist, went above and beyond the call of duty in tracking down images at the *Times* and elsewhere.

John Crotty, a lifelong resident of Stuyvesant Town, served as a guide to the customs and folkways of Stuyvesant Town. He introduced me to one resident after another who shared their stories with me at Quigley's, a pub at First Avenue and Eighteenth Street. He also introduced me to the Stuyvesant Town Little League's annual spring parade. Maybe not so coincidentally, John was a city housing official in 2006 and played a role in the drama behind the sale of his beloved complex.

I also want to thank Lee Lorch, a math professor and a founder of the Town and Village Tenants Committee to End Discrimination in Stuyvesant Town, who plumbed his remarkable memory for me. He is an admirable man and his lifelong dedication to justice was rewarded with a reserved seat on the 1950s blacklist.

Karen Smith, a former judge and a serious student of city housing, generously shared memories of her parents' involvement in the tenants committee in the 1940s and 1950s and the involvement of the Hendrix family. She graciously provided me with some of the committee's original leaflets and pamphlets, many of which were written by her mother, Esther. Her father, Dave Smith, led a rent strike at Stuyvesant Town. He later became a tenant leader at Penn South, after MetLife refused to give his family a new lease at Stuyvesant Town.

Al Doyle also provided a small trove of artifacts, ranging from original MetLife maps and pamphlets about Stuyvesant Town to a 1967 Stuyvesant-Cooper telephone directory. Marie Beirne, coproducer of the Peter Cooper Village-Stuyvesant Town Oral History Project and an old friend, provided me many leads, helpful phone numbers and good-humored support, as did Annie, Richie, and Debbie.

Jerilyn Perine, executive director, and Harold Schultz, senior fellow, of the Citizens Housing and Planning Council, a nonpartisan research organization, shared their knowledge of housing, affordable and otherwise. They also unlocked the files of the organization, which played a critical role in the debate over the building of Stuyvesant Town and MetLife's racial policies, as well as the crisis in affordable housing during the recent real estate boom and its aftermath. Likewise, Benjamin Dolchin at the Association for Neighborhood and Housing Development was kind enough to share his wisdom and a chest of loan documents that shed light on what he vividly described as predatory lenders and their practices.

Sydney P. Freedberg, a talented reporter for the *Tampa Bay Times*, was very kind to share with me documents and insight relating to her own 2009 investigation into how the Florida Board of Administration, a state pension fund, bet $250 million in public money "on a huge Manhattan real estate deal and lost every penny of it."

I also want to thank Rob Speyer for sitting for hours of interview questioning knowing that there was no chance he would emerge as a hero in this story. We have known each other for more than twenty years, ever since he was a fact checker at the *New York Observer*, where I was a senior reporter. He certainly had more fortitude than Larry Fink or Michael Bloomberg, who both rebuffed my requests for an interview for the book.

John E. Zuccotti was a consistent source of encouragement, as was a certain banker who was not directly involved in the deal but was an endless spigot of key documents, names, and phone numbers. Thanks to Richie, Debbie, Jay, Joy, Ann, Cathy, Bruce, and Alan for their support.

Finally, I want to thank my editors at the *New York Times*, who encouraged the project and allowed me to take a four-month leave from the paper to complete the first draft of this manuscript.

To the tenants, real estate executives, brokers and bankers who shared their observations and then repeatedly asked, "Where's the book?," here it is.

Notes

Chapter 1: "Negroes and Whites Don't Mix"

1 Transcript, April 18, 1943, WNYC broadcast, La Guardia and Wagner Archives, LaGuardia Community College.
2 Ibid.
3 Metropolitan Life Insurance Press Release, April 18, 1943, company archives.
4 Transcript, April 18, 1943, WNYC broadcast, La Guardia and Wagner Archives, LaGuardia Community College.
5 La Guardia to Salmon, memo dated April 22, 1943, La Guardia and Wagner Archives, LaGuardia Community College.
6 "West Side Housing Project Will Bar Negro Tenants," *New York Post*, May 20, 1943.
7 "Frederick Ecker, Financier, 96, Dies," *New York Times*, March 21, 1964.
8 Ibid.
9 MetLife, "Underwriting America's Success: 125 Years of Metropolitan Life."
10 "Metropolitan Life Makes Housing Pay," *Fortune*, April 1946; Henry Reed, "The Investment Policy of the Metropolitan Life," *Task Magazine*, undated, Citizens Housing and Planning Council Archives; Simon Breines, "Stuyvesant Town," *Task Magazine*, undated, Citizens Housing and Planning Council Archives.
11 "120-Acre Housing Will Rise in Bronx as Private Project," *New York Times*, April 8, 1938.
12 "Metropolitan Life Makes Housing Pay," *Fortune*, April 1946.
13 Ibid.
14 Robert Moses, *Public Works: A Dangerous Trade* (McGraw-Hill, 1970), 432.

15 Dominic J. Capeci Jr., "Fiorello H. La Guardia and the Stuyvesant Town Controversy of 1943," *New-York Historical Society Quarterly*, October 1978.

16 Charles Abrams, "The Walls of Stuyvesant Town," *Nation*, March 24, 1945.

17 Joel Schwartz, *The New York Approach: Robert Moses, Urban Liberals, and Redevelopment of the Inner City* (Ohio State University Press, 1993), 103.

18 Arthur Simon, *Stuyvesant Town USA* (New York University Press, 1970), 36.

19 "Housing Plan Seen as a 'Walled City,'" *New York Times*, May 20, 1943.

20 "Stuyvesant Town Approved by Board," *New York Times*, June 4, 1943.

21 Ibid.

22 Simon, *Stuyvesant Town USA*, 37.

23 Robert Moses, letter to the editor, *New York Times*, June 3, 1943.

24 Robert Moses to Frank C. Moore, 1943.

25 "Stuyvesant Town Approved by Board," *New York Times*, June 4, 1943; "City Approves Metropolitan's Housing Plan," *New York Herald Tribune*, June 4, 1943.

26 "Topics of the Times," *New York Times*, June 5, 1943.

27 Walter White to Mayor La Guardia, June 16, 1943, Manuscripts and Archives Division, New York Public Library.

28 Ecker to La Guardia, July 26, 1943, La Guardia and Wagner Archives, LaGuardia Community College.

29 La Guardia to Ecker, July 31, 1943, Manuscripts and Archives Division, New York Public Library.

30 Ecker to La Guardia, August 1943, Manuscripts and Archives Division, New York Public Library.

31 "Memo Concerning Stuyvesant Town, Inc.," Office of the Mayor, August 9, 1943, La Guardia and Wagner Archives, LaGuardia Community College.

32 Ecker to La Guardia, August 16, 1943, La Guardia and Wagner Archives, LaGuardia Community College.

33 Moses to Samuel Seabury, September 3, 1943, Manuscripts and Archives Division, New York Public Library.

34 "Memorandum for Mr. Ecker," from Moses, Re: Pratt vs. LaGuardia, February 25, 1944, Manuscripts and Archives Division, New York Public Library.

35 Moses to Ecker, February 28, 1944, Manuscripts and Archives Division, New York Public Library.

36 La Guardia to Ecker, April 5, 1944, La Guardia and Wagner Archives.

37 "Housing Project to Rise in Harlem," *New York Times*, September 18, 1944.

38 Ibid.

39 Informal Meeting on Riverton Project, October 25, 1944, Citizens Housing and Planning Council Archives.

40 Ibid.

Chapter 2: Thirty-Six Million Bricks

1 Interview with author.
2 Rosamond G. Roberts, "3,000 Families Move to Make Way for Stuyvesant Town: A Story of Tenant Relocation Bureau," Metropolitan Life Archives.
3 "The Rehousing Needs of the Families of the Stuyvesant Town Site," June 14, 1945, Community Service Society.
4 "Race Housing Plea Quashed by Courts," *New York Times*, July 29, 1947.
5 "Stuyvesant Town Ban on Negroes Upheld, 4–3, by Court of Appeals," *New York Herald Tribune*, July 20, 1949.
6 Interview with author.
7 Interview with author.
8 Lorch and Smith, interviews with author.
9 Daniel B. English, file marked "confidential," memo concerning meeting sponsored by East Side Tenants Council, August 29, 1949, Metropolitan Life Archives.
10 "Protests Voiced on Faculty Action," *New York Times*, June 9, 1949.
11 "Teacher Fighting Bias in Housing Faces Loss of Second College Job," *New York Times*, April 10, 1950; "Professor's Ousting Hit," *New York Times*, June 7, 1950.
12 "Estimate Board Votes Anti-Bias Bill on Housing," *New York Herald Tribune*, March 2, 1951.
13 Simon, *Stuyvesant Town USA*, 95–100.
14 Interview with author.

Chapter 3: The Golden Age

1 Interview with author.
2 Interview with author.
3 "City Seen Stunted by Lack of Housing," *New York Times*, June 17, 1947; "No Apartments Finished in 1946," *New York Times*, December 14, 1946.
4 Interview with author.
5 1960 Census, courtesy Andrew A. Beveridge, sociology professor, Queens College.
6 Interview with author.
7 Mary Roche, "New Housing Suite Is Copied in Store," *New York Times*, June 9, 1947; Ann Pringle, "New Ideas Seen in Stuyvesant Town Dwelling," *New York Herald Tribune*, April 16, 1948.
8 Allan Keller, "Stuyvesant Town: Where Hard Heads Made Dream Come True," *New York World-Telegram*, June 11, 1948.
9 "New York: New Nightmares for Old?," *Time*, December 13, 1948.
10 Interview with author.
11 Interview with author.
12 Interview with author.

13   Interview with author.
14   Interview with author.
15   Interview with author.
16   Interview with author.
17   Interview with author.
18   Interview with author.
19   Interview with author.
20   Interview with author.
21   Interview with author.
22   Interview with author.
23   Lotte N. Doverman, letter to the editor, *New York Times*, May 29, 1952.
24   Metropolitan Life leaflets, company archives.
25   Blaine Littell, "Stuyvesant Town Rent Increase Rejected by City, Goes to Court," *New York Herald Tribune*, May 20, 1952.
26   "Court Authorizes Stuyvesant Town to Increase Rent by $2.55 a Room," *New York Times*, July 3, 1952.
27   Steven D. Roberts, "Spiraling Rents Worry Officials," *New York Times*, July 31, 1967.
28   Joseph P. Fried, "City Charges Bias at Three Projects," *New York Times*, May 28, 1968.
29   Purcell, interview with author.
30   Interview with author.
31   Interview with author.
32   "Metropolitan Denies S.T. Sale Rumor," *Town & Village*, October 19, 1972; "Met May Not Renew Stuy Town's Policy," *Town & Village*, August 16, 1973.
33   Wendy Schuman, "Stuyvesant Town, with Tax Reprieve Enters New Era," *New York Times*, June 16, 1974.
34   Interview with author.
35   Angela Taylor, "Stuyvesant Town: Residents Are Still Singing Its Praise," *New York Times*, May 9, 1973.
36   Interview with author.
37   "Met May Not Renew Stuy Town's Policy," *Town & Village*, August 16, 1973.
38   "Met's President Says ST Not For Sale—Yet," *Town & Village*, September 1973.
39   "Stuy Town-Cooper Are Up for Sale," *Town & Village*, December 1973.
40   Frank M. Leiher, letter to Stuyvesant Town residents, January 10, 1974, Metropolitan Life Archives.
41   Wendy Schuman, "Stuyvesant Town, with Tax Reprieve, Enters New Era," *New York Times*, June 16, 1974.
42   "Poll Results: 59.7% Vote for a Tax Abatement," *Town & Village*, April 11, 1974.
43   "1,000 Rally for Abatement," *Town & Village*, undated, 1974, Metropolitan Life Archives.

44   Wendy Schuman, "Stuyvesant Town, with Tax Reprieve, Enters New Era," *New York Times*, June 16, 1974.
45   Interview with author.
46   "Met Asked to Hike Number of Guards," *Town & Village*, February 3, 1972.
47   Randy Young, "The City's Safest Neighborhoods," *New York*, October 19, 1981.
48   Jonathan Mandell, "New York's Best Landlords," *New York Sunday News Magazine*, October 10, 1982.

Chapter 4: Who Would Drive the Last Dollar?

1   Interview with author.
2   Real Capital Analytics. Office and residential sales of properties and portfolios greater than $5 million.
3   Participant interviews with author.
4   Interview with author.
5   Interview with author.
6   Interview with author.
7   Interview with author.
8   Interview with author.
9   Interview with author.
10   Interview with author.
11   Interview with author.
12   Interview with author.
13   Alan S. Oser, "The Upscaling of Stuyvesant Town," *New York Times*, January 28, 2001.
14   Interview with author.
15   Interview with author.
16   Oser, "The Upscaling of Stuyvesant Town."
17   Bruce Lambert, "2 Big Projects Deregulating Vacant Units," *New York Times*, July 13, 2001.
18   Interview with author.
19   Interview with author.
20   Speyer, interview with author.
21   MetLife pamphlet.
22   Interview with author.
23   Interview with author.

Chapter 5: Let's Make a Deal

1   Interview with author, 2006.
2   Mike Sheridan, "Manhattan Transfer: BlackRock Realty Acquires Landmark New York City Apartments," *National Real Estate Investor*, April 2007.

3   Barclay, interview with author.
4   "Deals of the Year," *Real Estate Forum*, March 2006; Les Shaver, "2006 MFE 50: Private Choices; Apartment REITs say Goodbye to Wall Street in '05 in Search of Higher Valuations," *Multifamily Executive*, May 15, 2006.
5   Beal, interview with author.
6   Real Capital Analytics.
7   "Shifting Assets," Private Equity Real Estate, October 2006.
8   Ibid.
9   Terry Pristin, "Square Feet; Real Estate Deals to Flip Over," *New York Times*, August 30, 2006.
10 "Broadway Partner Purchases 10-Building Portfolio for $3.3 Billion," *Mortgage Banking*, February 1, 2007.
11 Charles V. Bagli, "Default Talk and Frayed Nerves," *New York Times*, August 25, 2008.
12 Ibid.
13 Charles V. Bagli, "They Bet the Rent, and Lost," *New York Times*, May 29, 2010.
14 Pristin, "Square Feet."
15 Charles V. Bagli, "In Harlem Buildings, Reminders of Easy Money and the Financial Crisis," *New York Times*, June 10, 2011.
16 "N.Y. Firm Closes on Purchase of CarrAmerica Portfolio," *New York Times*, January 8, 2007.
17 Tom Shachtman, *Skyscraper Dreams: The Great Real Estate Dynasties of New York* (Little, Brown, 1991).
18 James Traub, "The Anti-Trump," *New York Times Magazine*, December 20, 1998.
19 Charles V. Bagli, "Era Closes at Rockefeller Center with $1.85 Billion Deal on Sale," *New York Times*, December 22, 2000.
20 Interview with author.
21 Traub, "The Anti-Trump."
22 Ibid.
23 Interview with author.
24 Charles V. Bagli and Robin Pogrebin, "New York's Cultural Power Brokers: Mixing the Real Estate Business and Everyone's Pleasure," *New York Times*, June 2, 2004.
25 Interview with author.
26 Interview with author.
27 Interview with author.
28 Interview with author.
29 Interview with author.
30 Interview with author.
31 Interview with author.
32 Interview with author.
33 Quinn, interview with author.

34   Interview with author.
35   Interview with author.

Chapter 6: For Sale

1   Charles V. Bagli and Janny Scott, "Housing Complex of 110 Buildings for Sale in City," *New York Times*, August 30, 2006.
2   Interview with author.
3   Garodnick to Henrikson, September 1, 2006.
4   Interview with author.
5   Interview with author.
6   Interview with author.
7   Interview with author.
8   Alistair Barr, "MetLife Has Seen 'Terrific' Interest in NY Properties, CEO Says," MarketWatch from Dow Jones, September 18, 2006.
9   Interview with author.
10   Interview with author.
11   CB Richard Ellis, Peter Cooper Village-Stuyvesant Town sales book
12   Interview with author.
13   Interview with author.
14   Interview with author.
15   Interview with author.
16   Interview with author.
17   Charles V. Bagli, "Tenants' Bid Among a Dozen for Complexes," *New York Times*, October 6, 2006.
18   Interview with author.
19   Janny Scott, "Complications of a For Sale Sign," *New York Times*, August 31, 2006.
20   Interview with author.
21   Interview with author.
22   Interview with author.
23   Interview with author.
24   Interview with author.
25   Interview with author.

Chapter 7: "The More You Spend, the More We Can Lend Against It"

1   Interview with author.
2   Interview with author.
3   Interview with author.
4   Interview with author.
5   Interview with author.
6   Transcript.
7   Interview with author.

8   Interview with author.
9   Interview with author.
10   Interview with author.
11   Interview with author.
12   Interview with author.
13   Lindenbaum, interview with author.
14   Interview with author.
15   Interview with author.
16   Interviews with author by three different executives who attended the
     meeting, including Dickey.
17   Interview with author.
18   Interview with author.
19   Interview with author.
20   Interview with author.
21   Interview with author.

Chapter 8: What $5.4 Billion Gets You

1   Interview with author.
2   "Peter Cooper Village-Stuyvesant Town Partners L.P.; Confidential Pri-
     vate Placement Memorandum," 40.
3   Interview with author.
4   Robert Siegel, "From Gashouse to Stuyvesant to Luxe Condos," *All
     Things Considered*, National Public Radio, October 18, 2006.
5   Interview with author.
6   Interview with author.
7   Doyle and Speyer, interviews with author.
8   Interview with author.
9   MetLife 10-K filing for 2006, Securities and Exchange Commission,
     March 1, 2007.
10   Speyer and Kandarian, interviews with author.
11   Interview with author.
12   Interview with author.
13   Interview with author.
14   Charles V. Bagli, "$5.4 Billion Bid Wins Complexes in New York Deal,"
     New York Times, October 18, 2006.
15   Damien Cave, "City Plans Middle-Income Project on Queens Water-
     front," *New York Times*, October 20, 2006.
16   Ibid.
17   Charles V. Bagli, "Brooklyn Tract Goes on the Block; Home to 14,000,"
     New York Times, December 1, 2006.
18   Ibid.
19   Charles V. Bagli, "Cuomo Says Investor's Past May Stop Starrett City
     Sale," *New York Times*, February 17, 2007.
20   Ibid.

21   Interview with author.
22   Wachovia and Merrill Lynch mortgage trust documents for Peter Cooper Village-Stuyvesant Town.
23   Term sheet for Stuyvesant Town-Peter Cooper Village investment, California Public Employees' Retirement System (CalPERS).
24   Interview with author.
25   "Rating Agency Presentation $3,000,000 First Mortgage on Peter Cooper Village/Stuyvesant Town Acquisition Financing," Wachovia Securities, Merrill Lynch, December 2006, 7.
26   Ibid.
27   Maha Khan Phillips, "Home Concerns from Abroad," *IPE Real Estate*, December 3, 2007.
28   Assembled from public sources and interviews with participants in the deal.
29   Erica Tay, "GIC Unit Seals $3b Property Deal with Tishman Speyer; Together, the Two Will Own Choice Real Estate in the US: 12 Buildings in 8 Cities," *Straits Times* (Singapore), December 3, 2004.
30   Interview with author.

Chapter 9: "What Do They Have Against Trees?"

1   "Peter Cooper Village-Stuyvesant Town Partners L.P.; Confidential Private Placement Memorandum," 2, 30.
2   Gabriel Sherman, "Clash of Utopias," *New York*, February 1, 2009.
3   "Rating Agency Presentation $3,000,000 First Mortgage on Peter Cooper Village/Stuyvesant Town Acquisition Financing," Wachovia Securities, Merrill Lynch, December 2006, 7.
4   Interview with author.
5   Charles V. Bagli, "After Sale, Rent Increases Give Some Sticker Shock," *New York Times*, January 16, 2007.
6   Ibid.
7   Housing documents provided by Horisk.
8   Bagli, "After Sale, Rent Increases Give Some Sticker Shock."
9   Nelson D. Schwartz and Vikas Bajaj, "Credit Time Bomb Ticked, but Few Heard," *New York Times*, August 19, 2007.
10   Ron Nixon, "Study Predicts Foreclosure for 1 in 5 Subprime Loans," *New York Times*, December 20, 2006.
11   Ibid.
12   Charles V. Bagli, "Suit Contests Rent Increases in Complexes MetLife Sold," *New York Times*, January 23, 2007.
13   Interview with author.
14   Interview with author.
15   Interview with author.
16   Interview with author.

17 Interview with author.
18 Terry Pristin, "Square Feet; A Warning on Risk in Commercial Mortgages," *New York Times*, May 2, 2007.
19 Mark Wellborn, "Stuy Town Is So Last Year Quinn, Speyers Make Nice," *New York Observer*, March 12, 2007.
20 Interview with author.
21 Interview with author.
22 Interview with author.
23 Interview with author.
24 Interview with author.
25 Interview with author.
26 Interview with author.
27 Interview with author.
28 Interview with author.
29 Tishman Speyer Properties.
30 Sherman, "Clash of Utopias."
31 Interview with author.
32 Author interviews with Tishman Speyer executives and lenders.
33 Charles V. Bagli, "At Eleventh Hour, Rivals Vie for Deal on West Side Railyards," *New York Times*, March 25, 2008.
34 Christine Haughney and Terry Pristin, "Wachovia's Big-City Splash Has a Sobering Aftermath," *New York Times*, January 23, 2008.
35 Interview with author.
36 Charles V. Bagli, "Deal to Build at Railyards on West Side Collapses," *New York Times*, May 9, 2008.
37 Interview with author.

Chapter 10: The Bubble Explodes

1   Interview with author.
2   Commercial Mortgage Alert, 2008.
3   Michael Barbaro, "As Bloomberg's Time Wanes, Titans Seek Mayor in His Mold," *New York Times*, July 7, 2008.
4   Charles V. Bagli, "Macklowes Sell G.M. Building for $2.9 Billion," *New York Times*, May 25, 2008.
5   Interview with author.
6   Interview with author.
7   Terry Pristin, "Risky Real Estate Deals Helped Doom Lehman," *New York Times*, September 17, 2008.
8   Mortgage documents and prospectus, Riverton Apartments, Ackman-Ziff Real Estate Group; *Wells Fargo v. RP Stellar Riverton*, New York State supreme court, 101491/2009; Charles V. Bagli, "Default Talk and Frayed Nerves," *New York Times*, August 25, 2008.
9   Interview with author.
10 Interview with author.

11 Interview with author.
12 Helen Kennedy, "You're the Villain, Pols Tell Fat Cat," *Daily News*, October 7, 2008.
13 Michael J. de la Merced, "Blackstone Group Reports $500 million 3rd-Quarter Loss," *New York Times*, November 7, 2008.
14 Standard & Poor's Stuyvesant Town release, September 26, 2008; Charles V. Bagli, "Failed Deals Replace Real Estate Boom," *New York Times*, October 1, 2008.
15 Interview with author.
16 Interview with author.
17 Interview with author.
18 Interview with author.
19 Seavey to Belkin, January 16, 1996; Martin J. Heistein of Belkin, Burden, Wenig & Goldman to Nathaniel Geller, Division of Housing and Community Renewal, June 22, 1995; Erik Strangeways of Division of Housing and Community Renewal to Heistein, September 28, 1995; Heistein to Marcia Hirsch, Division of Housing and Community Renewal, October 13, 1995; Geller to Heistein, October 19, 1995; Belkin to Geller, December 14, 1995.
20 Interview with author.
21 Interview with author.
22 J. Nardelli decision, *Roberts v. Tishman Speyer Props., LP*, March 5, 2009.
23 Transcript of SL Green, December 6, 2010.
24 Court filings in Roberts v. Tishman Speyer.

Chapter 11: How to Lose $3.6 Billion in Two Years

1 Monthly reports, Wachovia Bank Commercial Mortgage Trust Series 2007-C30 (Stuyvesant Town), Realpoint, a credit agency, 2009.
2 Interview with author.
3 Interview with author.
4 Charles V. Bagli, "With Rent Rollbacks and Refunds Looming, Landlords Fight Back," *New York Times*, March 15, 2009.
5 Interview with author.
6 Interview with author.
7 Interview with author.
8 Interview with author.
9 Interview with author.
10 Ann Segrest McCulloch, senior vice president, Fannie Mae, to Honorable Carolyn B. Maloney etc., November 12, 2009; Charles E. Haldeman Jr., chief executive officer, Freddie Mac, to Coalition of East Side Leaders etc., November 11, 2009.
11 Interview with author.
12 Interview with author.

13   Interview with author.
14   Wachovia Securities to PCV ST Mezz 1 LP and BlackRock Financial Management, January 11, 2010.
15   Interview with author.
16   Interview with author.
17   Interview with author.
18   Interview with author.
19   Interview with author.
20   Lingling Wei and Mike Spector, "Tishman Venture Gives Up Stuyvesant Project," *Wall Street Journal*, January 25, 2010; Charles V. Bagli, "Stuyvesant and Cooper Surrendered to Creditors," *New York Times*, January 25, 2010.
21   Interview with author.
22   Interview with author.
23   Interview with author.
24   Charles V. Bagli, "Hedge Fund Moves on Stuyvesant Town and Peter Cooper Village," *New York Times*, February 25, 2010.
25   Eliot Brown, "Taking Stuy Town," *Wall Street Journal*, June 8, 2010.
26   Oshrat Carmiel and Rob Urban, "Ackman Projected StuyTown Profits of $2 billion," Bloomberg News, December 3, 2010.
27   Interview with author.
28   Garodnick to Pershing Square; Charles V. Bagli, "In Latest Battle for Control of Stuyvesant Town, the Tenants are Wooed," *New York Times*, September 3, 2010.
29   Ackman and Ashner to Doyle etc., "Tenants Association Joint Venture," marked confidential, September 12, 2010.
30   Interview with author.

Chapter 12: Reckoning

1   Interview with author.
2   Interview with author.
3   Andrew Tangel, "Anatomy of an Implosion," *Record* (New Jersey), February 1, 2010.
4   Interview with author.
5   Interview with author.
6   Interview with author.
7   Interview with author.
8   Interview with author.
9   Interview with author.
10   Interview with author.
11   Interview with author.

Bibliography

Ballon, Hilary, and Jackson, Kenneth T., eds. *Robert Moses and the Modern City: The Transformation of New York*. W. W. Norton & Co, 2007.

Biondi, Martha. *To Stand and Fight: The Struggle for Civil Rights in Postwar New York City*. Harvard University Press, 2003.

Capeci Jr., Dominic J. "Fiorello H. La Guardia and the Stuyvesant Town Controversy of 1943." *The New-York Historical Society Quarterly*. October 1978.

Caro, Robert A. *The Power Broker: Robert Moses and the Fall of New York*. Alfred A. Knopf, 1974.

Freeman, Joshua B. *Working-Class New York: Life and Labor Since World War II*. The New Press, 2000.

Hamilton, Charles V. *Adam Clayton Powell Jr.: The Political Biography of an American Dilemma*. Atheneum, 1991.

Kessner, Thomas. *Fiorello H. La Guardia and the Making of Modern New York*. McGraw Hill, 1989.

Lewis, Michael. *The Big Short: Inside the Doomsday Machine*. W. W. Norton & Co, 2010.

Meyer, Gerald. *Vito Marcantonio: Radical Politician 1902–1954*. State University of New York, 1989.

Moody, Kim. *From Welfare State to Real Estate: Regime Change in New York City, 1974 to the Present*. The New Press, 2007.

Moses, Robert. *Public Works: A Dangerous Trade*. McGraw-Hill, 1970.

Schwartz, Joel. *The New York Approach: Robert Moses, Urban Liberals and Redevelopment of the Inner City*. Ohio State University Press, 1993.

Shachtman, Tom. *Skyscraper Dreams: The Great Real Estate Dynasties of New York*. Little, Brown, 1991.

Simon, Arthur. *Stuyvesant Town USA: Pattern for Two Americas*. New York University Press, 1970.

Sorkin, Andrew Ross. *Too Big to Fail*, Viking. 2009.

Zipp, Samuel. *Manhattan Projects: The Rise and Fall of Urban Renewal in Cold War New York*. Oxford University Press, 2010.

Index